GOD'S GREAT RESET

Assessing Covid, the Rapture & Yeshua's Body
in an END TIME Context

Yosef Rachamim Danieli

BookLocker
Trenton, Georgia

Paperback ISBN: 978-1-64719-958-6
Ebook ISBN: 978-1-64719-959-3

Artwork - Front Cover: Tod Angel

Design, Maps & Illustrations – Mr. Jonathan Parham

Published by BookLocker.com, Inc.

Printed on acid-free paper.

Library of Congress Cataloging in Publication Data
Danieli, Yosef Rachamim
"God's Great Reset - Assessing Covid, The Rapture and Yeshua's Body in an End Time Context," by Yosef Rachamim Danieli
Library of Congress Control Number: 2023901724

BookLocker.com, Inc.
2023

First Edition

Table of Contents

Thanks and Dedications xi

General Introduction 1

Chapter 1: Covid 19 – The Beginning of the End? 9

Introduction 10

The Big Picture - Part 1: Solo Night Navigation 15

Studying God's Navigation Map in Yeshua's Light 16
God's Compass 17
The Specific Timeframe on God's Prophetic Clock 18

The Big Picture - Part 2: Deception — The Main Characteristic
    of the End Times 27

Justice, Justice Shall You Pursue! 28
Turn Aside After Many to Pervert 30

Covid-19: The Official Version Accepted by the Vast Majority 36

Covid-19: The Non-Official Version Accepted by a Small Minority ... 39

Common Sense Questions and Musings 48

Covid-19, the Great Reset and the New World Order 53

Wealth and Power Ties 53
The Stated Goals of the Global Elite 58
The Fourth Industrial Revolution 59
The World's Elites and Their Aspirations 61
The Ruler of the Air 63

The Good News — God is One Hundred Percent Sovereign! 66

Satan — Only a Tool in the Hands of God 67

Great Resets in Scripture...68

Humanity's Problem and the Urgent Need for the Greatest
Reset of All 73

The Reign of the Anti-Messiah 76

Rom. 13 & 1 Pet. 2:13-17 in Light of Covid-19 79

Rightly Dividing the Word of Truth 80

Appointed by God 81

Science – The New God 90

Summary & Personal Conclusions...96

The Covid-19 Crisis is an Integral Part of a Much Bigger Thing 97

For the Coming of the Son of Man Will Be Just Like the Days
of Noah..98

A Great Deception & The Beginning of the End..........................100

A Personal Confession..104

Come Out of Her, My People...107

Non-Mainstream Media Sources 109

Websites that Give a Stage to Censored Doctors and Scientists 111

Websites With a Large Amount of Censored Material....................112

Researching the Efficacy of the mRNA Vaccine.........................113

Studies on Face Masks, Nano Technologies in the Vaccines
and More...113

Recommended Books..115

Chapter 2: The Doctrine of the Pre-Tribulation Rapture – The
Great Blessed Hope, or a Tragic Delusion?............................117

Introduction...118

Building the Foundations Part 1: The Origins and Concept of
Rapture in Scripture 120

Building the Foundations Part 2: Four Main Views 127

Main Claims of the Pre-Tribulation Viewpoint 127

Main Claims of the Mid-Tribulation Viewpoint *129*
Main Claims of the Post-Tribulation Viewpoint *130*
Main Claims of the Pre-Wrath Viewpoint *131*

Building the Foundations Part 3: Each of Us Needs Each Other
   So We Can See the Whole Picture 133

The Middle Eastern Hebraic Mindset 134

Logic and Mental Processing — Linear Versus Cyclical *135*
Numbers in the Middle Eastern Hebraic Mindset *137*

The Mindset and Background Behind the Pre-Tribulation
   Viewpoint 141

Reflections on the Pre-Tribulation View 145

The New Covenant Versus the Old Covenant *145*
Yeshua and the Old Covenant *147*
The First Century Believers and the Old Covenant *150*
But Didn't God Establish 'A New Thing' Through Yeshua? *151*
But Didn't Many in Israel Reject Their Own Messiah? *153*
Shaul (Paul) and the Nation of Israel *154*
Has God Cast Away His People Israel? *155*
The Olive Tree *157*
First The Fullness of the Gentiles and Only Then All Israel
   Shall be Saved *163*

The Good News and the Cyclical Hebraic Mindset 167

Our Fathers Under Moses and the Good News Message *167*
The Tabernacle, the Temple, and the Good News Message *170*

Israel and the Rapture 173

The First Rapture is Physical *173*
The Second Rapture is Spiritual *175*
The Third Rapture is Both Spiritual and Physical *177*

Noah, Lot, and the Rapture 181

A Summary 182

Assessment of Common Pre-Tribulation Claims 185

Assessment of Some Mid-Tribulation Claims................................209

Conclusions and a Call to Be Open-Minded 212

Chapter 2: Appendices..213

Appendix 1: Daniel's Seventy Weeks 214

Introduction *214*
A Short Summary of Related Historic Events................................*215*
Seventy Weeks Are Determined... ....*216*
Different Interpretations of Daniel's Seventy Weeks......................*218*
Different Presuppositions...*224*
The Birth of Preterism and Futurism *226*
Daniel's Seventieth Week, Messiah, and the Anti-Messiah
   Until the 17th-18th Centuries...*228*
Back to the Middle Eastern Hebraic Lens *228*
Author's Take..*239*
Messiah Yeshua and Daniel 9:24 ....*244*
Messiah Yeshua and Daniel 9:26-27 ....*244*
The Anti-Messiah and Daniel 9:26-27 ....*246*
Anti-Messiah attempting to imitate Messiah Yeshua *248*
Daniel's Seventy Weeks Has Multiple Progressive Fulfillments.......*249*

Appendix 2: Respected Traditional Commentaries on
   Daniel 9:24-27 Up Until the 19th Century CE 253

Appendix 3: Illustrations 257

Book of Daniel – Time Table...*257*
The Jewish Sages View...*260*
The Catholic View..*261*
The Seventh Day Adventist View...*262*
The Popular Protestant View *263*

Alternative Views..*264*

Chapter 3: A Call to Get Back to the Model Used By Yeshua's
   Body In the First Century 265

Introduction..266

The Middle Eastern Hebraic Roots of Yeshua's Body....................269

The Hebrew Behind the Greek *269*
Called Out from the Very Beginning..............................*270*
Hebrew Names of the Called Out and Their Deeper Meanings.......*272*

First Century Model of Yeshua's Body 279

Places of Gathering..*281*
Seating Arrangements *283*
Order of Service *285*
The Apostles' Doctrine *288*
Fellowship...*292*
Breaking of Bread *305*
Prayer *306*

A Call to Adopt the First Century Model 307

*The Covid Crisis and God's Calling for a Reset within His
   Own Body*..*307*
Home Gatherings..*308*
Community Living *309*
Home Gatherings' Size and Name..................................*309*
Everyone Should Participate *311*
Children, Young Adults and Community Living.....................*312*

The First Century Model — A Short Summary 313

Chapter 3: Appendices...315

Appendix 1: The Preferable Day of Gathering.....................316

Appendix 2: The Lord's Supper in the First Century.............322

Appendix 3: Water Immersion in the First Century 326

Appendix 4: Worship 329

Appendix 5: Suggested Order of Service...341

Appendix 6: Yeshua's Body and the Torah.....................................344

GOD'S GREAT RESET: Closing Words...369

Thanks and Dedications

This book went through many hardships, which required quite a few cleansings, modifications and polishings due to its very challenging approach to some controversial theological issues.

I would like to extend my thanks, gratitude and appreciation to all who came along side and helped me to arrive at this point.

First, I would like to extend my gratitude to **Shira,** for being the first to work on the original (pretty messy) manuscript. I thank you, Shira, for your encouragement, your patience and your professionalism in a way that made it much easier to read and understand!

Second, I would like to extend my gratitude to you all, my proofreaders, for inserting your valuable comments, recommendations and corrections, without which I would not have been able to arrive at this end point! Thank you, **Cookie**. Thank you, **Inge**. Thank you, **Liron**. Thank you, **Kees**, and lastly, but not less importantly, thank you, **Nirit** and **Maureen,** for putting the last touch on the final manuscript. Thank you all who preferred to stay anonymous! Forever grateful to each and every one of you!

I would like to thank you **Gabriela**, my precious wife, for continuing to stand with me throughout these last 38 years, even though I'm such an "out-of-the-box" person! ☺

Most importantly, I thank You O God - the God of my fathers - Abraham, Isaac, and Jacob, for Your abundant grace and mercies! Thank You mostly for Your only Begotten Son – Yeshua of Nazareth – the very Messiah, King of Israel, who saved me from my sins and failures, and welcomed me into His Kingdom, Your Kingdom precious Abba Father!

Yosef Rachamim Danieli.

General Introduction

Dear Reader,

Yeshua of Nazareth,[1] whom I consider to be the Son of the Living God and the greatest of all men who ever lived on Earth, said the following words two thousand years ago, when referring to the days approaching His glorious return (Second Coming):

Take heed that no one deceives you. For many will come in in My name, saying, 'I am the Messiah,' and will deceive many. And you will hear of wars and rumors of wars. See that you are not troubled for all these things must come to pass, but the end is not yet. For nation will rise against nation, and kingdom against kingdom, and there will be famines, pestilences, and earthquakes in various places. All these are the beginning of sorrows. Then they will deliver you up to teribulation and kill you, and you will be hated by all nations for My name's sake. And then many will be offended, will betray one another, and will hate one another. Then many false prophets will rise up and deceive many. And because lawlessness will abound, the love of many will grow cold. But he who endures to the end shall be saved. And this gospel of the kingdom will be preached in all the world as a witness to all the nations, and then the end will come...

Looking at the present-day world while pondering on Yeshua's above words, persuade me that we are indeed living in very interesting times, to say the least.

More than three years have passed since our world was introduced to what has been officially referred to as "the Covid-19 pandemic."

---

[1] *Yeshua* – The Hebrew name of Jesus. In Hebrew, it literally means *Salvation*.

1

In June 2022, it seemed as if this pandemic was finally behind us as life started going back to normal. However, recently we hear voices around the world from governmental officials that this pandemic is not over yet, and moreover, there is a high chance we will soon face "yet another Corona wave – much bigger than the previous..." Other than potential new Corona waves, different global experts predict new pandemics (such as tuberculosis), economic collapse, severe food shortages, increasing global warming due to a global climate change and more...

As if this weren't enough, our present world is experiencing *wars and rumors of wars,* such as the present Russian-Ukrainian war that some predict will lead to a third world war, which might lead into a nuclear exchange between the USA, NATO and Russia... add to it the growing tension between Israel and Iran, the tension between the East (led by China) and the West, and the overall picture is pretty clear, I think.

Could it be that the Covid-19 pandemic has been a major and integral part of the above end-time signs? Could it be that it even served as an important catalyst ushering in what I call "the beginning of the end?" Could it be that it actually served as a forerunner to events our world will soon face; events that will usher in the glorious return of our Messiah King?

Here, I would like to repeat one sentence from Yeshua's above statements:

Take heed that no one deceives you, for many will come in My name, saying, 'I am the Messiah,' and will <u>deceive</u> many (emphasis added).

These kinds of warnings about false messiahs and deception <u>in an end-time context</u>, are repeated time and again throughout Scripture.[2] The sad truth is that deception remains relevant not only within an end-time context, but also throughout the history of humanity!

Since that first sin took place in the Garden of Eden, it seems that the Serpent, Satan, has had permission to deceive and influence humanity. Satan has especially targeted those who wish to follow their Creator's commandments and holy principles, including Yeshua's own body of believers![3]

When describing *the Kingdom*, Messiah, who often spoke in parables, described *a fishing net* filled with all kinds of fish – kosher (clean) and non-kosher – which are separated <u>only at the end</u> of the process.[4] He also spoke of *wheat and tares,* which are also separated <u>only at the very end</u>, when the great harvest takes place![5] Thus, I do believe that Yeshua's body has always been comprised of both true, born-again, and fake, very fleshly believers! Our hope is to not be among the latter!

---

[2] See Matt. 7:15, 24:11; Mk. 13:22; 2 Cor. 11:13, 26; Gal. 2:4; 2 Pet. 2:1; 1 Jn. 4:1, and more. In Hebrew, "Messiah" (*Mashiach*), is one who is anointed with *Shemen Hamishchah* – the anointing oil with which kings and priests were anointed. *False teachers* and *false prophets* can be included in this description of *false messiahs* as they claim the anointing of Messiah upon their (false) words. More on that later...

[3] In the Greek manuscript of the New Covenant writings, "body of Yeshua" appears as the *ecclesia* (often translated as "the Church." See chapter 3 – "A Call to Get Back to the Model Used by Yeshua's Body in the First Century").

[4] See Matt. 13:47-51.

[5] See Matt. 13:24-30.

In 2020, an interesting book, *Covid-19: The Great Reset,* written by a man named Klaus Schwab, was published.[6] In his book, Schwab claims that our world is in urgent need of "a great reset." He continues to claim that Covid-19 should be utilized as a catalyst for this reset. In the opening chapter of *this* book, I deal in greater detail with this *great reset* and its close connection to what world leaders over many decades have referred to as, *the New World Order.*

I would like to raise a few challenging questions: Is Yeshua's body also in need of "a great reset," at least as it relates to some long-held man-made traditions and doctrines, which were never really based on Scripture? Has the time arrived to take an in-depth look at some of these man-made traditions and doctrines, especially as they relate to the end times in which we are living these very days?

It would be presumptuous to claim that the full content of this book is the whole truth and nothing but the truth. Nor do I, the author, possess all truth! It is my firm belief that we need one another if we wish to get to all the truths pertaining to the Good News of His Kingdom!

This book that you are about to read contains three chapters: (1) The opening one deals with the recent Covid-19 pandemic. In it, I attempt to objectively examine the commonly known and widely accepted official narrative, while considering also the not-so-popular narrative held by doctors and scientists, who claim to base their conclusions on true scientific evidence! I especially examine this new pandemic in the scriptural end-time context. (2) The second chapter deals with a pretty controversial doctrine in Yeshua's present-day body – the pre-

---

[6] See, https://www.amazon.com/COVID-19-Great-Reset-Klaus-Schwab/dp/2940631123/ref=sr_1_1?crid=3IYBEMQMP5B0G&keywords=covid+19+and+the+great+reset+klaus+schwab&qid=1666943534&qu=eyJxc2MiOiIwLjY3Iiwi cXNhIjoiMC41NCIsInFzcCI6IjAuNjIifQ%3D%3D&sprefix=Covid+19+and+the+%2Caps%2C288&sr=8-1 (more about Mr. Schwab and the organization he heads, in the opening chapter).

Tribulation Rapture. In it, I look at Scripture and carefully examine what it has to say regarding Yeshua's glorious Second Coming and *our gathering unto Him*, while attempting to answer some of the main claims[7] of those who hold to the pre-Tribulation Rapture doctrine and maintain its validity. (3) The closing chapter deals with some major differences existing between the present-day model in which Yeshua's body functions, as opposed to the one used by His followers in the first century, while suggesting an urgent need to get back to that first century prototype.

The connection between the three chapters is simple: If Covid-19 is indeed "the beginning of the end," is it not true that an integral part of the end is the soon reign of the Anti-Messiah (anti-Christ) over our world? Should we be reliant on the notion of an imminent (pre-Tribulation) Rapture experience? Is this doctrine really based on Scripture? What if we are not going to be snatched out of this world before the Anti-Messiah is revealed? Lastly, if Scripture indicates that we are going to remain here on earth while the Anti-Messiah reigns and inflicts his fierce persecution against Messiah's true followers, will we still be able to continue to fellowship using today's congregational model? Could it be that the sovereign God is urging all of us to get back to the first century model of fellowship, especially during the Anti-Messiah's rule over this world?

I am convinced that in order to fully understand the three topics dealt with in this book, one must first be acquainted with the Middle Eastern Hebraic Jewish mindset, or lens. After all, this is the only lens through which Scripture was written! Thus, all three chapters discuss and highlight different aspects of this original lens. The following is a small example.

---

[7] Claims that I have gathered from simple online surfing, as well as conversing with quite a few brethren who hold to this doctrine.

One of the main characteristics of the Middle Eastern Hebraic Jewish mindset is that it is *cyclical* in nature. As the wisest man proclaimed so long ago: *That which has been is what will be, that which is done is what will be done, and <u>there is nothing new under the sun</u>!*[8] Accepting that all of God's Word is true and that its very nature is *cyclical,* leads me to present you with the following questions:

If God is indeed holy and just, and if He expects us, His true followers, to follow His example and ourselves *be holy,* reject lies and fervently seek truth and righteousness, would it not be incumbent upon us to carefully examine what we are told by our authorities concerning Covid-19? Have we so quickly forgotten that this world operates in an antithetical way to true righteousness and justice?

What about the pre-Tribulation Rapture doctrine? If Yeshua rejected false teachings two thousand years ago, why would He accept a potential erroneous doctrine in our modern times, especially if it has the potential of misleading many within His body?

Lastly, if our present congregational model, by which Yeshua's body has functioned over the last 1600 years, has been permitted only temporarily by the Almighty (see more on that in the introduction to chapter 3), and if we seriously understand and accept that *there is nothing new under the sun,* wouldn't it be only logical that Messiah's perfect will for His beloved bride would be that she return to the way in which she was meant to function, as exemplified in the beginning?

My hope is that this book will challenge you to engage in critical thinking as you carefully consider the points outlined concerning these three topics. In fact, I encourage you to take them before our precious

---

[8] Ecc. 1:9. See also verse 10 and other references inside this book.

Savior in prayer to see what conclusions and needed actions He leads you to take.

A Few Words on the Front Cover Artwork

The front cover design was first envisioned by me, the author, and then was very skillfully and professionally designed by **Mr. Todd Angel** from the **BookLocker Publishing House.**

The artwork represents the three topics covered in this book: (1) Covid-19, which is symbolized by a few scattered protein spikes, (2) the doctrine of the pre-Tribulation Rapture, which is symbolized by the people who are caught up to heaven, and lastly, (3) Yeshua's body (the *ecclesia*), which is represented by famous medieval sculptures that depict two women: one representing "the enlightened ecclesia" (i.e., the church), while the other represents "the blinded synagoga" (i.e., Jews and Judaism). These statues can be seen on well-known Catholic churches and signify a complete separation between Israel and the ecclesia, as well as the erroneous doctrine of Replacement Theology.

Throughout this book, I present you with the biblical connection existing between Yeshua's body and the nation of Israel.

The backdrop of these three topics is the end of the age. It is symbolized by the dark sky, and fire and destruction on Earth.

I pray this book will be a great blessing to you!

Yosef Rachamim Danieli

Chapter 1:

Covid 19 – The Beginning of the End?

Introduction

As previously stated, more than three years have passed since our world was introduced to the Covid-19 pandemic.

Most of the world's nations, including Israel, responded to this new pandemic by imposing harsh restrictions, such as: lockdowns, limitations on the number of indoor gatherings, mandatory wearing of face masks[9], the cancelation of public events and the closure of all non-essential institutions and businesses.

These measures led to some terrible outcomes. What follows is only a very short list of the ramifications thus far:

- A lack of clarity concerning the future, leading to worry, fear, and anxiety

- An ever-increasing number of people needing psychological and psychiatric counseling

- A spike in domestic violence and abuse

- An increase in the number of suicide attempts, including a rapid rise amongst children and youth

- Growing inflation

- The collapse of numerous small and medium-sized businesses

- Separations and divisions among families, spouses, friends as well as among brethren in Yeshua!

---

[9] Israel is one of only a few countries that required its citizens to wear face masks even in open spaces until April 2021!

Indeed, this Covid-19 crisis has dramatically changed the world in which we live. Whether we like it or not, we can sense "a new normal" all around us. Moreover, we are told by different medical authorities, such as the World Health Organization – WHO – and local ministries of health, that the main and only effective solution for fighting this, as well as future pandemics, is new mRNA-based vaccines. Since the first dose of this new vaccine was implemented somewhere at the end of December 2019, people have been highly encouraged to take the second, third, fourth and even fifth dose, with the three last shots being described as "boosters."

Moreover, it seems that up until the beginning of 2022, the mainstream media throughout the world had been almost entirely occupied with one topic—new developments as they related to the Covid-19 pandemic. They painted a picture that claimed, "This dangerous pandemic is threatening mankind's very existence!" At the very start, somewhere around March 2020, they emphasized the number of new patients, newly added critically ill patients, the rising numbers of Covid deaths and so on. Day and night we heard reports about the great efforts of different vaccine companies to push forward and develop vaccines, which would hopefully be effective against both the original Covid-19 virus and its growing number of variants.

Yet, an increasing number of people around the world became suspicious, causing a growing trend of not blindly accepting the official (authorities') narrative. An ever-growing number of people throughout the world have claimed that one should not automatically trust the mainstream media, and that one should instead check "the real news" or "real scientific data" elsewhere. Where is that "elsewhere?" - on different alternative social media sites. Indeed, when "daring" to check these alternative sources, one can find a wealth of data related to this Covid-19 crisis.[10] Needless to say, the data there does *not* support the information we have heard via the mainstream sources.

Interviews with various doctors, professors, scientists, and world-renowned professionals have been published on many alternative sites. Most of them claim that the whole crisis has been "vastly overblown." Some of them state that the world governments' treatment of the crisis has *not* been professional *nor* based on true science! According to them, the Covid-19 disease has been "much lighter" than presented in the mainstream media and was treatable, even "easily curable," without the need for new mRNA-based vaccines! According to some of them, the lockdowns and social distancing never prevented the spread of viruses and in fact, did more harm than good.

Some world-renowned professionals have stated that these new vaccines (again, based on the new synthetic component—in the form of mRNA) have neither been approved by the FDA, nor tested using traditional methods as was done with past vaccines. Additionally, some of the ingredients in these new vaccines have been kept secret and thus, might even contain dangerous chemicals! Since these new vaccines have never been tested according to the traditional method, those world-renowned professionals say that there is no real way to check their short-term, and certainly not their long-term side effects. More on this later.

The two approaches above – the official authorities' narrative as well as the alternative perspective, have been so controvertibly different, that it has resulted in quite a bit of confusion, frustration, and division

---

[10] At the end of this chapter, I present you with a few alternative media sources for your own personal review and research.

in societies throughout the world. On the one hand, there are those who have chosen to fully believe and trust everything that has been said and presented to them by the authorities (using the mainstream media); while on the other hand, there are those who have completely lost their trust in both of these sources. Needless to say, as with any complex issue, some have also preferred to "sit on the fence and wait," rather than taking any side in this dispute.

This opening chapter is an attempt to address some very important questions:

- Is it at all possible to determine the truth about this recent world crisis?

- Is it possible to know where our world is headed in light of that specific crisis?

and, perhaps the most important question:

- Where should we, as followers of Yeshua, stand? Is there a certain position which we should hold, or can we just continue our lives "as normal" and keep our hands "clean" from any kind of involvement in this pretty fierce debate?

As many of you already know, I'm a tour guide by profession and, while it is true that I do have a small amount of basic medical training (a medic and later a psychiatric male nurse), I am certainly not a doctor, a professor or a scientist! The following is my limited attempt to shed mainly some *spiritual light* on this "hot button" issue. In other words: I would like to explain *the spiritual roots* of this recent crisis and its only true solution, or cure, that is provided in Scripture.

It is my hope that this opening chapter serves as a tool that will provide a small glimpse of how God sees these current world events.

Unless we see "the big picture," i.e., from God's heavenly perspective, we will never be able to get to the objective truth regarding the Covid-19 crisis nor other major crises which will undoubtedly follow and increase in magnitude, prior to Messiah's glorious return.

The Big Picture - Part 1:
Solo Night Navigation

Years ago, just as almost every other Israeli citizen, I served in the Israeli Defense Forces (IDF), as a combat medic. About midway through my three-year service, I was encouraged to join an officers' school, and so I did. At that school, my colleagues and I went through a lot of theoretical teachings as well as practical training, one of which comprised solo night navigations.

In preparation for this form of night navigation, we were required to study the navigation route during the day, down to the smallest details, as shown on the map. This *day preparation* included memorizing walking directions, studying the sky and its key stars (such as the North Star) and learning the exact distances between each of the path points.

A key to the success of our solo night navigation was studying *the big picture – the background details –* such as *the specific timeframe* allotted for the navigation, *the general direction* between the starting and ending points (North, South, East, or West), *the mountains and ravines within and around the route* and *the possible obstacles* we might encounter (neutral and/or hostile factors). If we were not familiar enough with the details of *the big picture,* our chances of successfully correcting mistakes made while on the actual night navigation would be very low.

Once night had fallen, we climbed aboard an army vehicle, and each of us was left alone at the starting point of his personal navigation route. We were all provided with *a sealed map* which we were permitted to open only in the event that we got completely lost; and *a sealed compass,* also to be used if we became completely disoriented!

Studying God's Navigation Map in Yeshua's Light

Our world can be pictured as *a big forest* (or *navigation area*), through which each and every one of us has to navigate their life. The forest of this world has many trees, different mountains, and ravines, as well as quite a few obstacles. Our Creator has also given each of us *a starting point*— the day we were born and *an endpoint*— the day we will die. Just as in the military's solo night navigations, so it is with our lives in this world. If we wish to finish our *solo night navigation* successfully, we must study hard and memorize a very specific "navigation map" for the task: God's Word – Scripture, which have been entrusted into our hands so that we can prepare for and have a very successful, blessed "navigation," while being *pilgrims and sojourners* in this present world.

Yeshua said, *I am the light of the world. He who follows Me shall not walk in darkness but have the light of life... As long as I am in the world, I am the light of the world!*[11] Allow me to elaborate on these very strong statements made by our Messiah Redeemer.

Darkness already entered this world as we see in Genesis 3, when Adam and Eve disobeyed God and were banished from the Garden! Yeshua, the One true Light, interrupted this spiritual darkness when He came into this world 2,000 years ago. When He left by ascending back to His Father's throne, "the darkness of the night" returned to

---

[11] See Jn. 8:12, 9:5. See also Jn. 11:10, 12:35-36.

this world! Yes, since then, the entire non-believing world has been in complete (spiritual) darkness!

As I needed to study and memorize all the details pertaining to my solo night navigation route, *during daylight*, we, true followers of Messiah Yeshua, need as well to study and memorize all the details pertaining to our own solo night navigation routes through this (*spiritually*) darkened world, doing it in *His daylight;* i.e., attuned to His Spirit, His voice, especially as portrayed to us in *His Holy Word—* our "navigation map."

God's Compass

What is the *compass* with which we were entrusted as followers of Yeshua? In Hebrew, there is a direct linguistic connection between the words for *compass* (*matzpen* — מצפן), *north* (*tzaphon* — צפון) and *conscience* (*matzpoon* — מצפון). Through and by the blood of the Lamb, our clean conscience serves as our *North Star.* As believers, His Spirit guides us in the direction in which we should go. If we really want to successfully finish our *solo night navigation* through this dark world, we must also equip ourselves with His conscience—His *compass.*

Beloved brothers and sisters, if our sincere desire is to continue to be and reflect Messiah's very light in this dark world, we must first *locate and identify* this recent Covid-19 crisis on *God's navigation map!* On the one hand, we have by no means been called to become delusional, anarchists, or God forbid, opponents of the authorities whom God has put over us. Yet, on the other hand, we were never called to be naïve, or to believe and trust everything we are told by mere flesh and blood! To the contrary, we were called to assess and weigh everything by His Spirit, and then take, or adopt, whatever is good and profitable for our spiritual walk and growth in Him, and discard, or reject whatever is a lie, deceitful or a stumbling block to our walk and growth in Him! We must carefully examine all evidence presented to us, while listening and being sensitive to the Holy Spirit, asking Him to guide us so that we can grasp how to see things in the way He, our gracious Creator, sees them!

So, let us now dive into *the navigation details* pertaining to this recent world crisis.

The Specific Timeframe on God's Prophetic Clock

As mentioned above, for soldiers in the IDF officers' school, one of the background details with which we needed to be familiar before getting started with our solo night navigation route, was the specific timeframe allotted for each of the navigation exercises. As we are already equipped with the *navigation map* and *compass* with which God has entrusted us, we now need to carefully check the timeframe in which this Covid-19 crisis appears.

Can we really know the timeframe that has been allotted to us by God for this specific Covid-19 night navigation route? Do we trust that God, who has already equipped us with His navigation map and compass, will also equip us with the relevant timeframe? Have we forgotten that God *does* wish for us to discern *the times and seasons* in which we are living?

Expectations for Messiah's Return

As we all know, there have been expectations for the return of the Messiah over the course of the last 2,000 years, throughout every generation. For instance, towards the beginning of the second millennium following His First Coming, there were very high expectations, both in Christianity (mostly Roman Catholicism), which led to the known Crusader journeys to the Holy Land (to cleanse and redeem it of its infidels); and within Judaism, where many rabbis, together with their dedicated disciples, immigrated to the Holy Land. During World War II, many (including some true believers) were sure that Hitler was the Anti-Messiah and thus, they were confident that Yeshua's glorious return was just around the corner!

Based on the above, many modern-day believers throughout the world have said, "Come on, you know that in every past generation people also thought He was coming in their time. It is simply impossible to really know when He will return. Actually, it is not even worthwhile to try to think or claim that we are really at the end of this age, lest we too become severely disappointed and mislead others as well!"

Now, it is very true that Yeshua stated: *Of that day and hour, no one knows, not even the angels of heaven, but My Father only!* Yet, in the very same context, He also said: *Now learn this parable from the fig tree … so you also, when you see all these things, know that it is near – at the door*[12] (emphasis added).

When we *lift our heads* and *look up*, in these very days, are we able to see certain background details that point to our Messiah's soon-to-come glorious return?

It is my understanding of God's "navigation map" which leads me to think that we are indeed very close to Yeshua's return! There are many signs or indications that prove, beyond any shadow of doubt, that we are living in the last days. In the following pages, I will present you with just a few of these.

---

[12] See Matt. 24:36. See also Mk. 13:28-29; Lk. 21:28-31.

The Latter Days

The above title (in Hebrew, *Acharit Hayamim* — אחרית הימים) appears many times on God's navigation map.[13] An in-depth study of God's Word reveals that these *latter days* began with Yeshua's First Coming, about two thousand years ago, and are about to end with His Second Coming.[14]

From the words of Messiah Himself, as well as His various apostles, it can be understood that there were high expectations for His return in their own time, i.e., the first century CE.[15] Thus, how much closer are we to the end of this period called, *the latter days* than they were?!

Our Lord, will you at this time restore the Kingdom to Israel?[16]

This question was asked by the disciples of Yeshua just before He ascended back to heaven right before their eyes. The immediate context is very important. It was the fortieth day since Yeshua had appeared to His disciples *as the resurrected Messiah*! As I mentioned above, as many others in their generation, Yeshua's disciples also thought and believed that Messiah would come in their own generation. Moreover, once Yeshua's true identity as *the Living Son of God* had been revealed, as they saw Him in His glorious, immortal, resurrected body, they were absolutely certain that during their

---

[13] See, for example, Gen. 49:1; Num. 24:14; Deut. 4:30; Isa. 2:2; Jer. 23:20, 30:24; Ezek. 38:16; Hos. 3:5; Micah 4:1; Dan. 10:14.

[14] See Acts 2:17; 1 Tim. 4:1; 2 Tim. 3:1; Heb. 1:1; 1 Pet. 1:20; 2 Pet. 3:3; Jude 18.

[15] See, for example, Matt. 10:16-25, especially verse 23; and 24:32-44, especially verse 34; Rom. 13:11; 1 Cor. 7:29; Jam. 5:8; 1 Jn. 2:18; and Rev. 1:3, 3:3.

[16] See Acts 1:6-7.

lifetime, He would bring about the end of the Roman occupation and finally establish the Kingdom of Israel over all the earth!

Nevertheless, what was Yeshua's clear answer? *It is not for you to know the times and the seasons which the Father has set in His own power.* To what exactly did these *times and seasons* refer? According to the immediate context, they referred to the establishment of *the Kingdom of Israel* here on Earth!

In the following verses, Yeshua instructs His disciples to return to Jerusalem (from the Mount of Olives) and wait there for the fulfillment of the promise concerning the Holy Spirit, who would help them preach and spread the gospel throughout the entire world. In other words, the good news (the gospel) of the Kingdom, was *first* to be proclaimed to both Jews and gentiles around the world, and *only then* would the Kingdom of Israel be fully established physically—here, in the Land of Israel.[17]

Now to the main point. Only a few minutes after Yeshua's response to the disciples' question, He ascended to heaven on a cloud, in front of their very eyes. About forty years later, the Romans destroyed the Temple and exiled most of the Jews from their land – an event that marked the longest Jewish exile ever of almost 2,000 years! Since that tragedy in 70 CE, there was *no generation* where it would have been possible to say that the establishment of the Kingdom of Israel was imminent! Why? Simply because for the Kingdom of Israel to have been established here on Earth, three main conditions would have needed to occur:

---

[17] See Acts 7-8. An idea closely related and similar can be seen in the following references: Matt. 24:14, 28:19; Lk. 21:24; Rom. 11:25.

a. The return of the King Himself, who, since that event on the Mount of Olives, has been sitting at the right hand of the Father.

b. The return of the people of Israel back to their ancient Promised Land, and finally,

c. The people of Israel themselves being sovereign over their inheritance—the land of Israel.

Condition *b* began to take shape about one hundred and fifty years ago through what is known as *modern Zionism*—the means by which God started to gather His covenant people from *the four corners of the Earth* back to the land He promised to give them forever and ever. Condition *c* was fulfilled in 1948, when Israel became sovereign over her Promised Land. Now, since conditions *b* and *c* stand – after almost two thousand years – I believe the stage for Yeshua's return (condition *a*) has been fully prepared; thus, Yeshua's glorious return to *restore the Kingdom to Israel* is truly at the door!

This might raise the following legitimate question: Why should anyone think it will happen in our own generation? Why not in future generations? Why not during the generation of our grandchildren or even great-grandchildren? In other words, why not in another hundred or even hundreds of years? I believe the following points will provide the answer.

After two days He will revive us, on the third day He will raise us up and we shall live in His sight.[18]

In chapters two and three, I will discuss in great detail the Hebraic/Jewish Middle Eastern mindset and culture, by which

---

[18] See Hos. 6:2.

Scripture was written and given to us all. Here I would like to outline some primary points.

In the general introduction, I said that one of the main characteristics of this mindset and culture is that *there is nothing new under the sun* and that almost everything is *cyclical* (i.e., repetitive). Here I would like to add: Prophecies usually have more than one fulfillment. The Old Covenant writings – the *Tanach*[19] are filled with *pictures, foreshadowings* and *patterns*. Lastly, *numbers* are understood not merely as quantities but also as spiritually significant.

When the Book of Hosea is read through the Middle Eastern or Hebraic lens, a few interesting things emerge. The prophet says that God is going to revive His Chosen Nation *after* two days and that, *on the third day,* He will raise her up.

In Scripture, the number 3 is very significant. It was on the *third* day of Creation that God declared twice, *it is good!*[20] It was at *the beginning of the third* decade that our ancestor Jacob was restored by God back to his homeland.[21] It was at *the beginning of the third* decade that

---

[19] *Tanach,* (or "Tanakh"). A Hebrew acronym of three words: *Torah* (the teachings of Moses, the five first books of the Bible); *Nevi'im* (the Prophets) and *K'tuvim* (the Writings).

[20] See Gen. 1:9-13. This is the very reason why some Orthodox Jewish groups have developed the concept of "twice as good," and prefer their wedding celebrations to take place on the third day of the week. Please note that the famous wedding at Cana of Galilee also took place *on the third day* (Jn. 2).

[21] From his *long exile* in Haran (see Gen. 31:36-42).

Joseph made himself known to his brothers in Egypt.[22] It was *at the beginning of the third* day that Yeshua rose from the dead.[23]

We also know that as far as God is concerned, *one day is as a thousand years, and a thousand years as one day.*[24] So, allow me to ask you: How many *days*, i.e., thousands of years, have passed since Yeshua ascended back to Heaven? Almost two! Plus, if we start our counting at the birth of Yeshua (somewhere around 4 or 5 BCE[25]), we are now at the very beginning of *the third day!*

Based on the above pattern, that relates to the number 3, here are some interesting insights:

    a. The nation of Israel is following in the steps of her forefather Jacob, as she is being restored to her own Promised Land *at the beginning of the third day* (millennium) since Yeshua's First Coming.

    b. Messiah Yeshua – following His prototype, Joseph, is going to reveal Himself to His beloved nation *at the beginning of the third day* (millennium).

    c. Israel is going to be resurrected from her spiritual *sleep* – or death – *at the very beginning of the third day* (millennium), on God's prophetic calendar, which fits perfectly with our own time period.[26]

---

[22] Gen. 37:2; 41:46, 53; 45:6.

[23] Matt. 16:21, 17:23, 20:19; and the parallels in the other Gospels, as well as in the writings of the Apostle Shaul (Paul).

[24] See Ps. 90:4 and 2 Pet. 3:8.

[25] BCE - Before Common Era. CE – Common Era.

[26] See Ezek. 37.

***Assuredly I say to you that this generation will by no means pass away until all these things take place!*[27]**

Yeshua proclaimed these words within the immediate context of His description concerning the End Times, which will include His glorious return. In chapter two, I will discuss this specific statement which He made in greater detail. Here, I would like to discuss only the following:

Since Yeshua spoke of *this generation,* it is pretty clear that He was indeed pointing to *one specific generation*! Yet, if read and understand Scripture while using the Hebraic/Jewish lens – or thought processes (i.e., the cyclical or repetitive manner of this perspective), and acknowledge the simple fact that He did not return in the first century, it is clear that Yeshua's words were aimed both at *His own first century generation* and at *the very last generation*, which will welcome Him when He returns.

What is *a generation* (Hebrew, *dor* - דור)? How many years is *a generation?* Scripture offers more than one answer. In fact, when read in Hebrew, *dor* does not speak of someone's age, but rather of someone who is born *to dwell* in this world (in Hebrew, *la-dur* - לדור). Thus, a *dor* can last from only a few years all the way up to one hundred or more years.[28] There can be a few generations living side by side at the very same *dor* (parents, children, grandchildren, great-grandchildren and so on). This is not the place to expound on it, but when Yeshua talked about *this generation,* there were at least four of them in existence (fathers, sons, grandsons, and great-grandsons). Thus, I believe it will also be as such in the *last generation*. When exactly will Yeshua return? Will it be in our *dor?* Will it be in our

---

[27] See Matt. 24:34.

[28] See, for example, Gen. 15:13-16; Ex. 12:40; Ps. 90:10 and others.

children's *dor?* Does this *dor* already include our parents and their parents? Does it include our children? Does it include our grandchildren? It might very well be that the answer to all the above questions is, *yes.*

My personal opinion is that we *are* living in this timeframe of *the last generation* and that we are the ones who are going to see His glorious return, soon, in our time.

The Big Picture - Part 2:
Deception — The Main Characteristic
of the End Times

Some of the main things which characterize the end of *the latter days* period – i.e., prior to Yeshua's glorious return – are: <u>deception</u>, <u>lies</u> and <u>falsehoods</u>, which are instigated by the greatest liar of all— Satan![29] Going back to the analogy of this world as *a big forest* (or *a navigation area*), and our need to *navigate through its dark night*, we can assume that the different *obstacles* on our solo night navigation route will be likewise characterized by deception. The following are only a few of the many Scripture references to these *obstacles*.

When asked about His return and the end of the age, the first thing Yeshua said was, *take heed that no one <u>deceives</u> you!*[30] Of course, the immediate context of this sentence relates to *false messiahs* who would appear, saying, *I am he.* In my understanding, Yeshua was speaking of the false teachers and prophets <u>within</u> His very body, who say, "come to me, listen to me; Messiah's anointing oil is upon me..."[31] Yeshua also said, *false prophets will arise and deceive many;* and, worst of all, they will try to deceive *even the elect!*[32]

---

[29] See Rev. 12:9, 20:2.

[30] See Matt. 24:4.

[31] As most of us know, *Christ* comes from the Hebrew word *Mashiach,* which comes from *shemen haMishchah* — the *anointing oil* with which priests and kings were anointed. Needless to say, this anointing oil symbolized the Holy Spirit.

[32] See Matt. 11:24; Mk. 13:22.

The Apostle John in his first epistle, warns against those false prophets and encourages us all not to believe any spirit, but rather to *examine the spirits, [as to] whether [they are] from God or not!*[33]

Generally speaking, God's navigation map – Scripture - clearly states that in this world there are actually only two kingdoms: 1) *the kingdom of darkness*—in which most of the world operates, and 2) *the Kingdom of His Beloved*, or *the kingdom of light*, in which only true followers of Messiah Yeshua operate![34] This same map also tells us that *our citizenship is in Heaven*; and thus, our thoughts should not be directed toward this physical world, but rather upwards—toward Heaven.[35] True followers of Israel's Messiah who are well-acquainted with His navigation map are supposed to know the identity of the one who rules the hearts and minds of the unredeemed people of this world.[36]

Justice, Justice Shall You Pursue!

Isaiah cried out, *and the truth is absent, and the wicked departed from the fear of the Lord, and it is evil in His sight, for there is no judgment.*[37] The Torah explicitly admonishes, *justice, justice shall you pursue!* (In Hebrew, *tsedek, tsedek tirdof* —צדק, צדק תרדוף).[38] "Justice" is a term usually associated with courtrooms, where it is supposed to be handed down. Judges are supposed to hear *both sides* and only then

---

[33] See 1 Jn. 4:1.

[34] See Col. 1:13.

[35] See Phil. 3:20; Col. 3:1-4.

[36] See Lk. 3:5-7. Note that Yeshua did not argue with Satan when he stated, *All the kingdoms of this world were given to me...*

[37] See Isa. 59:15.

[38] See Deut. 16:20. Other translations read: *That which is altogether just shalt thou follow.*

decide which side is telling the truth, thus administering true justice! *Justice can only exist if it is based and founded upon truth!* Needless to say, as believers we know who the greatest and most just judge of all is—the God of Israel! We also know who the One Righteous Man is, the One who paid the just price for humanity's sin—Yeshua the Messiah!

We who believe in Yeshua have been called to side with and hold onto *the truth and the truth alone!* We are exhorted to discern between the spirits. We are not called to be mixed with, nor influenced by this world. We are called to follow our forefathers – the children of Israel – who, while living in Egypt (a picture of this world), did not completely mix with its pagan Egyptian inhabitants, but rather lived in Goshen. Following their example, we should know that even though we live in this world, *Egypt,* we are not really part of it!³⁹

Yeshua said to His disciples, *you shall know <u>the truth</u> and <u>the truth</u> shall set you free!* Yeshua further said, *and the <u>Spirit of Truth</u>, when He shall come, will guide you into <u>all truth</u>; for He will not speak of Himself, but whatever He hears, that He will speak...* And moreover, *you say that I am a king. For this purpose, I was born and for this purpose I have come into the world—to bear witness to <u>the truth</u>. Everyone who is <u>of the truth</u> listens to my voice!*⁴⁰ (emphasis added).

The Apostle Shaul⁴¹ said, *for the wrath of God is revealed from Heaven against all ungodliness and <u>unrighteousness</u> of men, who hold <u>the truth in unrighteousness</u>.* He added, *therefore let us celebrate the*

---

³⁹ See Gen. 46:28–47:6; Jn. 15:18-19, 17:13-16; 1 Cor. 5:9-13; and more.

⁴⁰ See Jn. 8:32, 16:13, 18:37.

⁴¹ "Shaul" – The Hebrew spelling and pronunciation of *Saul* (in this specific case, Paul the apostle).

feast, not with old leaven, neither with the leaven of malice and wickedness; but with the unleavened bread (matzah) of sincerity and truth ... [Love] ... does not rejoice in injustice, [but] rather rejoices in the truth. Speaking of the weapons of God, the famous apostle said, *by truthful speech, and the power of God; with the weapons of righteousness for the right hand and for the left; Because we can do nothing against the truth but for the truth; and, stand therefore, having fastened on the belt of truth.*[42] (emphasis added).

It is clear to me that some of the above-mentioned references speak of absolute divine truth, that which relates directly to the gospel of the kingdom—the salvation and redemption by the precious and atoning blood of Israel's Messiah. At the same time, I do not think it would be accurate to say that our belief in God's absolute divine truth is limited only to the spiritual realm. The opposite is true. Our belief in the absolute truth of Scripture is supposed to lead us, true believers, to desire and cling solely to every truth—in *every* realm of our lives! If we believe in absolute divine truth, how can we in the same breath accept lies—even though they might be "white" or "small lies?" The writers of God's Word were very clear and uncompromising as to the need of the believer who fears His Master to hold fast to *the truth and nothing but the truth*![43]

Turn Aside After Many to Pervert...

Many precious brothers and sisters in Yeshua claim that since there are hundreds of thousands of doctors and scientists who hold to the official narrative regarding the Covid-19 crisis, while only a few

---

[42] See Rom. 1:18; 1 Cor. 5:8, 13:6; 2 Cor. 6:7, 13:8; Eph. 6:14.

[43] See a few examples: Ex. 20:16, 23:7; Lev. 19:11; Isa. 28:15, 59:3; Jer. 7:8; Ps. 101:7, 119:29; Prov. 10:18; Eph. 4:25; Col. 3:9; 1 Jn. 2:21; and many more.

thousand oppose it, we should follow and fully trust the majority. They go on to say, "We should heed the Word of God, which explicitly instructs us to 'obey the authorities!'"[44] Some add, "As believers, we must not relate to any of these 'conspiracy theories' which have been presented on unofficial media channels. We must submit, trust, and accept whatever the authorities tell us, and most of all, we must pray for the people God has put in these positions, continuing our routine as much as possible under these difficult circumstances, until everything works out for the best, by God's Grace!"

Per my understanding of Scripture, while we are called to pray for those who are in authority, the approach described above is incorrect, and is in complete opposition to *the big picture*—God's *navigation map.* Allow me to elaborate.

God's Torah, which is *holy, just and good,*[45] declares: *You shall not follow a crowd to do evil; nor shall you testify in a dispute so as <u>to turn aside after many to pervert</u> (justice).*[46] Some of these very words (*to turn aside after many*) have often been quoted throughout the generations by rabbis who explained that in the case of a dispute between rabbis concerning a specific rabbinical interpretation or instruction, a decision made by the majority should always be honored and completely obeyed! One does not need to be a rabbi or a great theologian to see that these rabbis did not consider the words immediately following – *to pervert* – and actually took this phrase (*to turn aside after many*) completely out of its immediate context! In fact, when the whole verse is read within context, one cannot escape

---

[44] See a detailed discussion on Rom. 13 and 1 Pet. 2 towards the end of this opening chapter.

[45] See Rom. 7:12.

[46] See Ex. 23:2.

the opposite conclusion: *The majority is <u>not</u> always right!* The majority can at times be very wrong, and as a direct outcome, deceive and turn people away from true justice. In other words, the majority can at times pervert justice!

Further, throughout Scripture, those who believed and followed God with their whole hearts, <u>were always a small minority</u>! Most of the time they were looked down upon and considered to be strange, dreamers, rebels against the authority and even mentally ill! The following are only a few examples:

- Moses was forced to flee for his life after trying to execute justice. After returning to Egypt to redeem his people, following God's direct command, he encountered considerable obstacles, objections, and persecution — both in Egypt and later on in the desert journey to the Promised Land.[47]

- At the foot of Mount Sinai, it was only *a minority* who answered Moses' call.[48]

- Elijah the prophet, in his great frustration due to the spiritual condition of his people, cried out to God, complaining that he *remained alone…* God, in His great mercy, assured him that there were others — *a minority of seven thousand,* who followed Him wholly.[49]

---

[47] See Ex. 2:11-15, 5:20-23, 14:11, 16:2-3, 17:2-7; Acts 7:35.

[48] See the Levites, in Ex. 32:26.

[49] See 1 Kings 19:9-18. See also Rom. 11:4-5 — *Even so then, at this present time there is <u>a remnant</u> according to the election of grace.*

- David, having already been anointed as the next king, was persecuted, and suffered greatly at the hand of *the ruling authority.*[50]

- The prophet Isaiah, in the greatest divine revelation that he experienced in his life, received a scary message: A great majority of the chosen people, due to their sins, would not be able to see, hear or understand God's Word until just before the very end! And even then – at the very end of the age – only *a tiny minority, a tenth, a small remnant* would be saved![51]

- Jeremiah the prophet, discouraged and frustrated by the spiritual condition of his people, cried out, *oh, that I had in the wilderness a lodging place for travelers, that I might leave my people and go from them!* The same prophet prophesied that it will be only *a remnant* who will be saved![52]

- The Apostle Shaul, when speaking of his nation Israel, addressed the issue of the *remnant based on grace/election...*[53]

- Yeshua clearly pointed out that it would only be *a minority (a remnant)* who would enter His Kingdom! He said: *Enter through the narrow gate, for wide is the gate and the road*

---

[50] See 1 Sam. chapters 19–30.

[51] See Isa. 6. See also 10:21-22, 11:16, 37:32. For these who think now of *all Israel shall be saved* (see Rom. 11:26), I would highly recommend taking a simple concordance and check the word *all* throughout Scripture. All I can say at this point, is that (unfortunately) *all* does not mean each and every individual, but rather, these who are present in the specific given time.

[52] See Jer. 9:2, 23:3, 24:8, 31:7; and more.

[53] See again Rom. 11:2-10.

leading to destruction, and many are those walking on it, but narrow is the gate, and narrow is the road leading to life and <u>few</u> find it![54]

- Yeshua also told us that if we choose to follow Him, we might not always have a comfortable life. At least some of His true followers need to prepare for and expect persecution—even unto death! Those who choose to follow Him need to first *calculate the costs* and choose *death to self,* and so on.[55]

- All the apostles, except for John, died as martyrs for their faith in Yeshua! Most of Yeshua's body, for at least the first two centuries, were persecuted and paid a heavy price for their faith!

History as well supports the above principles within God's navigation map. It was and still is, <u>a remnant</u>, <u>a minority</u> who, at the end – even long after they pass away, have been found to be right after all! One can think of examples such as Martin Luther,[56] Martin Luther King Jr., and many others.

Why are some of us so surprised when we find ourselves in a minority? Why are we shocked when the majority around us think that we are weird, extreme, conspiracy theorists, etc.? In what way are we truly different from all the above examples? Are we really called to join

---

[54] See Matt. 7:13-14.

[55] See Matt. 16:24-27; Lk. 14:25-33; Rom. 6:6; Gal. 2:20, 5:24.

[56] I'm well aware of Martin Luther's turning against the Jews towards the end of his life. Yet, in the beginning, he was for sure within a minority, resisting the majority within the Roman Catholic Christianity of his time.

those who go *after many to pervert (justice)* — or are we rather called to be *the salt* and *the light* of this world?

Now, after having considered *the big picture* (God's *navigation map, compass, the timeframe,* the different *obstacles* on *the navigation route* etc.), it's time to delve deeper and look at the recent Covid-19 crisis in greater detail. We shall carefully examine the official narrative, the opposing non-official one, and in the end, I will give my own personal take on it.

Covid-19: The Official Version Accepted by the Vast Majority

It was during February-March 2020 that we were all introduced to this new pandemic — mainly by the mainstream media. The following is a summary of the main points presented to us by government officials:

- Covid-19 – known principally by two names, Covid-19 and Sars-Cov-2 – has been "a global pandemic." Its first outbreak occurred in China sometime in November-December 2019 (hence the suffix -19).

- The virus originated from infected animals in an open market in Wuhan, China.

- Since then, the virus has continued to mutate and, as of April 2022, two "variants" in particular became the most prominent: "Delta" and "Omicron."

- As of August 2022, there have already been 598,434,664 Coronavirus cases with 6,464,974 deaths.[57]

- The disease was very serious, dangerous, and fatal. Therefore, it was a huge threat to humanity's very existence!

- There was a real fear that hospitals were going to be at full capacity due to an increasing number of new Covid patients.

---

[57] See *https://www.worldometers.info/coronavirus/*

The entire health care system was said to have been in real danger of collapsing.

As said previously, the vast majority of the world's nations, including Israel, responded to this new pandemic by imposing harsh restrictions, such as lockdowns, limitations on the number of indoor gatherings, mandatory wearing of face masks, the cancelation of public events and the closure of all non-essential institutions and businesses. In addition, efforts have been made to locate and isolate patients, protect medical staff, and increase the capacity of hospitals including the construction of special hospitalization facilities for Covid patients.

At least nine drug companies have been working on the development of vaccines against Covid and its different mutations. To this day, a few companies, such as Pfizer, Moderna and AstraZeneca, as well as Russian and Chinese companies, have developed the vaccine and have been marketing it mostly since Jan.-Feb. of 2021.

Here, in God's Promised Land, since February-March 2021, there has been a very well-orchestrated campaign in the mainstream media regarding the Covid vaccines. The officials, along with their experts have been telling us from morning to evening, "the FDA tested and approved the new mRNA-based vaccine," and "it is very safe" and with only "minor side effects." Moreover, they have told us, "There is no other effective and efficient way to help Covid patients or to eradicate the new pandemic other than through these new vaccines!"

As of October 2022, here in Israel, 6,719,313 people have been vaccinated with the first dose of the Pfizer vaccine; 6,155,492 have gotten the second dose; 4,512,697 received the third dose; and 863,438 have taken the fourth![58]

Additionally, the Israeli government established the privacy clause of *a confidentiality act* for thirty long years, as it relates to both protocols within the special Corona Cabinet discussions, as well as for the (almost entire) redacted parts of the agreement it entered into with Pfizer for their vaccine supply.

---

[58] It is a known fact that some Israelis got the fifth shot as well. Yet, on the Israeli ministry of health dashboard they do not show their number yet. See *https://datadashboard.health.gov.il/COVID-19/general*

Covid-19: The Non-Official Version
Accepted by a Small Minority

Before I present you with the non-official version, allow me to start with a brief personal confession: In the first two months of this pandemic (March-April 2020), I, along with my family, believed and clung to some of the official claims above. We had been following the mainstream media channels and were spending quite a lot of time in front of the TV every day. We tried our best to fully obey the repeated instructions recommended by the authorities, especially regarding excessive hygiene, wearing masks and disposable gloves, disinfecting any surfaces we or others had touched (using the well-known Alco-Gel), etc. I must admit that as most of the population here in Israel, we too were afraid and even anxious concerning this "new extremely dangerous virus."

It was not until a while later, sometime into May-June of 2020, that we noticed that a few things were not adding up within the official narrative. Thus, we started to ask some questions and looked into a few non-official sources. Friends and family members, as well as brothers and sisters in Messiah around the world, began to share the same suspicions along with us and started to send us articles and short video clips, where some top world doctors and scientists claimed that what the different global authorities had been presenting to their people was far from being factual or scientifically based.

The following are the main points of this "non-official version," presented by doctors, renowned scientists, and professors from around the world:

- The new coronavirus is the seventh in a very well-known series called *the Corona Family*, of which medical authorities have been aware as early as the 1960s. The series includes over sixty coronavirus types and subtypes. Scientifically, the structure of the new virus and its properties are remarkably similar (about seventy-eight percent) to the previous ones.

- The symptoms of those infected with the new virus are also remarkably like those of past seasonal flus: fever, cough, fatigue and, at times, also a temporary loss of taste and smell!

- The new virus is *not* as deadly as has been presented by the authorities, neither does it pose a threat to humanity! It affects very specific populations, such as adults over seventy, as well as individuals who suffer from chronic illnesses. Nevertheless, just as with any other disease, there is *a minority* (i.e., an exception) who are under 70 – including children and teenagers – who, once infected, have been severely affected by this virus. Moreover, according to these doctors and scientists, the probability of full recovery from this new virus, absent any treatment other than "some rest, hot tea and the like" (which we also employ when we have a cold or the flu), is close to ninety-nine percent, on average!

- There are known *scientifically and clinically approved* drugs, which have already been used for several decades, that are very safe to take and whose effectiveness in the full recovery of this new illness is extremely high! Surprisingly, the World Health Organization (WHO), together with health authorities around the world, have banned the use of these drugs for the treatment of new Covid-19 patients! Not only that, but this sweeping and comprehensive ban, also forbade the distribution and sale of these drugs in pharmacies throughout the world! If the authorities had permitted access to these specific drugs, large numbers of those who died from this specific virus, undoubtedly would have been saved! Further, had a large number of critically ill patients taken these safe (yet banned) drugs, they would not even have needed to be hospitalized from the beginning![59]

- The instructions and guidelines given by the WHO to doctors around the world, were at times very strange, confusing, and even contradictory. First , they did not match the medical condition of Covid patients — especially those in need of hospitalization. Second, *in contrast to the situation prior to the outbreak of the disease*, the WHO now instructed doctors on how to write death certificates for the purpose of inflating the number of alleged Covid-19 death rates. According to some doctors who were willing to speak out, the new guidelines were not in keeping with the objective scientific truth by which they were accustomed to writing death certificates prior to Covid-19! For example, after the onset of a disease, terminal patients, such as those with serious diabetes, cancer sufferers

---

[59] Known drugs such as Hydroxychloroquine, taken with Azithromycin and Zinc (in addition to vitamins D and C) in the early stages of the illness; and/or Ivermectin and others. I would highly recommend watching and listening to Dr. Zelenko (known for his "Zelenko Protocol," and unfortunately, deceased since July 2022), Dr. Peter McCullough and others, at: *https://www.clarkcountytoday.com/news/dr-zelenko-we-could-have-ended-pandemic-long-ago/.* To hear Dr. Peter McCullough, go to: *https://www.clarkcountytoday.com/news/dr-peter-mccullough-official-covid-narrative-has-crumbled/*

or those with heart or kidney diseases, who died from complications caused by various infections such as different flus (which is a very well-known phenomenon), were never described as having died as a result of the flu, on their death certificates. Their death certificates had always stated the terminal disease from which they had suffered, as being their cause of death! According to the new WHO guidelines, any deceased person, even if only suspected of being infected by the new virus (i.e., without actually having ever been tested) was categorized as "Covid-deceased." In addition, the WHO also changed the guidelines concerning how to determine and categorize a patient as critically ill. Before the new virus appeared, only patients with an oxygen saturation of 90 and under were defined as critically ill. Now the doctors were instructed that this would be changed to "under 94," which would naturally recategorize "moderately-ill" patients as "critically-ill," thus causing the numbers of the critically- ill to rise rapidly![60]

- Doctors and scientists throughout the world have claimed there is no transparency whatsoever on the part of the governmental health ministries regarding the identity of new patients, their ages, their medical background, etc.

- Speaking of transparency and telling the truth, it should be noted that according to some doctors and scientists, the much-touted PCR test, *upon which this whole pandemic has been based*, was *not* invented *nor* intended to diagnose infectious

---

[60] Later, the WHO changed their guidelines back to what they had been previously (a saturation of 90 and under). Interestingly, the Israeli health system still kept the new guidelines, at least through Feb. 2021!

diseases! In a video interview, its inventor (Dr. Kary Mullis, who actually won the Nobel Prize for his invention) admitted this by saying that *the results of the PCR test can be easily manipulated to fit any desired result!*[61]

- Speaking of the PCR test, more and more doctors around the world have confessed that the new Covid-19 virus has never been isolated, or differentiated, from the other Coronaviruses in a traditional, purely scientific way![62]

- And what about the new mRNA-based vaccine? Doctors and scientists throughout the world have said that this new vaccine does not at all fit the traditional definition of "a vaccine," and should be more properly defined as "a gene therapy!"[63]

- They have continued to say that these "vaccines" have *never actually been approved by the FDA,* but rather only been permitted for emergency use![64] In other words, the only approval pertained to a measure given in "an emergency," and

---

[61] The results are depending on how many "cycle thresholds" each test went through – As more they are, as inaccurate the test is! It is a known fact that, at least here in Israel, the number of these "cycle thresholds" were much higher than they were supposed to be, if seeking truthful and reliable results! Also, see interview with Dr. Kerry Mullis at: *https://t.me/hisunim/1333*

[62] See a response by the British Health Ministry, published on Oct. 28, 2020, to a petition filed by Marc Horn (request-679704): *https://www.whatdotheyknow.com/request/679704/response/1666239/attach/ht ml/4/IR%201243364.pdf.html* — see also *https://principia-scientific.com/irish-government-admits-covid-19-does-not-exist/*

[63] In fact, in recent months, these "vaccines" <u>are</u> defined, in many health ministries around the world, as "gene therapy."

[64] See the complete document Pfizer admitted to the FDA in Dec. 2020: *https://www.fda.gov/media/144245/download*

this would be its status until all the aspects of this experimental gene therapy could be assessed — hopefully some time in 2023 or even 2024!

- Doctors and scientists throughout the world have warned of the side-effects of this new *gene therapy*. They explicitly have said that its side effects in the mid-term (two to five years) and long-term (ten years or more) have never been tested, nor can they practically be tested! As of October of 2022, it is already known worldwide that among the billions who recieved these shots, there are many who already are experiencing serious side effects. Most of them have to do with the cardiovascular system, such as blood clots, heart attacks and myocarditis - especially among youngsters. Moreover, chronic, and terminal diseases, such as cancer and diabetes, and autoimmune issues have increased tremendously![65]

---

[65] See only a few examples in the following links:
https://childrenshealthdefense.org/defender/vaers-cdc-covid-vaccine-injuries-kids-5-to-11-pfizer-vaccine/

https://www.nature.com/articles/s41467-022-31401-5

https://dailyexpose.uk/2022/01/27/bbc-news-wont-tell-you-vaccinated-suffering-ade/

https://expose-news.com/2022/05/29/70k-dead-28-days-covid-vaccination-2/

https://www.lifesitenews.com/news/covid-jab-side-effects-are-like-a-nuclear-bomb-us-pathologist/

https://www.gospanews.net/en/2022/05/07/covid-vaccines-huge-holocaust-43898-deaths-in-the-eu-27758-in-the-us-more-than-5-million-injured/

https://vaccineimpact.com/2022/covid-19-vaccine-massacre-68000-increase-in-strokes-44000-increase-in-heart-disease-6800-increase-in-deaths-over-non-covid-vaccines/

- There are doctors and scientists who strongly claim that this new gene therapy (as well as a few previous "traditional vaccines") contains very dangerous substances that can cause side-effects - mostly in the long term! They claim that certain vaccines also contain embryonic particles, which in the-long term, can affect the DNA of those who have taken them!

- There are some doctors who declare that this gene therapy also contains nanoparticles of certain metals (such as graphene oxide) which, beside the fact that they cause blood clots, they also have the potential of turning us into a type of live antenna, which can receive and transmit information about us![66]

---

https://brightlightnews.com/wp-content/uploads/2022/10/deaths-doctors-80-canadian-william-makis-2022-10-15-CMA-Letter-FINAL.pdf

https://rumble.com/v1pi7tw-dr.-robert-malone-says-the-annual-flu-vaccine-program-is-built-on-a-lie.html

https://www.the-people-committee.com/english

https://aflds.org/news/post/israel-health-ministry-knew-of-adverse-effects-yet-continued-to-push-booster/

https://www.israelnationalnews.com/news/328529

[66] See examples: https://www.ncbi.nlm.nih.gov/pmc/articles/PMC8580522/

https://zeeemedia.com/interview/exclusive-australian-whistleblower-scientists-provide-evidence/

https://www.naturalnews.com/2022-06-12-blood-clots-microscopy-suddenly-died.html

https://archive.fo/2022.01.29-225016/https://masksaredangerous.com/nanotech-in-the-shots/

https://www.orwell.city/2022/02/new-images.html

https://telegra.ph/TECHNOLOGICAL-GENOCIDE--19-02-03

- There is at least one renowned scientist who has expressed that this new gene therapy contains some of the original HIV, and that those who have been fully vaccinated for Covid-19 should test for HIV and then sue their governments![67]

- It is now a known fact and publicly acknowledged by top government figures, that Israel served as the experimental laboratory for the rest of the world. Our government made an agreement with Pfizer, the pharmaceutical company, to be the provider of Covid-19 vaccines to the population of Israel.[68]

- The Helsinki Committee in Israel has also voiced concerns, saying that they believe experimental testing on humans (including the use of these "vaccines") should be done with complete transparency and only according to the law, which requires health providers to explain all the risks and side-effects any vaccine might have. Needless to say, none of this was practiced by health authorities since the inception of this pandemic.

- Doctors and scientists have pointed to the very non-kosher financial arrangement, as well as other connections between

---

[67] *https://www.who.int/standards/classifications/classification-of-diseases/emergency-use-icd-codes-for-covid-19-disease-outbreak.* — See an interview with the Nobel Prize-winning French professor, who died meanwhile, for his discovery of the HIV virus (!) at: *https://t.me/Israel_is_Awakening/5220*

[68] Our prime minister, Mr. Benjamin Netanyahu, stated this in an interview he gave at the last World Economic Forum conference in Davos, Switzerland. The interview is 33 minutes long, and his admission is between minutes "4" and "8": *https://www.youtube.com/hashtag/worldeconomicforum*. Pfizer CEO Albert Bourla also admitted it publicly! See also another interview he gave, from minutes "30" and onward: https://www.redvoicemedia.com/video/2022/12/the-israeli-genetic-database-and-friends-xmas-special-jason-bermas/ref/17/

the various drug and vaccine companies (Big Pharma) and some of the world's richest people, including politicians and physicians. We will discuss this later.

- As stated at the beginning of this chapter, there are many doctors and scientists here in Israel and throughout the world who have claimed that the measures taken by government officials in dealing with this pandemic – namely the frequent lockdowns and mask-wearing mandates – are not only scientifically incorrect, but are measures that will eventually achieve the exact opposite effect: they will cause other illnesses, frustration, depression, suicides and so on; not to mention the huge negative economic effect on society in general!

Physicians and scientists here in Israel have already written a number of formal letters to government officials in which they have requested full transparency, especially on the side of the Health Ministry of Israel. They have offered their help based on their many years of experience but have received almost no serious response from the authorities.

It should be noted that any top physician or scientist who has dared to express a different opinion other than the one presented day and night by the mainstream media, or who has had the courage to go against the tide, was almost immediately censored, defined as a "Corona-denier" (like a "Holocaust-denier"), a "delusional conspirator" and one who is "endangering public health!"

Common Sense Questions and Musings

After having read a number of articles and watching several videos in which those top, renowned doctors and scientists were interviewed, and, as I noticed the draconian laws which were being established by our government here in Israel and throughout the world, supposedly to fight the new pandemic, I could no longer keep silent and ignore the voices sounding the alarm. I began to ponder the statements of those aforementioned doctors and scientists as well as question and doubt the official narrative that had been so well orchestrated by the mainstream media. Some of the following questions came to mind by simply using my healthy, God-given common sense:

- Why is the mainstream media presenting such a unified and one-sided narrative about this new virus? Why are they repeating it from morning to evening, seven days a week, while ignoring almost every other professional or scientifically based opinion?

- Why are many top well-known doctors, professors and scientists being censored on almost every mainstream platform? Why are most of these doctors excluded from our various Knesset (Parliament) committees and, most notably, from the discussions behind the closed doors of the Corona Cabinet?

- If there is indeed a new "worldwide pandemic," why has the data published by the world's statistics bureaus (including here in Israel) through the end of 2020, shown no significant increase in the death rate as compared to the previous five years? If this is indeed a worldwide pandemic that is "threatening humanity's very existence," is it not a bit strange to see no significant increase in the total annual mortality rate?

- Why does the Israeli Corona Cabinet, headed by our prime minister, need a minimum of thirty years' confidentiality for all its discussions, sessions, and protocols? Why are its respected members discussing *our public health issues* behind closed doors? I'm sure they are not discussing the Iranian nuclear program or the threats on our Southern and Northern borders, are they? What is the real reason for this huge lack of transparency? *What exactly are they hiding from us?* Just to remind you, a "confidentiality act" is always set in place to hide crucially important data from... the enemy! Are we, the public, really "the enemy" of the authorities whom we have elected in a democratic process?

- Why are most of the pages of the contract between Pfizer and our authorities, redacted? What are they really trying to hide from us?!

- Why has Israel, and most of the other world authorities, mandated the wearing of face masks, even if only in enclosed places? Are they not aware of other opinions as it pertains to the effectiveness of these masks?[69]

---

[69] It's important to note that there are some renowned doctors and scientists whose studies claim the exact opposite regarding the effectiveness of these face masks! See an example about face masks, lockdowns and more: *https://dailyexpose.uk/2021/12/16/more-than-400-studies-show-lockdowns-and-face-masks-dont-work/*. See also "Investigating the current status of COVID-19

- Why have we been so aggressively pushed by our authorities to be tested with a (PCR) test that was never intended to identify viral infections, and whose inaccuracy is a known scientific fact? Furthermore, how can this test be accurate at all, when top world-renowned doctors and scientists claim this specific Sars-2 Covid strain has never really been identified or isolated?

- Why have we been encouraged (or better say, *pushed and greatly manipulated*) from morning to evening, to go and get vaccinated? Why have officials in Israel and throughout the world put such pressure on us with great help from the mainstream media, to get vaccinated with *an experimental "vaccine,"* which actually has been officially defined as nothing more than *a gene therapy* - one which has been doubted by top, well-known professionals as to its scientific effectiveness and, even more importantly, have warned of its potentially dangerous short and long-term side effects! Why should we be injected with a "vaccine" that is (supposedly) ninety-five percent effective, when the probability that those of us who are healthy, with no chronic illnesses, are going to recover without any special treatment, is well over ninety-nine percent?[70] Why have they never applied the same pressure regarding other diseases such as the seasonal flu, which has an even higher death rate? Why?

---

related plastics and their potential impact on human health" at *https://doi.org/10.1016/j.cotox.2021.08.002*

[70] New data released due to an American court order, of the Pfizer documents provided to the FDA, clearly shows that the effectiveness of the "vaccine" never reached 95% in their trials!

- Why don't they shut down the entire world, as they did during 2020 and 2021, following a yearly seasonal flu or the like?

- Why have Israeli and other authorities around the world implemented *a green pass* to allow the vaccinated into public places and events while preventing the unvaccinated from accessing them? It is a known fact that the world is moving rapidly toward establishing a global "digital health pass," a passport that will enable the vaccinated to freely enjoy basic human rights of entering public places such as restaurants, hotels and gyms, as well as flying on commercial planes, while the unvaccinated (i.e., those who do not possess the special digital pass) will be precluded from enjoying those same benefits? Does this not sound an alarm or cause a red flag to be waved in the minds of, at least those who read and are familiar with God's *navigation map*?!

As time passed and I was exposed to more and more opinions and voices of doctors and scientists, I had a growing sense that something was very wrong. Something was going on behind the scenes, something of a very sinister nature, something that stinks to high Heaven! I continued pondering:

- Are there some hidden players who are directing everything that relates to this pandemic?

- Is there a secret agenda behind the official narrative portrayed to us by the mainstream media?

These and other questions have led me to look even deeper into the wonderful *navigation map* that God has entrusted into our hands—Scripture, His Holy and ever trustworthy Word! Is there any chance that this excellent navigation map includes some clues, some background details, which can help us better understand this pandemic and better locate it within *the bigger picture?* In the following pages I will present you with some other crucially important discoveries I made while delving even deeper into all that I discussed above.

Covid-19, the Great Reset, and
the New World Order

Previously, I stated that some doctors and scientists testify that there is a very non-kosher financial arrangement between various drug companies and a number of the world's richest elites, politicians, and physicians. In the following paragraphs I would like to elaborate on these non-kosher arrangements.

Wealth and Power Ties

Most Israelis are aware of the saying, *He who is close to the plate* (another way of saying – whoever is in the right place), *has a much greater chance of success in this world, than someone who is not.*

It is estimated that in today's world, there are approximately eight thousand to then thousand outstanding wealthy elites, who have complete control over almost every area of our lives, whether directly or indirectly. These elites own and control the entertainment and film industries (Hollywood, Walt Disney, etc.), the global media (including the print and digital press), the economy (banks and financial systems) and big corporations as well as key figures, including prime ministers, governmental ministers, presidents of sovereign nations and others.[71] In Israel alone, it is a known fact that there are about twenty to thirty tremendously wealthy families who have complete control over almost everything that pertains to our daily lives!

---

[71] See *https://www.stopworldcontrol.com/monopoly/*

The common belief is that people living in western democracies are free people. However, when one becomes aware of facts that are not presented or promoted by the mainstream media, one discovers that this "freedom" is nothing more than a mirage! Anyone who has eyes to see will notice that the mainstream media, supposedly "the watchdog of democracy," is <u>not</u> doing its job faithfully, to say the least! The mainstream media is likewise controlled or governed by these same global elites; so naturally, it is *not* the voice of public opinion. Rather, it serves its owners by shaping and engineering public opinion! This form of brainwashing has been going on through various means over the course of many decades. It has been done through the advent of TV, mobile phones, credit cards, digital systems and films which contain subliminal messages, promoting and advancing narratives by those who wish to promote them.

Surfing the Internet, not limited to independent private sites, unveils the following points:

- Among the world's leading elites who have a huge impact and influence on humanity, are the *Rothschild, Rockefeller,* and *Ford* families. In recent decades, they have been joined by other wealthy figures, such as *George Soros, Bill Gates, Elon Musk,* and *Mark Zuckerberg.*

- The above-named wealthy families and individuals are on the top of this "elite pyramid." As such, they possess both wealth and power ties with key politicians, presidents, and prime ministers. They also possess close ties to well-known international organizations, such as *the United Nations* (UN) and *the World Health Organization* (WHO). They are known for their wealth and power ties with top pharmaceutical and vaccine companies as well. For example, did you know that almost everything pertaining to the modern world health system, including the curriculum used in different medical schools around the world, is closely connected to the Rockefeller family?[72]

- The pharmaceutical industry, especially those which are involved in the development of various vaccines, is a thriving business! It is one of the world's leading industries as it relates to revenues, and that involves many billions of dollars each and every year! Indeed, there is a lot of money flowing into the pockets of those who are "close to the plate."

- There are also direct financial and power ties between the vaccine industry and Bill Gates (usually operated through the Bill and Melinda Gates Foundation with its various affiliated companies). Bill Gates has registered patents on the Coronavirus, both in Europe and the USA! One of a few other patents registered in his name (relating to "Cryptocurrency & Body Data") is very interesting and should alarm any person who is familiar with God's navigation map. Its registration number ends with 060606...[73]

- There is a strong friendship between Bill Gates and the present head of the WHO. Gates is also one of the biggest donors to this organization. The current head of the WHO, originally from

---

[72] See "Health & Well-Being" by the Rockefeller Foundation — *https://www.rockefellerfoundation.org/wp-content/uploads/Health-Well-being.pdf*

[73] See "1. WO2020060606 - CRYPTOCURRENCY SYSTEM USING BODY ACTIVITY DATA" — *https://patentscope.wipo.int/search/en/detail.jsf?docId=WO2020060606*

Ethiopia, has been accused in that country of "crimes against humanity" (more specifically, against his own people)![74]

- Could there be a connection between the various new mRNA-based "vaccines" for Coronavirus and the aspiration of some of these global elites to *depopulate the world's population?* In at least one lecture given by Bill Gates, he spoke about the ways and means by which the world's population *must be controlled and even reduced by ten to fifteen percent.* He clearly stated that one of the ways this can be done is by using vaccines! Recently, Mr. Gates also expressed his hope that at least *seven billion people would be vaccinated over the next few years.*[75]

- The same Bill Gates, together with the current head of the WHO, has been un-welcomed in at least two countries (India and a specific country in the continent of Africa) due to their direct involvement in the administration of vaccines, which had been proven to cause irreversible damage to many citizens there—including female infertility![76]

---

[74] See, for example, from Dec. 2020 in *The Times*: "Tedros Adhanom: WHO chief may face genocide charges" — *https://www.thetimes.co.uk/article/who-chief-tedros-adhanom-ghebreyesus-may-face-genocide-charges-2fbfz7sff*

[75] Almost immediately, different "fact checkers" published their own "assessments" and unanimously concluded: "False! Fake news!" There is only one problem with these "fact checkers"—the vast majority of them are owned by the global elite, of which Mr. Gates is one of the leading figures.

[76] See "Why are Indians So Angry at Bill Gates" at *The Diplomat* — *https://thediplomat.com/2021/06/why-are-indians-so-angry-at-bill-gates/*

— See "Controversial Vaccine Studies: Why is Bill-Melinda Gates Foundation Under Fire From Critics in India" at India's *Economic Times* — *https://economictimes.indiatimes.com/industry/healthcare/biotech/healthcare/co*

- Each January, there is a well-known gathering of the world's top elites called the World Economic Forum (WEF). It is held in a Swiss village called Davos and was founded by a man named Klaus Schwab. In these annual gatherings, present, future, and potential world leaders are invited as guests of honor. During the January 2021 gathering, held via Zoom due to the Covid crisis, Prime Minister Benjamin Netanyahu was one of the key guests of honor. I highly recommend visiting the WEF site and listening to Netanyahu's 33-minute interview, and in particular, the segment between the 4 to 8-minute mark, where he proudly speaks about the *very successful vaccination campaign in Israel*, stating that Israel has indeed become the biggest laboratory in the world for this (experimental) injection![77] Needless to say, once Naftali Bennett took over the role of Israel's Prime Minister in June 2021, he too was included as one of the guests of honor at the WEF 2022 gathering.

- Interestingly enough, the WEF also teaches and trains future world leaders in what they call "Young Global Leaders School." Known young leaders of the present day, such as Canada's Prime Minister (Justin Trudeau), the President of France

---

ntroversial-vaccine-studies-why-is-bill-melinda-gates-foundation-under-fire-from-critics-in-india/articleshow/41280050.cms?from=mdr

[77] See "Netanyahu to Davos: Israel is 'world's laboratory for immunity'" by Zev Stub in *The Jerusalem Post* —

https://www.jpost.com/israel-news/netanyahu-to-davos-israel-is-worlds-laboratory-for-immunity-656901

— See YouTube video: "PM Netanyahu Addresses World Economic Forum 2021-Davos" at

https://www.youtube.com/watch?v=TkgX6FPLcC4

(Emmanuel Macron), the Prime Minister of New Zealand (Jacinda Ardern) and many others are graduates of the WEF Young Global Leaders training program.[78]

- Another such gathering of world elites, to which both present-day leaders and future candidates for leadership are invited, is *the Bilderberg Conference*, also known as *the Round Table.* Its gatherings are heavily secured and confidential.[79]

The Stated Goals of the Global Elite

For at least three decades now, well-known world leaders, such as some of the United States' presidents (i.e., Bush Sr., Clinton, Obama), along with our Prime Minister Benjamin Netanyahu, have been engaged in speaking about the urgent need for "a New World Order"—an order that will be established mainly through "advanced technology" such as high-speed Internet, communication networks, artificial intelligence (AI) and more. Another name closely associated with this "New World Order" concept is "the One World Order."

Others (such as Klaus Schwab of the WEF) are loudly calling for "A Great Reset" in our world; a reset that would be an integral part of this "One World Order." Some of them go on to say that this current pandemic must be exploited to the fullest as a *catalyst* for this very much needed reset.

---

[78] See the WEF's Forum of Young Global Leaders —
https://www.younggloballeaders.org/ as of January 2023, Ms. Ardern stated she will step down from office in Feb. 2023.

— See: *https://www.linkedin.com/pulse/schwabs-young-global-leaders-school-anthony-laing-nomad-*

[79] See Bilderberg Meetings, official website — *https://bilderbergmeetings.org*

The UN, through its many proxies, published a long detailed document in 1992 known as "Agenda 21."[80] It was signed by some 197 states around the world, including Israel. Towards the end of 2020, yet another document – "2030" – was published.[81] Both documents (and others) describe, in great detail, the steps that are needed to bring about this New World Order. It includes the need for *sustainable living*, establishing *control over the growth of the world's population* and more. Using smooth and politically correct terminology, they state that we need to protect the world in which we are living, as it is rapidly and dangerously warming due to (the supposed) *Climate Change* and *Over-Population.*

How do they plan to control the global population? Well, not very differently from what is already known and being practiced throughout the entire world as *nuclear family planning*, i.e., the abortion industry. The emphasis is placed upon girls and women who have gotten pregnant and are unable to take care of their unplanned babies; and, through the use of various contraceptive pills which enable a sexually active lifestyle for the unmarried. Needless to say— all this in addition to the use of vaccines to manage "global pandemics," of course.

The Fourth Industrial Revolution

One of the main things which is unclassified that will be incorporated into this New World Order, is what the world's elites call "The Fourth Industrial Revolution." According to Schwab, the founder and head of

---

[80] United Nations Department of Economic and Social Affairs: Sustainable Development, *Agenda 21* —
https://sustainabledevelopment.un.org/content/documents/Agenda21.pdf

[81] United Nations Department of Economic and Social Affairs: Sustainable Development, "Transforming our world: the 2030 Agenda for Sustainable Development" — *https://sdgs.un.org/2030agenda*

the World Economic Forum, this "revolution" will include the *connecting of humankind to advanced computer technologies*—in the form of what I like to describe as *transhumanism*! (See the following).[82]

It is known that in recent decades there have been several very advanced *nanotechnologies*, which use nanoparticles implemented into different types of factory machines as well as pharmaceutical drugs!

Could it be that these new mRNA-based "vaccines" are part of advancing this specific aspiration for the Fourth Industrial Revolution? If the answer is "no," then what is the reason for the lack of transparency, such as disclosing the different ingredients contained in these new vaccines? Why are huge portions of the Pfizer-Israel agreement (as well as agreements with other countries) redacted? Why have all of the protocols of the Israeli Corona Cabinet been classified for a period of thirty long years? Again, what are they trying to hide from us?

---

[82] See Mr. Schwab's vision for "The Fourth Industrial Revolution: what it means, how to respond" at
https://www.weforum.org/agenda/2016/01/the-fourth-industrial-revolution-what-it-means-and-how-to-respond/

— See "What is the Fourth Industrial Revolution?" —
https://www.youtube.com/watch?v=kpW9JcWxKq0

— See "Will the Future Be Human? - Yuval Noah Harari" —
https://www.youtube.com/watch?v=hL9uk4hKyg4

— See "[Dialogue Session] Klaus Schwab: Global Leadership needed in the Era of Fourth Industrial Revolution" —
https://www.youtube.com/watch?v=HTmzbSFNK2c

— See also, "What is the Internet of Bodies" —
https://www.youtube.com/watch?v=-0bXUxRqy8g

Is there any chance, even the smallest one, that these mRNA-based *gene therapy* can affect our human DNA (our genome)? There are scientists who have been censored by the mainstream media who claim that they can![83]

The World's Elites and Their Aspirations

A question often raised is: Why do the world's elites need more wealth, power and control? After all, they, their children, grandchildren, and great-grandchildren can enjoy the huge fortunes they have gathered without the need for one day of hard work! What follows is my attempt to connect the many dots upon which we have touched thus far, while adding a few more. Doing this will hopefully present you with a more complete portrait of *the big picture.*

As we dive deeper, we find that some of the hobbies, preferences, and passions of the global elites, regardless of their cultural or geographical location, are the following.[84]

These tremendously wealthy and powerful people often like to use their unlimited resources to satisfy their own uncontrolled *lusts of the flesh.* Shockingly, more and more exposés (mostly through alternative, independent social media) reveal the close ties of these global elites with international sex-trade and trafficking networks. I'm talking specifically about the trading and trafficking of women and youngsters, including little boys and girls, for the purpose of a vast

---

[83] See at the end of this chapter, alternative news medias, which provide a stage to censored doctors and scientists; such as Dr. Jessica Rose, a known immunologist.

[84] I highly recommend watching a series called *The Fall of the Cabal*, by Janet Ossebaard, where all these points and more are presented and backed by evidence — *https://www.bitchute.com/playlist/kcgRt6O0v6Sn/* — and *https://www.bitchute.com/search/?query=the%20fall%20of%20the%20cabal%20p arts%2011-22&kind=video*

network of different types of prostitution. A significant portion of these wealthy and powerful elites (including some government officials) attend private parties in which these unfortunate women, boys, and girls, serve as their sex slaves. It's nothing more than unconscionable!

Many of you have undoubtedly heard of one specific example that was exposed through private social media, and admitted, albeit unwillingly, by the mainstream media as well: The facts surrounding the private island dubbed "Orgie Island," owned by the disgraced, deceased Jeffrey Epstein, where he hosted such private parties. His guests of honor on this island included billionaires, former and present-day prime ministers, presidents, owners of Internet networks, famous TV show hosts, celebrities, and others.[85]

In Israel, one man exposed no fewer than thirty pedophiles, some of whom are thought to be "high ranking individuals," who hold political, financial, and even judicial positions! Strangely enough, the mainstream media reported that the State Prosecution reached an agreement with the suspected pedophiles, promising them not to expose their names to the public, in exchange for witnessing against the man who exposed them! The outcome: the man was prosecuted and sentenced to ten long years in prison![86]

---

[85] See, for example, "'THE GIRLS WERE JUST SO YOUNG': THE HORRORS OF JEFFREY EPSTEIN'S PRIVATE ISLAND" — https://www.vanityfair.com/news/2019/07/horrors-of-jeffrey-epstein-private-island

[86] For Hebrew readers, see " פדופילים זוכים לחיסיון שערורייתי בתמורה לעדות נגדשלושים הצייד שסחט אותם" —

https://www.news-israel.net/2021/08/02/30-בתמ-שערורייתי-לחיסיון-זוכים-פדופילים/
and

Many who belong to this global elite are also proud members of one or more "secret societies" or "clubs," such as the Free Masons, the Illuminati, the CFR, and others.

When glancing even deeper into what is actually happening behind the closed doors of these secret societies, one can be in for quite a huge shock! I know that it is really hard to believe that in today's "modern, developed and intellectual world," the very same type of idol worship described in Scripture, is still practiced. Yes, behind these closed doors, the participants are involved in rituals that even include the sacrifice of children!

What is the reason for this shocking phenomenon described above? What is behind this uncontrolled greed for money, power, and the satisfaction of the lusts of the flesh, which involve actual idol worship? One does not need to hold a PhD or be a seminary graduate to comprehend the only answer to the above questions. One need only to turn back to God's navigation map, where it is plainly portrayed.

The Ruler of the Air

The one who controls the hearts of the unbelievers, or unsaved in our world, is what Scripture defines as *the ruler of the air.*[87] Yes, the unfortunate truth is that the vast majority of people who live on Earth are ruled and directed by Satan! The people of this world, for the most part, walk in complete spiritual darkness, and unfortunately, there is no "middle path," or "gray area" in which to walk. In truth, not "all roads lead to Rome!" In this world, there are only two very distinct kingdoms: (a) *the kingdom of light*, in which God rules through His only

---

"פרשת הפדופילים :כמו אצל קצב ,אבל להיפך" — *https://zets.co.il/law/55789/*

[87] See, for example, Eph. 2:2.

begotten Son, Yeshua, who practically rules through His body, or members, and (b) *the kingdom of darkness*, which is controlled by that *ruler of the air* - Satan!

As already stated, ever since Adam and Eve sinned in that magnificent garden, our world has fallen into deep spiritual darkness! When Yeshua walked here on Earth 2,000 years ago, He illuminated that darkness, but only for a short time—after which it fell back into its spiritual "dark night."[88]

Those at the top of the world's pyramid – the extremely wealthy elites – whether knowingly or unknowingly, are nothing less than faithful servants of Satan! It is evident that the spirit of the *liar, thief, and murderer from the very beginning* guides and leads them in all their wicked ways.

Speaking of Satan's ways, it is important to note that an integral part of the world elites' plans is to have <u>absolute</u>, <u>complete control</u> over the people who remain after their desired "depopulation plans" are accomplished. This totalitarian type of control includes every aspect of life and can be achieved through advanced technology, such as the 5G network, artificial intelligence (AI) and the implantation of nanoparticles of certain metals into the human body through mandatory vaccines—particles that would turn people into a type of "small antenna" by which a One World Government would be able to determine our whereabouts as well as what we are doing at any given moment!

In my understanding of Scripture, this is yet another attempt of the devil to imitate the One true God, who is Omniscient, able to see us anywhere we go and through every possible situation we face—even

---

[88] See Jn. 1:5, 1:9, 3:19-20, 11:10, 12:35-36; Acts 22:9; and more.

our thoughts are not hidden from Him! Yes, Satan's true agenda that he strives assiduously to accomplish through these world elites who serve him so well, is to eventually be worshiped as "god!"

The coming New One World Order is the very means through which Satan hopes to have complete and full control over the entire world's population. In fact, this same One World Order is nothing less than his attempt to re-build the Bible's infamous Tower of Babylon.[89] As a reminder, the Tower of Babylon (often referred to as "the Tower of Babel") was a city-building project which was cooperatively pursued by the entire known world (which then spoke only one language), with the express goal of *making a name for themselves*. More about that tower later.

---

[89] See Gen. 11.

The Good News — God is One Hundred Percent Sovereign!

He who sits in the Heavens laughs, the Lord scoffs at them.[90] Yes, as the global elites look forward to their soon-to-be established New World Order, with its one centralized government, one banking system, one currency, one religion, etc.; as they employ this Covid "pandemic" to be the very catalyst by which they aim to lead this modern world into their "Great Reset," it's easy to imagine God, sitting securely on His Heavenly throne, addressing the one who is trying his utmost to imitate Him and take His place, with the following words:

Satan, you know that your time is very short, don't you? So, you are trying to take down with you as many as you possibly can. You promise them the very same things I had promised my faithful remnant long ago: A new world order with one central government. Yes. This is exactly what I promised them I'd do at the very end! Indeed, there will be a new world order—it will be __MY__ New Order! There will indeed be one central government run by only One King – My only begotten Son – Yeshua of Nazareth! You want to institute your one world order from Jerusalem? That's exactly from where my Son will reign! Yes, you fallen and rebellious angel, the day will come when you discover that everything you have done in this world actually served my original, intended plans! Yes, I used you, devil, as My tool! You will be shocked to discover that I literally used you and your servants on Earth to carry

---

[90] See Ps. 2:4, 37:13; Habak. 1:10.

out *My original plans; plans that I established before the foundation of this world!*

Satan — Only a Tool in the Hands of God

In God's *navigation map,* one can see that He uses Satan and his servants (both the fallen angels, or demons, along with unsaved men and women), as *tools,* or as Scripture often refers, as *a disciplining rod.* For example, the God of Israel has used His enemies to discipline and redirect His children toward the right path, as a good father who chastens his sons. Once His children have repented, setting themselves on the right track, He forgave them and turned His punishment toward the very disciplining rods He had used against them. Why? Simply because the disciplining rods departed from their original God-given authority! Many times, God has shown His great mercies to individuals who were part of the devil's kingdom, or part of these *disciplining rods*, ultimately accepting them into His Kingdom. The following are only a few examples of the above phenomenon:

- Just before He delivered His Chosen People out of Egypt, the Lord *hardened Pharaoh's heart* so that *the Egyptians shall know that I am the Lord, I have set my Hand upon Egypt...* And indeed, among those who left Egypt, there was *a mixed multitude,* probably comprising Egyptians and non-Israelites who dwelt in Egypt at the time.[91]

- The Assyrians, who exiled the Northern Kingdom of Israel (in the eighth century BCE), are described as *the rod of My anger, and the staff in whose hand is My indignation...*[92]

---

[91] See Ex. 7:4-5; 12:38, 14:4, 18.

[92] See Isa. 10:5-19. Look also at verse 31.

- God calls the pagan king of Persia *Cyrus My Shepherd,* and also, *My anointed one,* and uses him as a great tool to send His Chosen ones back to their Promised Land.[93]

- God uses the evil aspirations of Haman, which was to kill all the Jews in the Ancient Persian Empire, to eventually lead the Jews into a deep repentance and deep desire to seek His Face wholeheartedly, with fasting and supplication. God, then, judged Haman by the very same means through which he planned to kill Mordecai, the Jews' leader![94]

Great Resets in Scripture

As mentioned before, the worlds' elites openly speak about the need to lead this world into *a Great Reset,* which will eventually serve their goal of establishing their desired *New World Order.* We have already established that as far as God is concerned, *there is nothing new under the sun!* This is very true also as it relates to the current satanic, sinister plan for this modern-day reset. While it seems to be a new idea, a new "technique," Scripture clearly shows it is not! Let me explain.

The concept of "resets" is usually connected to the world of computers. When a computer stops working optimally, the manufacturer's representative strongly recommends "resetting" it to return it to the manufacturer's original settings. Needless to say, the main reason for the computer's urgent need for a reset is that it was misused or abused by its careless user, who overstepped the boundaries of its original manufacturer settings.

---

[93] See Isa. 48:28, 45:1.

[94] See Esther. 5:14, 7:10, 8:3-17.

And so it is with the "original manufacturer's settings" that God, in His great Wisdom, placed into "the big computer" called "the world." Since mankind has failed, time and again, to take good care of this "computer," and in fact has done everything possible to wreck the world's "original manufacturer's settings," God has needed to put it into "a reset mode" more than once. The following are a few famous Bible references for such *divine resets:*

Genesis 1 — God's First Great Reset

In the beginning, God created the Heavens and the Earth. Knowing that God is GOOD (the only One who fits the description of *good*[95]), and that everything He does must be good and in perfect order, why does the next verse say, *the Earth was formless and void, and darkness was over the surface of the deep...?*[96] Throughout history, Bible scholars have debated this issue. The following are two possible explanations:

- There was an unknown timespan between Gen. 1:1 and Gen. 1:2, during which Satan fell from his very high position before God and caused the chaos on Earth (notice that the description of *formless and void, and darkness* only applied to the Earth). Thus, God put everything into "reset mode" by putting His settings and order back into it, as seen in verses 3 to 31.

- God created the raw materials (*Heaven and Earth*) first , and in verse 3 began to insert His "original manufacturer's settings" into the Creation.

---

[95] See Matt. 19:17.

[96] See Gen. 1:1-2; Matt. 19:19.

Whatever the correct explanation is (and there are more than just two), one thing is crystal clear: God is <u>not</u> *a God of confusion!* Rather, He is a God of (divine) order. [97] Thus "a reset" was indeed needed at that time.

Sin and the Need for A Second Great Reset — The Flood

In Genesis 3, something crucially significant went wrong, something that interrupted and disrupted God's Divine Order—His "original manufacturer's settings" for the world.[98] The following are only two of many points worth mentioning:

1.   Eve (and then, Adam) ate from the fruit of the only tree God forbade them - *the tree of the <u>knowledge</u> of good and evil.*[99] What was one of the main things that attracted Eve to that tree after being deceived by the serpent's manipulations? She saw that *the tree was desirable to <u>make one wise</u>.* The Hebrew word used here for *wise* is *lehaskil* (להשכיל). It is based on the Hebrew root *Sa-Ka-L* (or *Sa.Cha.L* — ש.כ.ל). It is used close to seventy times in Scripture (depending on which English translation you read), and its main meanings are: "To be (causatively make or act) circumspect and hence, <u>intelligent</u>; to be an <u>expert</u>; to have good success; to <u>teach</u>; (to have, make to) <u>understand</u>; <u>wisdom</u>; and (consider, make) <u>wise</u> (emphasis added).[100]

---

[97] See 1 Cor. 14:33, 15:23; and more.

[98] See Gen. 1:2–3:5.

[99] See Gen. 2:16-17, 3:6.

[100] See Strong H-7919.

2.   Adam and Eve's sin had horrible consequences. God drove them out of the Garden and away from His very presence![101]

Failure to trust the complete love and goodness of the One who created her, and the attempt to be on an equal footing with God's wisdom and intelligence, had terrible repercussions: (a) she and Adam suddenly knew both good *and* evil, without any real ability to deal or cope with it (until that time, it seems they only knew *good*); and (b) they lost their special eternal position before God, having consequently been ejected from His presence and being doomed to return to the dust from which they had been taken.

In the following chapters of the book of Genesis, we see that as far as knowing how to deal or cope with this new knowledge of *evil*, Adam and Eve's descendants did not fare much better.

To the contrary, their life conduct became so evil and so disgusting that God declared, *I will blot out man whom I have created from the face of the land, from man to animals to creeping things and to birds of the sky, for I am sorry that I have made them!*[102] (emphasis added). What was "the straw that broke the camel's back?" What made the Creator of all things decide, "enough is enough?"

Bible scholars are still debating whether or not it was the intermingling between *the sons of God* and *the daughters of man,* which was mentioned just before God chose Noah and his family to be the only survivors of His impending severe wrath.[103]

---

[101] See Gen. 3:23-24.

[102] See Gen. 6:7.

[103] See Gen. 6:1-4.

In the non-canonized book of *First Enoch* (probably dated back to the 3rd Century BCE), *the sons of God* were "fallen angels" who, by intermingling (engaging in sexual intercourse) with *the daughters of men,* <u>spoiled humanity's genome</u>, and "<u>dehumanized mankind</u>!" Their sinful act brought about monster-like creatures—the *nephilim* and the *mighty men.* According to Enoch, another outcome of this gross intermingling was the emergence of giants, as well as demons and evil spirits.[104] During the 4th-5th Centuries CE, both Judaism and Christianity rejected Enoch's interpretation, and only during the Middle-Ages did Bible commentators start to reconsider it. I sense that Enoch's interpretation was indeed correct, and that this incident was likely "the straw that broke the camel's back" as far as God was concerned. More about this later.

The Flood was the means by which the Creator of all walked the ancient world through yet another great reset. Yes, this ancient world had completely lost its "original manufacturer's settings" and thus needed "a great reset." God used the Flood as that "great reset." In His great mercy, He left <u>a remnant</u> of eight people: Noah, his wife, his three sons and their wives. This remnant received God's same original manufacturer's settings, that Adam and Eve had received from Him.[105]

Mankind's Aspirations to be Like God leading to yet another 'Great Reset' in Babylon

Not surprisingly, the descendants of Noah and his family did *not* live in accordance with the original manufacturer's settings. This brings us to the ancient city of Babylon.

---

[104] See Gen. 6:4. See also Deut. 1:28, 2:10, 21, 9:2; Josh. 11:21-22; see Goliath the Philistine in 1 Sam. 17.

[105] See again Gen. 1:28-30, 9:1-7.

What was the straw that broke the camel's back this time? Scripture is clear: (a) *let us build <u>for ourselves</u> a city, and a tower <u>whose top will reach into Heaven</u>, and <u>let us make for ourselves a name</u>* and (b) *<u>otherwise we will be scattered</u> over the face of the whole Earth...*[106] (emphasis added).

God's great reset in this particular instance, had to do with the Babylonians' aspirations to do <u>their own thing</u> (*for ourselves a city, for ourselves a name*), while completely ignoring that there was a Creator, a true "boss" in the world they were living in. What were some of God's original manufacturer's settings, which would have been clear even in that generation? (a) God's Holy Name is the only one deserving all glory and honor; He will not share His Glory with any other entity (flesh or spiritual being); and (b) mankind is specifically commanded to *<u>be fruitful</u> and <u>multiply</u> and <u>fill the Earth</u>!*[107] (emphasis added).

And so, God confused their language and dispersed them throughout the Earth, hoping that this time, given that they could no longer unite under one order, one government and one language – they might seek Him and Him alone! We know this was not the end of the story, don't we? So, the question is, "Since that infamous incident in the garden, what is the real problem of mankind?" The following is my take on this crucially important question.

Humanity's Problem and the Urgent Need for the Greatest Reset of All

Since the tragic incident in the Garden of Eden, the source of all problems has been <u>mankind's heart</u>! *The wickedness of man was great*

---

[106] See Gen. 11:3-4.

[107] See Gen. 1:28, 8:17.

in the Earth, and every intent of the thoughts <u>of his heart</u> was only evil continually![108] And so, the Creator of all things needed to plan on yet another great reset, one which would be the greatest of them all! It would contain three stages and address the very source of humanity's problem—the heart!

The First Stage:

Centuries after the incidents of the Flood and the Tower of Babylon, the same manufacturer of this "supercomputer" - the world - sent His only begotten Son, Yeshua of Nazareth—also known as *the second Adam.*[109] Yeshua, born of a virgin, came into our world to conduct "transplant surgery" on the most complex problem of all —man's deceitful heart! Yeshua was sinless and died as such for us. He was buried and resurrected on the third day, and gave to all who believed in Him, *a new heart!*[110] Yeshua also promised *everlasting life* that starts at the moment one decides to believe in Him! He said, *I Am the Resurrection and the Life. He who believes in Me will live even if he dies! And whosoever lives and believes in Me shall never die!*[111]

Needless to say, we, the present-day believers and disciples of Yeshua, as were all of those who walked before us over the last two thousand years, are still living in this body of flesh (or, *vessel of clay*), which will one day return to the dust from which it was taken. Nevertheless, in the spiritual realm, we are already *a new creation!*[112] All we must do at this point, is to submit ourselves and lay at His feet any thought that

---

[108] See Gen. 6:5.

[109] See Rom. 5:18-19; 1 Cor. 15:21-22, 47.

[110] See Rom. 12:2.

[111] See Jn. 11:25. See also Eph. 2:6; Col. 1:13; and Heb. 12:22-24.

[112] See 2 Cor. 5:17.

refuses His authority in our lives. Our struggle is *not with flesh and blood.* Rather, it is against *rulers and authorities* in the heavenlies; therefore, our weapons of war are radically different from these used by the non-believers![113] But is this where the story ends? Will this be our state for all eternity —a state where we are in continuous spiritual warfare, while at the same time in a very fleshly, imperfect body? By no means! Praise be to God—the second stage of this greatest reset of all is just around the corner...

The Second Stage:

The second stage is going to take place when Yeshua returns to our world to *restore the kingdom to Israel,* and reign as the King of Kings over all the Earth for a thousand-year period![114] Satan will be bound and cast into a pit, while this world will experience and enjoy the greatest Sabbath it has ever known - the seventh millennium! Yeshua will reign here, together with His true followers, who will realize not only a spiritual redemption or salvation, but also a physical one—once they receive their completely new body with its immortal glory and await the final stage of this greatest reset of all time.

The Third and Final Stage:

This thousand-year period will lead to the eighth millennium (from the creation of mankind). This is a millennium that will herald the beginning of a completely new era, *the new Heavens and the new Earth!*[115] I do not pretend to understand all of the details surrounding this *new Heavens and new Earth*—what they will look like or what the main changes will be by comparison to the world in which we

---

[113] See 2 Cor. 10:1-6; Eph. 6:10-18; Phil. 3:20.

[114] See Acts 1:6-8; Rev. 20:1-6.

[115] See Rev. chapters 21–22 and Isa. 65:17-25.

presently live. All I can say is that the world with which we are acquainted will indeed experience the third and final phase of the greatest reset of all!

As mentioned above, *resets* are *not* something that is *new under the sun!* Knowingly or unknowingly, these global elites who probably think they are "inventing the wheel" with their evil aspirations, are actually being used by the Almighty to bring us to the very fulfillment described long ago in God's navigation map, especially as it concerns HIS soon-to-come New World Order!

Nevertheless, before God's New World Order will be established here on Earth, something else must precede it.

The Reign of the Anti-Messiah

I do think that the Covid-19 crisis was an integral part of the establishment of the Anti-Messiah's reign. In fact, his system has already been in place for quite a few decades—if not longer! What we have been seeing since this global crisis that began in March 2020, is an exponential increase in the revelation of this system. It is not hidden any longer, and its ugly face is becoming clearer and clearer as the days go by!

Is the current mRNA-based coronavirus "vaccine" connected to *the mark of the beast* that is mentioned in Rev. 13? It really depends on the following: (a) Can it indeed change the human genome? (b) Will it lead to a worldwide "digital health pass," without which you will be unable to travel from one place to another or even to enter a grocery store or other essential places, such as pharmacies to acquire medical treatments?

If the answer to both questions is yes, then this *gene therapy* does have the potential to eventually lead to the infamous *mark of the beast!* If the answer is no, then it is for sure a precursor for the mark, as slowly but surely it has accustomed people to the idea that we are totally dependent on whatever the authorities tell us to do in order to maintain our most basic, God-given, freedoms and rights!

I am well aware that there are many brothers and sisters in Messiah, who wholeheartedly believe that they will not be here at all, nor even see the Anti-Messiah and his seven-year rule… They rather believe that they will be "snatched out" (Raptured) before all of this actually starts. Well, as you read further, you will become more familiar with my reasoning regarding this specific pre-Tribulation Rapture doctrine.

In this stage of the book, let me present you with the two following points:

a. If there is even a slight chance that this doctrine of the pre-trib Rapture is untrue (i.e., not biblically based), there is a danger that those who believe in it might be swept up into submitting to the system of the beast, simply as a result of being unaware that they are actually living in the midst of it!

b. As we will discuss in chapter two, troubles and at times even terrible suffering (including unto death) have been and continue to be an integral part of the lives of true and faithful followers of the God of Israel. This can clearly be seen throughout Scripture! Tribulations and sufferings were experienced by the very first apostles and other followers of Messiah in the first century and onwards. It's crucial to know that tribulations and sufferings are an integral part of the believer's lifestyle when he or she chooses to walk through that *narrow gate* and in that *difficult way* of which Yeshua spoke![116]

Before closing with a short summary and my own conclusions, I would like to address the following legitimate questions:

Is it not true that Scripture instructs us to obey the authorities God has placed over us? And, what about science? Don't you believe it helped to improve our lives, especially our health and longevity?

Are you up for a different take, an "outside-the-box" kind of approach to these critical important issues?

---

[116] See Matt. 7:13-14; Lk. 13:22-24; and many more.

Rom. 13 & 1 Pet. 2:13-17 in Light of Covid-19

Beginning in November 2000 and ending in June 2005, my wife and I, together with our four children, had been living and ministering in the USA. Gaby and I were sure that the best education for our children would be in one of the many Christian schools or academies spread throughout the entire country.

When comparing the American culture with the Middle Eastern, Israeli culture, which we had left, we, as well as our children, faced various cultural differences and needed to overcome some challenging bumps in the road while living there. I remember the day one of our daughters came home and said that while she had been at school, they were discussing World War II and the tragic Holocaust of the Jews. She told us that during one of the classes, a question was raised, "What would you do as a Christian who wished to help Jews during that time, if you had chosen to hide them in your home, and had been asked by Nazi police knocking at your door, whether or not you had Jews in your home?" A difficult one, hmm? Our daughter was shocked to hear her teacher say, "As believers, we can never lie! We should always tell the truth, the whole truth and nothing but the truth! Thus, our answer should have been, 'Yes, sir, we do have some Jews here in our home.'"

Well, I don't know about you, but I had a hard time agreeing with that specific teacher's statement. In fact, what immediately came to my mind when hearing my daughter's report, was, "Wow, how disconnected this very sincere and respected believing teacher is from her Middle Eastern Hebraic roots!"

I don't think it would be a stretch to say that the main scriptures this teacher was basing her conclusion on were Rom. 13 and 1. Pet. 2:13-17. The vast majority in the present-day body of Messiah use these very scriptures as the basis for their desire to be in total submission to *the authorities,* which were *appointed by God,* and to avoid dealing with any of the "conspiracy theories" that an insignificant minority holds.

Rightly Dividing the Word of Truth

Both Shaul and Simon the apostles grew up as Israeli Jews. Yes, they were typical Middle Eastern men. Let's speak specifically about Shaul: Before he met Yeshua on the road to Damascus, he was a devout Pharisee and faithful disciple (or student) of the renowned Rabbi Gamaliel![117] I don't think it would be too much of an exaggeration to say that Shaul was not a typical Greek philosopher or the like. He was a Jew, a rabbi, and thus, the lenses he used were *not* Western but rather Middle Eastern. We are going to continue to discuss the enormous differences between these lenses in the following chapters.

All I'm trying to say is that Shaul was very familiar with that Jewish/Middle Eastern document that he had in his hands—the *Tanach* (the Torah, the Prophets, and the Writings).[118] Shaul was certainly familiar with the wisest man's words contained therein, *to everything there is a season, a time for every purpose under Heaven...*[119] Shaul was not a Christian theologian who held to a particular set of dogmatic doctrines. He knew quite well what every

---

[117] See Acts 22:3.

[118] At that time there were no other canonized New Testament Scriptures. These were canonized much later.

[119] See Eccl. 3:1.

true Bible teacher should know – that we cannot take a specific scripture and establish a dogma from it, without first considering other scriptures which might contradict that new dogma. As Bible teachers, we indeed have a great need and obligation to *rightly divide the word of truth!*[120] Shaul knew that there was *a time and a season for everything under the sun,* including the application or non-application of a certain scripture or scriptural principle to any given situation.

Any theological dogma must be tested by other scriptural references! For example, would it really be considered a sin not to expose or betray someone whom the authorities are after, simply because those authorities were appointed by God Himself? Are we allowed, at certain times, to disregard the dictates of authorities and purposefully disobey them, especially when we know that their laws go against those of God and men? To answer these important questions, we need to first assess the phrase...

Appointed by God

God is a sovereign God! Nothing in this world happens without Him first allowing it—nothing! We have already discussed this when we dealt with the issue of how God uses Satan himself to accomplish what He has been planning since before the foundations of the world. We have seen how, at times, He has used kings and kingdoms as *a disciplining rod* to chastise His children, and then has chosen to punish them because they have overstepped the boundaries of their God-given authority! In my understanding of Scripture, this is the real meaning behind being *appointed by Him.*

---

[120] See 2 Tim. 2:15.

God is *LOVE!* God is *GOOD!* He is *the Father of Lights, with whom there is no variation or shadow of turning!*[121] As such, He is never to be blamed for the sorrows, hardships, difficulties, and temptations that this evil, sinful world, offers us in abundance! There is a saying which may be appropriate to help illustrate this perfectly: "Every generation gets what it deserves!" In other words, God allows (or *appoints*) bad, cruel, or idol-worshiping kings and rulers when a given generation deserves it—due to their own sins!

Disobeying Authorities?

Am I stepping out of my responsibility as a teacher of God's Holy Word when claiming that there are times when we, as true followers of Israel's Messiah, are actually called to disobey the very authorities whom He has appointed over us? If you think so, then what would you say about the following people of the Bible?

- *Shiphrah and Puah:*[122] These two respected women were Hebrew midwives who were directly commanded by Pharaoh, the king of the most powerful empire of the time—yes, <u>one who was *appointed by God*</u>, *when you do the duties of a midwife for the Hebrew women, and see them on the birth stools, if it is a son, then <u>you shall kill him</u>...* Well, Scripture clearly shows that Shiphrah and Puah disobeyed this explicit and direct command of the king! Do you think there is even a slight chance the following thought crossed their minds: "Well, God is sovereign, and He certainly allowed Pharaoh to be king over all of us at this time. Thus, we should obey him so that we don't disobey God's will...?" I don't think so! In fact, had they

---

[121] See Jam. 1:17.

[122] See Ex. 1:15-21.

obeyed the authorities, many innocent Israelite boys would have perished, Including Moses himself (!), and this would have been considered <u>a much greater sin</u>!

- *Jochebed, Moses' Mother:*[123] Jochebed certainly knew that the king was in hot pursuit of all the Israelite/Jewish newborn males in order to kill them! Yet, she did not heed Pharaoh's command and instead, hid her son—the very one who would be used by the Almighty as the redeemer of Israel! During the three months that Jochebed concealed Moses, had by chance representatives of Pharaoh knocked on her door and asked whether someone had just given birth to a boy, do you think that Amram, her husband or Miriam, his daughter would have said: "Yes, Sir! We believe in the God of Israel, who is the One who appoints all the authorities of the world, and we would never lie; come in and see the baby?" Do you assume that later Miriam revealed the whole truth and nothing but the truth, regarding the identity of the crying baby in the small ark, to Pharaoh's daughter, when she found him by the riverbank?

- *Moses:*[124] Contrary to what some Bible teachers think, Moses was not "a very impulsive, immature man" when he killed the Egyptian. According to the Book of Hebrews, Moses was very aware of who he was and to which nation he belonged. Actually, *he refused to be called the son of Pharaoh's daughter, choosing rather to suffer affliction with the people of God than to enjoy the passing pleasures of sin, esteeming the reproach for Messiah greater riches than the treasures in Egypt, for he*

---

[123] See Ex. 2:1-9.

[124] See Ex. 2:10-15.

looked to the reward.[125] Moses was aware that by killing this cruel Egyptian officer, he actually had rebelled against the authority that God had appointed over him. He saw unrighteousness being committed on one of his Israelite brethren and acted in accordance with a sense of righteous indignation that God had already put in him.

- *Daniel and his three friends:* Shadrach, Meshach and Abednego disobeyed the explicit command of the authorities to bow down to the infamous statue erected in honor of the king.[126] Daniel disobeyed the clear command of the authorities when he did not offer prayers to King Darius but continued to pray only to the God of Israel![127] I do not think for a moment that Daniel and his friends were unaware of the fact that King Nebuchadnezzar, and then Darius, had actually been *appointed by God.*

- *Mordechai and Esther:* Both Mordechai and Esther, at times, disobeyed the authorities of their day. Mordechai did this with regard to Haman, who had the legal authority to command everyone to bow down to him. Esther disobeyed the king's clear regulations regarding the appointed times that anyone was permitted to approach him.[128]

- *The apostles:* When standing before the religious authorities of their time, who had also been *appointed by God,*[129] they

---

[125] See Heb. 11:23-26.

[126] See Dan. 3.

[127] See Dan. 6.

[128] Est. 3:1-5, 4:16–5:1.

[129] See Matt. 23:1.

refused the explicit command to stop preaching and teaching in Yeshua's Name![130]

These are only six examples from Scripture which show that, at times, we will have to obey God and disobey the authorities. A careful and deeper look at Scripture will reveal that the above examples are not the only ones. Most of the prophets in the Tanach, on occasion, needed to go and speak out directly against the authorities whom God had appointed during their specific time, and on occasion, they even disobeyed them.

However, when any of these God-fearing people chose to disobey the authorities, they also had to be aware that they might need to pay a price for their refusal to obey.

The Hebrew midwives, as well as Moses' mother and sister, took a great risk upon themselves, and without God's provision of grace, they would have surely paid a high price. Moses suffered the consequences of killing the Egyptian - forty long years in the wilderness! Daniel and his three faithful friends were ready to pay any price for their refusal to obey. They all trusted God's perfect sovereignty and will for their lives! Mordechai and Esther also took on the risk of losing their very lives! The apostles paid a high price as well, first by being beaten and humiliated, and later by being killed for their unwillingness to obey!

I'm sure you have noticed above that I used the words "on occasion" and, "at times," quite often. This is an indication that I'm neither teaching nor encouraging anyone who reads this book to adopt a lifestyle of disobeying the authorities! Yet, I believe that on occasion during our lifetime, and as true followers of Israel's Messiah, we might need to choose between obeying or disobeying the authorities which

---

[130] See Acts 4:18-20, 31; 5:40-42.

God has appointed over us, so that we, similar to the above six examples, will also be remembered as godly people who were found to be on the right side of history.

Let us recall some of Shaul's and Peter's words in Rom. 13 and 1 Pet. 2:

For rulers are not a terror to good works but to evil… do what is good, and you will have praise from the same. For he is God's minister to you for good. For he is God's minister, and avenger to execute wrath on them who practices evil. For because of this you are also to pay taxes… and do this, knowing the times, that now it is high time to awake out of sleep, for now our salvation is nearer than when we first believed. The night is far spent, the day is at hand, therefore let us cast off the works of darkness and put on the armor of light. Therefore, submit yourselves to every ordinance of man for the Lord's sake, whether to the king as supreme, or to governors, to these who are sent by Him for the punishment of evildoers and for the praise of those who do good[131] (emphases added).

Here is the key! As long as the authorities really do their God-appointed job, which is to *administer what is good* (in God's eyes) and to *execute wrath on those who practice evil* or to *punish evildoers,* all will be well. In that case, we should praise God for them, pray on their behalf and wish for their best; knowing that God is *a God of order* and certainly not interested in anarchy! In such circumstances, we are indeed called to be good witnesses to the world around us while practicing model citizenship. We should pay our taxes on time, give honor to whom honor is due, and so on.

---

[131] See Rom. 13:3-4, 6, 11-12; 1 Pet. 2:13-14.

Yet, when the authorities exceed or come against their (godly) authority <u>to do good and execute (His) righteousness</u> over us; when instead of doing good, they do evil; when they are corrupt to the core of their being; when they call evil good and good evil, light darkness and darkness light; when they promote clear deception and sin to the degree that they become dangerous to their own people, our duty as true believers is to boldly oppose them, while being ready to pay the price—any price! To make it crystal clear once again: I'm *not* speaking of disobeying our authorities on *everything* they say or mandate!

History is filled with evil authorities who were all *appointed by God!* We see this starting with Pharaoh at the time of Moses and continuing with Haman in Persia and some of the Roman emperors. Herod and Stalin also come to mind, and the list goes on and on. What did they all have in common? They were <u>wicked</u> rulers who aspired to do evil to their own people only to exalt themselves. They meet the Scriptures' exact description of *false shepherds!*[132]

I started the discussion on Rom. 13 and 1 Peter 2 by mentioning one of my daughters' teachers and her opinion as it pertained to believers during the time of the Holocaust. Allow me to finish with a reflection on this same tragic time in our recent history.

It's important, as horrible as it sounds, to understand that Hitler and his Nazi regime were also *appointed by God!* Unfortunately, the majority of non-Jewish believers chose to stay in their comfort zones, while doing nothing to help those who were taken to the slaughter!

Mature and faithful followers of Israel's Messiah should know how to discern the times and seasons in which they live! We should all

---

[132] See Ezek. 34. See also a discussion on the Hebrew meanings of "shepherds" in the closing chapter of this book.

remember that delivering, helping, and saving *those who are headed toward death,* as well as *those going to the slaughter,* is a much higher and nobler act of obedience to the Lord than blindly and naively *submitting to authorities!*[133]

Do we really live in a world where most of the authorities who, although appointed by God, are actually doing evil, even extreme evil, in His sight? I believe that we are! I am also convinced that we are facing a new holocaust in our day, this time not only against God's Chosen Nation, but against all of humanity – God's very creation![134] Satan, who knows that his time is short, is enraged. He has therefore begun to reveal his ugly face more and more through the present-day rulers of this world—those who are highly dedicated to worshipping him, whether they know it or not!

Please let us not forget, Satan *was a murderer from the beginning... there is no truth in him... for he is the father of lies!*[135] The authority over all the kingdoms of this world was given to him![136] The human heart is evil from the core— *every intent of the thoughts of his heart*

---

[133] See Prov. 24:11-12.

[134] For these who are shocked by the comparison of our times to the terrible Holocaust, under the Nazi regime, please listen to what Holocaust survivors, such as Vera Sharav and others, have to say about it — *https://play.anghami.com/episode/1025388702*

— Also, read the excellent article "Lessons from Nazi history," written by a dear Messianic brother living here in Israel: *https://davidstent.org/lessons-from-nazi-history/*

— See also "On the Subtlety of Monsters: We have to Talk about Nazism. How Our Times Do Indeed Echo an Earlier Totalitarian Era", by Dr. Naomi Wolf — *https://naomiwolf.substack.com/p/compartmentalization-bureaucratization?s=r*

[135] See Jn. 8:44-45.

[136] See Lk. 4:6.

was only evil continually![137] This world is *not* a good world, but rather an evil one![138] None of us should be putting our trust in man, but in God alone!

Scripture is very clear that just before Yeshua's glorious return and the establishment of His kingdom – the kingdom of Israel here on Earth – there will be a certain ruler, *a man of sin,* who, together with his *beast* governing system, will demand that people bow down to *an image* as well as take *the mark of the beast.*[139] I would like to end with some very challenging questions, especially aimed at those who still think we should *at all times* obey the authorities:

- How do you assume you will recognize the Anti-Messiah? Do you think someone will knock on your door one day and introduce himself as the Anti-Messiah or his servant, and politely ask you to submit to his authority?

- Is the Anti-Messiah's authority also *appointed by God*—or by Satan?

- If you are really convinced that you should obey the authorities, *no matter what,* are you going to submit to the Anti-Messiah's authority as well? Are you going to take his mark?[140]

---

[137] See Gen. 6:5.

[138] See Gal. 1:4; Tit. 2:12.

[139] See Dan. 7–12; Rev. 13.

[140] See Rev. 13. See also 14:9-11.

Science – The New God

One of the well-known axioms accepted in our present-day world is that "everyone with a head on their shoulders must believe in science!" In fact, those of us who have had a hard time accepting the official Covid narrative are often accused of and referred to as "science deniers." In the following paragraphs, I would like to challenge this widely accepted axiom, which is unfortunately also accepted among most members of Yeshua's body.

What is "science" really? From where did it originate? Does it truly fit in with God's navigation map? What follows are a few excerpts taken from Wikipedia (intentionally in different font. All emphases and edits have been added for clarity):

The word 'science' comes from Latin (*scientia*), and its main meaning is knowledge. It is a systematic endeavor that builds and organizes knowledge in the form of testable explanations and predictions about the universe.

The earliest roots of science can be traced to <u>ancient Egypt and Mesopotamia</u> in around 3000 to 1200 BCE. Their contributions to <u>mathematics</u>, <u>astronomy</u> and <u>medicine</u> entered and shaped <u>the Greek natural philosophy of classical antiquity</u>, whereby formal attempts were made to provide explanations of events <u>in the physical world based on natural causes</u>. After the fall of the Western Roman Empire, knowledge of Greek during the early centuries of the Middle Ages was preserved in the Muslim world during the Islamic Golden Age. The recovery and assimilation of <u>Greek works and Islamic</u> inquiries into Western Europe from the 10th to 13th centuries revived '<u>natural philosophy</u>,' which was later transformed by <u>the Scientific Revolution that began in the 16th</u>

century, as new ideas and discoveries departed from previous Greek concepts and traditions. The scientific method soon played a greater role in the knowledge of creation, and it was not until the 19th century that many of the institutional and professional features of science began to take shape, along with the changing of 'natural philosophy' to 'natural science.'

Modern science is typically divided into three major branches that consist of the natural sciences (i.e., biology, chemistry and physics, which study nature in the broadest sense); the social sciences (i.e., economics and psychology), which study individuals and societies, and the formal sciences (i.e., logic, mathematics and theoretical computer science), which deal with symbols governed by rules.

New knowledge in science is advanced through research by scientists who are motivated by curiosity about the world and a desire to solve problems. Contemporary scientific research is highly collaborative and is usually done by teams in academic research institutions, government agencies and companies. The practical impact of their work has led to the emergence of science policies that seek to influence the scientific enterprise by prioritizing the development of commercial products, armaments, health care, public infrastructure, and environmental protection.[141]

As you can see, I intentionally emphasized a few specific words and terms used by Wikipedia: *knowledge, the physical world, natural, a desire to solve problems, engineering and medicine, environmental protection, Greek natural philosophy* and, finally, *Greek works and Islamic inquiries.* I don't think it would be wrong to say that the main interests of science are: (a) gaining knowledge of the natural, i.e., the things that can be seen, touched, smelled, etc., and (b) solving problems in the natural, such as health, medicine, and environmental

---

[141] See "Science" at *https://en.wikipedia.org/wiki/Science#cite_note-webster-4*

protection. And what are the roots of all of this? They go back to ancient Egyptian, Greek and Muslim philosophies and methods.

As you will see, throughout this book I discuss our great need as true followers of Messiah, to get in touch with our Middle Eastern, Hebraic/Jewish roots. Is the above description of science based upon, or somehow connected to, our true historical and Biblical roots? Let's examine that.

Above, we discussed God's great resets, which included the Flood. There, we said it was a direct outcome of the gross increase of sin, which originated in the ancient Garden of Eden! Before we continue our discussion about science, let me remind you of a few important points that we have previously talked about.

Eve ate the fruit of the only tree from which God forbade her and her husband to eat - *the tree of <u>the knowledge</u> of good and evil.*[142] What was one of the main things that attracted Eve to that tree? She saw that *the tree was desirable to make one <u>wise</u>...*

As we already discussed above, the Hebrew word used here for *wise* is, *Lehaskil* (להשכיל). It is based on the Hebrew root, Sa.ka.l (or, Sa.Cha.L – ש.כ.ל), and its main meanings are: "To *be* (causatively *make* or *act*) circumspect and hence, <u>intelligent,</u> <u>expert</u>, have good success, <u>teach</u>, (have, make to) <u>understand</u>, <u>wisdom</u>, and (be, behave self, consider, make) <u>wise</u>" (Emphasis added).[143]

It is very interesting to note that the Hebrew word for *the knowledge* in this verse is *haDa'at* (הדעת). In Hebrew, *the tree of the knowledge good and evil* is, *etz haDa'at tov v'ra* (עץ הדעת טוב ורע)!

---

[142] See Gen. 2:16-17, 3:6.

[143] See again, Strong H-7919.

Precious brothers and sisters, one of the clear End-Time signs is that *knowledge will increase...*[144] We must remember that <u>true</u> *knowledge,* <u>true</u> *wisdom,* is found only in our Messiah Redeemer![145] Thus, we should all strive for *His* wisdom, *His* knowledge, rather than the wisdom and knowledge of this world!

We were never called to idolize "natural science" nor blindly trust whatever we are told by modern-day "experts," professors and doctors, who have been given lots of space and screen time and are entrenched in the mainstream media! We are supposed to acquire <u>spiritual</u> knowledge and wisdom that usually cannot be found at schools, universities and even in theological seminaries!

As those who have been *born from above,* followers of Messiah should strive to be led by the *One from above* – God's very Spirit! True followers of Yeshua should not *lean on your own* (Adamic-inherited) *understanding*— or on our own *sechel,* (or *sekhel* – intellect and wisdom)![146]

Now let's continue with science. According to my understanding of Scripture, God does not seem to be pleased with people's attempts to replace Him with what I consider as this 'new god' – science - especially as it pertains to the following factors:

- *Knowledge*: As far as God is concerned, all that mankind really needs is to have HIS knowledge! i.e., to know HIM personally, to follow His ways, to keep His commandments! All of this can

---

[144] See Dan. 12:4.

[145] See Col. 2:3.

[146] See examples: Prov. 3:5; 1 Cor. 1:18-31, 2:1-9; and many more.

93

never be achieved through <u>natural</u> knowledge alone! Mankind urgently needs <u>spiritual</u> knowledge![147]

- *Health issues:* Once things have been understood through the spirit, and people truly follow Him and Him alone, He is very well able to protect their health and perfectly heal them, in perfect accordance with His timing and will. After all, is He not our One true Healer?[148]

- *Environmental issues:* As the Creator of ALL, God is the only true "environmental protector!" Once humankind seeks His face, His knowledge and wisdom, once we truly follow Him, we do not need to worry about environmental issues, such as (fake) "global warming," famine, lack of food supplies, earthquakes and so on...![149]

Is there anything wrong with the new scientific ways that are attempting to improve our health and protect the world we are living in? Not at all! *As long as we don't use the natural knowledge He allows us to acquire, against Him and His creation!* As long as we do not use the knowledge we have acquired to exploit, to bribe and to advance our own manipulated and false narrative.

How many of us are aware of the huge differences between what I refer to as "science BC" (Before Corona) and "science AC" (After Corona)? Have we noticed that up until around February-March of 2020, science looked quite different than the way it looks today? Up

---

[147] See examples: Job. 38–39; 1 Cor. 1:18-31; Col. 2:3; and many more.

[148] See Ex. 15:26, 23:25; 2 Kings 1:1-4; and many more.

[149] See Gen. 8:22, Deut. 28:1-15; Isa. 51:15; Jer. 5:22; Ps. 89:8-12; and more. See also what the famous man of God – <u>C.S. Lewis</u> said about the great danger of an uncontrolled and abused "science" at: https://youtu.be/WDPBashRONI

until the beginning of the Covid-19 crisis, science (at least outwardly) did its best to stay empirical and debatable, while showing more than only one possible side. Science, up until then was more or less transparent and open for discussion and criticism. And what about science AC? Am I the only one who has noticed that, suddenly, it promotes only one narrative while censoring and threatening scientists who dare to voice a different opinion? Woe to those scientists who try to criticize the mainstream narrative! They are publicly rebuked, ridiculed and censored from any possible respected scientific forum.

As long as we do not try to replace God and what He says throughout Scripture, with this new god, or *a new golden calf* named science, we are okay. Once we try to put science above Him or – God forbid – instead of Him and His Holy Word, we should be very worried, as He sees everything, even our most hidden thoughts! We must remember that the God of Israel is never going to share His glory with *other gods!*

Our present world seems to be taking the last steps needed to rebuild the new *Tower of Babylon.* What is "Agenda 21" and "2030" about, if not the establishment of this ancient city and its tower? What is behind the modern-day digital and scientific advancements, if not clear attempts made by a number of idolatrous elites, who wish to be wiser and more intelligent than God Himself? What is it, if not attempting to *make a name for ourselves?*

May our heavenly Father grant us all <u>His</u> wisdom, knowledge and much-needed spiritual discernment to differentiate between good and evil, even when it comes in the form, or under an umbrella, of something called "science."

Summary & Personal Conclusions

When viewing the world over the last two to three years and comparing it with the way it looked up until 2020, we can see it is truly a changed world! It seems that most of us have really gotten used to a new normal—one which is characterized by fear of the unknown and a growing dependency on the wisdom of authorities as they decide on whether to ease or to double down on the multiple restrictions they have placed on us, due to this 'new very dangerous pandemic...'

On the one hand, there are those who, through God's great mercies, can see into *the depth of Satan* (more on that later) and thus better discern between the truth and lies, good and evil, light and darkness, etc. On the other hand, some are not yet able to see, read and understand what I refer to as *the writing on the wall.*

And so, we will all need to take responsibility for our own perspective on this whole issue, conduct our own research concerning the things which I have presented in this chapter, as well as the following chapters, and reach our own conclusions. Let us analyze and assess the actual scientific facts which relate to this Covid-19 crisis, in addition to the openly expressed aspirations of known world leaders (including ours here in Israel) along with renowned and influential elite figures who have memorialized it into their well-written articles and books.[150]

---

[150] See again, *Covid-19: The Great Reset* by Mr. Klaus Schwab, the founder and head of the WEF.

The following is my own view and summary of the Covid-19 pandemic within its broader context.

The Covid-19 Crisis is an Integral Part of a Much Bigger Thing

In this opening chapter, I tried to present the Covid-19 Crisis within its broader context, what I kept calling, *the big picture.* I have presented my personal convictions while using the Word of God as *a navigation map,*—a map that He has given each one of us to help us successfully navigate our lives within this dark world.

What follows are the main points that have been discussed in this chapter:

- We are unquestionably living in what Scripture defines as *the Latter Days* or the End Times! Messiah Yeshua is indeed right at the door.

- One of the main characteristics of these interesting and challenging *Latter Days* is a great increase in deception— deception which is fueled directly by *the father of all lies, the murderer,* Satan himself, who is very much aware that with each passing day, his time is running out.

- According to Scripture, true followers of Yeshua belong to a small minority—*a small remnant!* As such, we are called to do our very best to hold on to God's absolute truths, while distancing ourselves, as much as possible, from anything that does not line up with His principles!

- The remnant's responsibility is to *pursue justice*—even if it involves swimming against the (world's) currents and paying a high personal price!

- There are two sides to almost everything in this world. This includes and relates to the Covid-19 crisis as well! In other words, while world authorities are doing their very best to present only one narrative, there are actually other ways to see and interpret the situation.

- In our present-day world, there are a number of extremely wealthy people, elites who are situated at the apex of the pyramid and control almost everything that we know and see around us.

- These elites have *wealth and power ties* with pharmaceutical companies and the mainstream media, as well as with key figures in governments and world authorities. Furthermore, some of them possess several satanic hobbies, which they practice as members of different secret, idol-worshipping societies.

- These world elites aspire to lead our world into a great reset, which will bring about their desired New/One World Order.

- Finally, these global elites are actually being used by the Creator, to advance His original master plan, which is the establishment of <u>HIS</u> New World Order—the kingdom of Israel ruled by Yeshua of Nazareth, the King of the Jews—from Jerusalem.

For the Coming of the Son of Man Will Be Just Like the Days of Noah...

When describing *the end of the age*, and to help His first century disciples discern the *times and seasons,* Yeshua mentioned two

Biblical narratives; those that relate to the lives of *Noah* and *Lot*.[151] I would like to briefly examine the main characteristics of those days, as well as the days of ancient Babylon.

In both Noah and Lot's generations, sin was abundant in such a grotesque way, to the extent that unrighteousness, lies, deceptions and corruption had consumed all the areas of their lives. The Jewish sages explained that most of the sins in Noah's generation had to do with (a) idol worship or paganism (in Hebrew, *avoda zara* — עבודה זרה), and (b) forbidden sexual relations, i.e., incest (in Hebrew, *gilluy arayot* — גילוי עריות). These were expressed and manifested mainly after being drawn into materialism, wealth and power, which were then used to practice the above sins at the expense of the poor, needy, feeble and vulnerable of the time!

As mentioned above, there was a clear corruption of the human genome itself through the mingling of the *sons of God* with *the daughters of man!* Could it be that the Covid-19 *gene therapy* (incorrectly labeled as "vaccine") does contain ingredients, such as nanoparticles, which are purposed to change the actual human genome? It is my personal view, based on my extensive research, that the answer to this specific question is a resounding YES, comporting with the fact that *there is nothing new under the sun!*

In Babylon, the above sins were grouped with a few more pagan aspirations. The Babylonians wished to have a more concentrated governing power so that they could *make a name for themselves.* At the same time, they also wished to physically reach the Heavens, to not only be materialistically elevated but also spiritually. They were not satisfied with only physical wealth and power but desired to be

---

[151] See Matt. 24:37; Lk. 17:28-32.

like God Himself—to be where He is and to possess whatever He possesses! In short, during the times of Noah, Lot and Babylon, the rich and powerful devil-worshipers aspired to get rid of the Creator, taking His place, while attempting to be gods!

I would like to ask the following questions:

a. Are we able to see and discern certain major similarities between the times in which we are living today and the above description of the days of Noah, Lot, and Babylon?

b. Are we aware of the rapid modern-day increase of idol worship and paganism, as well as the practice of forbidden sexual relations, including incest?

c. Are our eyes open and able to recognize the aspirations of world elites to change the God-created human genome, to be *as God,* in order to make a name for themselves, by attempting to unite the world under a One, New World Order, and spiritually rebuilding the ancient Tower of Babylon?

A Great Deception & The Beginning of the End

When looking at the various arguments, opinions and claims concerning the Covid-19 crisis *in the light of Scripture,* I could not arrive at any other conclusion except to side with the not-so-popular-or-accepted minority. I choose <u>not</u> to go *after the many to pervert justice!* I have decided to examine with a suspicious eye, everything that the authorities (as they use the mainstream media) are trying to convey to me.

It is my understanding that the recent Covid-19 crisis is nothing more than a very well-thought-out and pre-meditated satanic plan. For those of us who have *eyes to see and ears to hear,* we can easily see that from the very beginning, this crisis has been characterized by a great lack of transparency on the side of the authorities, who have practiced lies, deception and the misleading of so many. If there is "a terrible global pandemic" that threatens humanity's very existence, it is more likely *a global pandemic of deception!* In fact, I see it as the greatest deception which has ever taken place throughout human history!

I am not a Corona-denier—no! I'm aware that there might be *a virus called Covid-19*. Yet, I also know that it is remarkably similar in its structure and symptoms to some other, previous, and well-known coronaviruses. It is my understanding that the source of this new coronavirus was *not* natural, as has been presented to us by the authorities (i.e., animals in the open Wuhan Market)! It was rather well-engineered—initially in a U.S. lab (led by none other than the infamous Dr. Fauci) and later, in a lab in Wuhan, China. It was engineered with one main purpose: to serve as a tool – a catalyst – through which the Great Reset can take shape and manifest in our world—a Great Reset that will eventually lead to the establishment of their much-desired New World Order. In other words: This Covid-19 Crisis is nothing but the beginning of the end – Something like a snowball that gains more and more speed as the days pass by, till it will be stopped by the glorious appearance of Yeshua the Messiah Redeemer!

If world governments would have invested the same enormous amount of resources that they have invested into this Covid-19 crisis, in, for example in building new hospitals throughout the world, conducting research into better treatments for existing chronic illnesses, and so on, the world in which we are living would be greatly improved!

The fact that there is no real transparency on the side of the authorities should grab our attention as true seekers of truth and righteousness! Given that the Israeli Corona Cabinet is under a thirty-year act of confidentiality, covering all its sessions and protocols, should sound an alarm! The fact that the voices of top doctors, professors, virologists, epidemiologists, and other scientists have been silenced and censored on almost every possible stage, should also send off some huge signals in our minds! The proven and well-known phenomenon of wealth and power ties leads me to seriously doubt all these repeated mainstream media reports as it relates to new developments regarding the Covid-19 pandemic. This would include the rising numbers of new variants, deaths, critically ill patients and so on, presented especially during the years 2020 and 2021![152]

The following is a summary of the main points which convinced me that that this entire Covid-19 crisis is a huge scam which has been blown out of proportion – to usher in the Anti-Messiah's reign:

- ***The PCR Test*** - The test upon which virtually this entire global pandemic has been based! A test that is unreliable, to say the least! A test that was never intended by its inventor to detect

---

[152] As stated, there is great suspicion that many who have died from so-called "Corona deaths" were not really killed by Covid-19, but simply died while "with" (or infected by) Covid-19! There is ample evidence from Israel and around the world that many people – too many – have had "Corona death" recorded on their death certificates without any confirmation or scientific proof that supported it! Part of the problem with this disingenuous reporting has likely been due to hospitals, throughout the world, including in the United States, having received extra federal funding for every coronavirus case they have treated and certainly for any Covid-19 *deaths* that have occurred at their facilities.

infectious diseases! A test that can easily be manipulated to serve the official narrative.[153]

- ***The Green Pass:*** As of June 2022, it became clearer and clearer by the day that these green passes were not established based on pure scientific health data! All they have tried to achieve, up until very recently, was to coerce all of mankind into taking the experimental injection erroneously called "a vaccine!" Moreover, despite the fact that these mRNA-based *gene therapy* have had a myriad of side effects already reported[154] (without yet knowing the mid and long-term side-effects), world governments are still considering making it mandatory!

---

[153] Note, the new "antigen test" is even less accurate! See the recent FDA report admitting the inaccuracy of this the PCR test via *https://t.me/Israel_is_Awakening/4369* — An excerpt shared on Telegram by UK Lawyer "Anna De" states: "A document, just released by the U.S. Food and Drug Administration (FDA), openly admits that the infamous PCR test for the Wuhan Coronavirus (Covid-19) was developed not with actual samples, but, rather, with what appears to be genetic material from a common cold virus. From the document: *'Since no quantified virus isolates of the 2019-nCoV were available for CDC use at the time the test was developed, and this study conducted, essays designed for detection of the 2019-nCoV RNA were tested with characterized stocks of in vitro transcribed full-length RNA (N gene; GenBank accession: MN908947.2) of known titer (RNA copies/µL) spiked into a diluent consisting of a suspension of human A549 cells and viral transport medium (VTM) to mimic clinical specimen.'* ... Another revelation in the document is the admission by the FDA that test results are 'pooled' together to produce numbers that are inaccurate. The FDA is quite literally manufacturing data to support a false narrative."

[154] See one example from the United States: The Vaccine Adverse Event Reporting System (VAERS): *https://wonder.cdc.gov/vaers.html*

- **Pfizer's dubious past:** Did you know that this pharmaceutical company received the highest fine ever imposed in an official court for fraud and other malfeasance?[155]

- **The Israeli Corona Cabinet:** The act of confidentiality for thirty long years. What are they trying to hide from us?

- **The redacted Pfizer-Israel agreement:** Again, highly classified for thirty years. Why?

- **The urgent need for the mRNA-based vaccines:** Since Pfizer itself admitted that its vaccine only helps to relieve some of the difficult symptoms of the virus, and that it does not prevent its transmission to others, why should people run to take them?

A Personal Confession

Over the last two to three years, I have come to a few personal convictions. One of them is that God has graciously chosen to use this Covid-19 crisis to open my own spiritual eyes to a number of shocking events on the world backstage, (i.e., behind the scenes), which I might have ordinarily ignored...

I'm grateful that He has clearly shown me the dark side of this world, including the unfathomable depth of Satan's evil.[156] Part of this has

---

[155] See, for example *Drug Dangers* — *https://www.drugdangers.com/manufacturers/pfizer/* — and from the U.S. Department of Justice: "Justice Department Announces Largest Health Care Fraud Settlement in Its History: Pfizer to Pay $2.3 Billion for Fraudulent Marketing" — *https://www.justice.gov/opa/pr/justice-department-announces-largest-health-care-fraud-settlement-its-history*

[156] See Rev. 2:24.

involved getting a glimpse into how Satan actually controls the minds of his servants (whether or not they are aware of it), many of whom are the elites we previously discussed. I've been able to see how Satan uses them to achieve what he thinks will end up becoming his victory over the one true God – the One who threw him out of His presence.

I'm grateful to be part of a very small minority within a minority! As I'm sure some of you know, here in Israel, true followers of Yeshua make up about 0.3-0.5% of the entire population! That means that I not only belong to a small minority of believers in Yeshua, but to an even smaller minority within that minority! I admit that life would be so much easier for me and my family had I not been exposed to all that I have shared with you in this opening chapter. Having understood Covid-19 in its true broader context, I felt compelled to share it with you, and that can definitely have its pitfalls among those in the body who do not share these revelations!

Not only is it possible that I may be seen as an outcast here in Israel among some body members, but I have also had to pay a price in the form of personal freedoms for living according to what I believe God has been speaking to my conscience. For example, had I taken the jab, I would have been able to go and visit two of my precious daughters who remain in America with their children (our grandchildren).[157] I could have continued preaching and teaching His Word in many home gatherings, churches and Messianic synagogues all over the English-speaking world. I would have been able to partake in life's everyday activities, during the first one a and half years of this pandemic, such as going to the movie theatre, the gym, a restaurant, or other indoor events, all of which were forbidden to the unvaccinated.

---

[157] As of Nov. 2022, the USA is the only western country (as far as I know) that did not lift the restriction that forbids the unvaccinated tourists from entering the country. I surely hope this will change soon, as it was changed here in Israel, in Canada, Australia and other countries around the world.

But then I had to ask myself —should I, a disciple and teacher of His Holy Word, be at all surprised by what has taken place? Have not all the surprising truths that I've discovered in my research already been revealed in the *navigation map* which God has entrusted into our hands? So, what or who could have hidden these truths from my sight?

I am persuaded that if there was anything which could have caused me to elude these truths, it would have been the fact that I had gotten too used to, and even addicted to the goodies this modern world has been able to offer me, as well as others, who live in a Western, developed and materialistically saturated world. The God of Israel has blessed me with a wonderful wife, four beautiful children, five grandchildren, an abundance of food, a lovely home and an excellent job filled with so many bonuses. Working as a tour guide has allowed me to meet many wonderful people throughout the English-speaking world. It has also afforded me to make annual visits abroad, the ability to teach and preach the Word to various audiences and even enjoy a few nice vacations in those venues.

Yet, something dramatically changed within the course of less than three years. I am so very grateful to the sovereign God who has allowed me to see all that I have shared with you here. This pandemic has forced me to turn back to some of the eternal truths that are presented in His Holy Word.

This crisis has caused me to ask difficult questions regarding my own personal relationship and walk with the Lord, such as: Would I be willing to pay the price – any price – for standing on the Bible's eternal truths and principles (standing on God's side as it relates to this satanic, invented crisis)? Would I be willing to give up my basic human rights in this world? Am I willing to forego any future green pass, which will prevent me from enjoying the same normal life I had enjoyed up until March 2020? Am I willing, as many men and women of God in the past, to swim against the tide? Am I willing to belong to a minority within a minority—one which is being ridiculed and labeled delusional, fanatic, conspiratorial and the like?

Being aware of *the big picture,* the background details along my navigation route, such as the UN agendas 2021 and 2030, the hidden and highly classified reasons behind the new "vaccines," etc., I can no longer stick my head in the sand. I don't see any good reason why I should collaborate with the global, idol-worshipping and psychopathic elites of this evil world, who along with their leader, the serpent of old, are God's very enemies!

Come Out of Her, My People

Beloved, Yeshua proclaimed that *every plant our Heavenly Father has not planted will be uprooted!*[158] None of us in Yeshua's body can doubt that every element of darkness and deception will indeed be *uprooted!* Yet, we have the responsibility to discern what has been planted by our Heavenly Father and what has not. It was not in vain that Shaul the Apostle admonished the faithful in Ephesus, *put on the whole armor of God, that you may be able to stand against the wiles of the devil.*[159]

As God's faithful, we are called to *stand against the wiles of the devil—*not to coast along on the easy currents of deception that are so quickly accepted by the majority. We are called, as Yeshua prayed over us, to be *in the world, not of it.*[160] We are further admonished to *come out* from the frameworks of deception that define the satanic kingdom of this world. Could it be here, too, as referred to concerning Babylon, that we are to *come out of her, my people, lest you share in her sins,*

---

[158] See Matt. 15:13.

[159] See Eph. 6:11.

[160] See Jn. 17:16.

and lest you receive of her plagues?[161] May we not be caught up in the very system our Father is going to eventually uproot!

As the Heavenly Father destroys and judges all man-made practices, global systems and deceptions, including the Covid-19 pandemic, which has manipulated multitudes into quick and total submission, are we willing to *be sanctified by the truth — to withstand in the evil day, having done all, to stand?*[162]

I wouldn't dare tell any of you, precious brethren in Yeshua, how to act or what to do! Each and every one of us must one day stand-alone before the throne of God! It is not my job to judge you for your own personal walk and convictions! The only thing I humbly ask you to do is to consider what I have shared with you here, bring it before the Lord and ask HIM to guide you by His gentle Spirit to the right path on this *solo night navigation route*, which we are all called to take. I pray and beseech the Lord that all of us eventually reach the endpoint of this *night navigation,* whole, safe and with great success!

---

[161] See Rev. 18:4.

[162] See Eph. 6:13.

Non-Mainstream Media Sources

Introduction

Let me start with a disclaimer: Most of the following non-mainstream sites are run by individuals and private organizations that are *not* supported or controlled by the global elites! Many of them are *not* run by believers in Yeshua, and thus are also not one hundred percent biblically accurate, and I do *not* agree with all that they say or present! According to Scripture, we need to carefully discern the spirits and are not to fall for everything we see or hear, whether from fellow believers or non-believers. The gift of discernment is needed more these days than ever! It is our responsibility to distinguish between recognized facts and someone's interpretation of those facts. For example, we must distinguish between what doctors, professors, virologists, epidemiologists and other professionals and scientists say, on the one hand, and the personal interpretation of those who interview them, on the other.

It's important to acknowledge that the suggested news sources that follow do not and cannot present all the details pertaining to *the big picture* regarding the Covid-19 pandemic. Just as children and even adults do jigsaw puzzles or play with Legos, connecting one piece to another, so too, should we try to assemble the different parts and dots of the facts presented to us on the sites below, so that we will be able, with God's help, to see the complete puzzle.

On each site below, there are many links to other sites, as is customary on the web. You are encouraged to browse and expand your search accordingly, as He leads you to do so.

You will find that there are lots of videos featuring interviews of doctors, professors and other scientists—many of which have been censored and taken off the web, and thus are no longer available. I fully trust the Lord to help you locate the ones which will magnify the important scientific material supporting the viewpoints I have presented to you in this opening chapter.

Many private scientists, doctors and others have been forced to open alternative online outlets - platforms such as *Rumble* and *NewTube* podcasts on applications such as *Telegram* and *Signal*, and so on... Some of these new news platforms require you to sign up to join them to be able to view their content and do your own research. I highly recommend doing so, as it is very well worth your time and effort.[163]

---

[163] Out there, in the non-mainstream media, there are also a few ultra-Orthodox rabbis, who share the same convictions regarding this covid crisis. I am aware that for some believers in Yeshua, rabbis and their opinions are not relevant. However, my personal conviction is that we should never throw out the baby with the bath water. I personally believe that unsaved rabbis often have relevant contributions which add to the understanding of *the big picture*, the broader context of the Covid-19 crisis. Here are a few names that you can look up for yourself, if you feel led to: *Rabbi Daniel Asor* — A rabbi, known as a vigorous activist against those who believe in Yeshua, but, at the same time, has a very deep understanding of cults, secret societies, modern idol worship, and more. What he shares is highly recommended for those of us who can overcome and forgive his ignorance concerning his own Messiah, while remembering that *the veil* is still on his heart! *Rabbi Yoav Alon* — Formerly a scientist in the Israeli defense industry. He, too, understands *the big picture,* without (yet) recognizing His Messiah Redeemer. *Rabbi Chananya Weissman* — An Orthodox rabbi, who speaks openly against the Corona Deception, and has a real gift of writing—a very interesting man, indeed! I highly recommend reading what he recently entitled as, *the thirteen articles of Scientific faith,* where he sarcastically compares the thirteen articles of faith by the famous Rambam (Maimonides), and the blinded faith of many orthodox Jews in

Lastly, as we all surf the web at times, I'm sure you are aware of Fact Checking sites such as *Snopes* for English speakers and *Mida'at* for Hebrew speakers. My suggestion is not to fall into the trap of believing all that they say! For the most part, these Fact Checkers themselves are associated with the mainstream media and are strongly connected to the wealth and power ties system discussed earlier! We must not be naïve! Let us use our God-given discernment when navigating all of these popular "Fact Checking" sites.[164]

Websites that Give a Stage to Censored Doctors and Scientists

America's Frontline Doctors — *https://aflds.org* — Hundreds of American doctors are making harsh allegations against the official version of the U.S. administration regarding the coronavirus crisis. It is highly recommended to listen to some of the fascinating lectures by the founder of this association—a Jewish doctor (as well as a lawyer) by the name of Simone Gold.

World Doctors Alliance — *https://worlddoctorsalliance.com* — A group of doctors, professors and others who stand for the truth and provide a stage for censored information relating to the Covid pandemic. You can find good articles and other important data on their website.

Doctors for COVID Ethics — *https://rumble.com/c/c-1238333.* Hundreds of doctors, professors, lawyers and scientists, mostly from

---

modern-day Science. *Rabbi Alon Anava* — A rabbi who broadcasts in a high level of English, whose opinion regarding this current crisis is very clear.

[164] For example, some of these "Fact Checking" sites are strongly connected to the Bill and Melinda Gates Foundation (or their affiliates by their various names)! Would any reasonable person expect them to criticize their boss or write a negative article about the Gates?!

Germany, set up a committee to arouse public interest in the failure of their government in handling this crisis.

Grand Jury — *https://odysee.com/@GrandJury:f/Grand-Jury-1-EN:0* — Not long ago, Doctors for Covid Ethics launched the Grand Jury court of public opinion, which I highly recommend watching and listening to, as they present scientific evidence that proves, beyond a shadow of a doubt, that this pandemic orchestration is a hoax.

Red Voice Media with Stew Peters — *https://www.redvoicemedia.com/stew-peters-show/* — A highly recommended show, where scientists are interviewed and expose the Covid hoax.

The Highwire with Del Bigtree - https://www.audible.com/pd/The-Highwire-with-Del-Bigtree-Podcast/B08JJNXRNR - As with the above "Red Voice Media," I highly recommend this show, hosted by Del Bigtree - an American television and film producer.

Websites With a Large Amount of Censored Material

Rav Hanistar (Hebrew for: *Much is Hidden*) — *https://www.ravhanistar.net/en*

The SGT report — *https://sgtreport.tv*

Health Impact News — *https://healthimpactnews.com*

The Daily Expose — A U.K.-based website — *https://dailyexpose.uk*

The Israeli Civil Committee — Dealing especially with the many side effects of the mRNA vaccines— *https://www.the-people-committee.com/english* — See also:

Vaccines Impact — *https://vaccineimpact.com*

Child sex slavery and the Elite — *https://rumble.com/vwfjex-boys-for-sale-child-sex-slavery-and-the-elite.html*

Banned Doctors — *https://covidvaccinedeaths.org/banned-doctors* — Or:

Covid Vaccine Deaths — *https://covidvaccinedeaths.org* OR *www.lovecantstaysilent.com*

The Defender — A site by Robert F. Kennedy, Jr. Highly recommended! https://childrenshealthdefense.org

Expose News (Steve Kirsch) at - https://expose-news.com/

Researching the Efficacy of the mRNA Vaccine

Unacceptable Jessica: I don't know what to say — https://jessicar.substack.com/p/i-dont-know-what-to-say?r=2wvfu

Efficacy of the mRNA-1273 SARS-CoV-2 Vaccine at Completion of Blinded Phase — *https://www.nejm.org/doi/full/10.1056/NEJMoa2113017* — **and its Supplementary Appendix** https://www.nejm.org/doi/suppl/10.1056/NEJMoa2113017/suppl_file/nejmoa2113017_appendix.pdf

Studies on Face Masks, Nano Technologies in the Vaccines and More

More Than 400 Studies Show Lockdowns and Face Masks Don't Work https://dailyexpose.uk/2021/12/16/more-than-400-studies-show-lockdowns-and-face-masks-dont-work/

Masks are Dangerous and Ineffective: Nanotech in the Shots? https://archive.fo/2022.01.29-225016/https://masksaredangerous.com/nanotech-in-the-shots/

Do musk mandates work? New York Times: https://www.nytimes.com/2023/02/21/opinion/do-mask-mandates-work.html?smid=nytcore-ios-share&referringSource=articleShare

*Investigating the current status of COVID-19 related plastics and their potential impact on human health https://doi.org/10.1016/j.cotox.2021.08.002 **Or:** https://www.sciencedirect.com/science/article/pii/S2468202021000 371*

Orwell City: New Pfizer vaccine images: Self-assembling microstructures — https://www.orwell.city/2022/02/new-images.html

Technological Genocide — 19 — https://telegra.ph/TECHNOLOGICAL-GENOCIDE--19-02-03

EXCLUSIVE: Australian Whistleblower Scientists Provide Evidence of Nanotech & Graphene Oxide in COVID-19 Injections! https://zeeemedia.com/interview/exclusive-australian-whistleblower-scientists-provide-evidence/

Tim Gielen, Monopoly: Who Owns the World? https://www.stopworldcontrol.com/monopoly/

Telegram channel of Sergeant Robert Horton, sergeant in the U.S. Army as a Psychological Operations Warfare Specialist from 1999-2012 in the U.S. Special Operations Command/U.S. Army — *https://t.me/SergeantRobertHorton/14857*

A Place to Know —https://en.knowheretoknow.com — This is the site of Raphael Ben Dor, a dear Israeli man who greatly cares for the Israeli people and is very close to seeing *the big picture.* Raphael downloaded and saved many censored movies and articles, making them easily accessible here on his site which is a valuable and plentiful treasure trove of resources. For example, many episodes in a series entitled, *The Fall of the Kabal* deal with many of the behind-the-scenes global activities, such as the entertainment world (Hollywood and the like), the main news outlets as well as who really controls them, etc. You can also find a two-episode series called *Bill Gates: Smashing the Conspiracy.* This gives a completely new perspective of Bill Gates (compared to the one which has been presented to us by the mainstream media) and is related to what he really believes. It also explains why he contributes so much of his time and money to vaccine research, as well as why he (and his friend, the head of the WHO) are not welcomed in India and Africa anymore.

Avi Barak News: ab-news.net

Recommended Books

The truth about Covid-19, by Dr. Joseph Mercola & Ronnie Cumins
https://www.amazon.com/Truth-About-COVID-19-Lockdowns-Passports/dp/1645020886

The Great Reset and the war for the World, by Alex Jones
https://www.amazon.com/Great-Reset-War-World/dp/1510774041/ref=d_pd_vtp_sccl_3_2/131-2831879-4343332?pd_rd_w=saL2V&content-id=amzn1.sym.484e9db3-40a7-48ee-b5b0-d31beb157daa&pf_rd_p=484e9db3-40a7-48ee-b5b0-d31beb157daa&pf_rd_r=NBDQ5R57KJNC5H812TW8&pd_rd_wg=4lk Rl&pd_rd_r=5dbfdd5c-a6ee-4640-8aa0-f149aa9fa7e5&pd_rd_i=1510774041&psc=1

The Great Reset, by Glenn Beck
https://www.amazon.com/Great-Reset-Biden-Twenty-First -Century-Fascism/dp/163763059X/ref=d_pd_sbs_sccl_3_2/131-2831879-

4343332?pd_rd_w=nrPhV&content-id=amzn1.sym.3676f086-9496-4fd7-8490-77cf7f43f846&pf_rd_p=3676f086-9496-4fd7-8490-77cf7f43f846&pf_rd_r=Z676BBNWTKHR8WSASJ55&pd_rd_wg=aCfEv&pd_rd_r=36c5578a-77ac-44ed-b9a7-f1062af37d25&pd_rd_i=163763059X&psc=1

Corona False Alarm, by Karina Reiss and Sucharit Bhakdi
https://www.amazon.com/Corona-Sucharit-Covid-19-Michael-Collection/dp/9124084395/ref=sr_1_1?qid=1667836964&refinements=p_27%3ASucharit+Bhakdi+MD&s=books&sr=1-1

Chapter 2:

The Doctrine of the Pre-Tribulation Rapture – The Great Blessed Hope, or a Tragic Delusion?

Introduction

As I wrote in the opening chapter, I am persuaded that we are living at the very end of what Scripture defines as *the Latter Days.* I am convinced that Covid-19 has been the starting point, the catalyst, or as I called it, "the beginning of the end." I do believe that the signs we are witnessing in today's world clearly reveal that we are indeed entering the time which will usher in the very *end of the age.*

This second chapter deals with one of the most controversial topics in the body of Messiah today, especially as it relates to eschatology—namely, the pre-Tribulation Rapture. My goal is to assess what Scripture really tells us about the return of Messiah and our gathering unto Him.

Is the study of the Rapture and its timing important at all? Why should we invest time in it? Millions and millions of sincere followers of Messiah throughout the world (including here in God's Promised Land) believe they are not going to live through what Scripture defines as *the Great Tribulation.* Not only this, but they also claim that they will not even witness the revelation of the Anti-Messiah in this world. They believe, instead, that they will be snatched up and out of this world just before his public appearing.

Now, if they are correct, none of us should be troubled or even look into this study, as there is no real need for it. Yet, if they are wrong and followers of Yeshua are going to not only witness the revelation of the Anti-Messiah, but also go through (even a part) of the great Tribulation, then studying this subject should be of crucial importance to all of us!

If our gathering unto the Lord takes place *after* the Anti-Messiah is revealed, many millions among the worldwide followers of Yeshua will find themselves in great confusion. They are going to be disappointed and, as a direct outcome, at risk of losing their faith in Messiah Yeshua! Their confusion might lead them to anger towards God, as the realization sets in that they were neither spared from the great Tribulation nor did God fulfill "His promises" to them. They might seriously doubt His goodness, mercies and even His very salvation through Yeshua of Nazareth! In more scriptural terms, some of them might find themselves as those who are part of *the great falling away.*[165]

The following are the main points I will address in this chapter:

- From where does the concept of *a Rapture* emanate? Is it a biblically based concept?

- Does Scripture tell us *when* the Rapture of the true believers will take place?

- The Rapture as seen and interpreted through Hebrew Middle Eastern lenses

- Biblical patterns of Rapture

- Responding to some known claims held by believers in the doctrine of pre-Tribulation Rapture

---

[165] Or *apostasy.* See 2 Thes. 2:3. See also Jn. 6:66.

119

Building the Foundations Part 1:
The Origins and Concept of Rapture in Scripture

The word *Rapture* does not exist in the original Greek manuscripts of the New Covenant writings. *Rapture* originated from the first translation of the Bible into Latin in the fifth century CE.[166] There, in 1 Thes. 4:17, the Greek word *harpazō* (*har-pad'-zo*)[167] was translated as *rapio* (*to catch up* or *take away*) and made its way into the English translations as *Rapture*.

Yet, the concept of Rapture, in the sense of an individual or a group of people (even a whole nation) being *taken away* (or "transferred") from one place to another or from one position and condition to another, is very much biblically based! To better understand this concept, we first need to become familiar with a few other words in Scripture, both in Hebrew and in Greek, which allude to the idea, or concept, of a *Rapture*. Before we do, it's important to note that in ancient Hebrew, as well as in the Greek, there is often more than one possible translation for words! To make it easier, I have included all the different possible translations for each of the following words, in specific footnotes.

In the Tanach, we have two main words that allude to the concept of Rapture:

---

[166] *The Vulgate*, by Hieronymus.

[167] G726 (Strong), ἁρπάζω, *harpazō*—*to seize* (in various applications): *catch (away, up), pluck, pull, take (by force)*. This use is also seen in other texts, such as in Acts 8:39; 2 Cor. 12:2-4; and Rev. 12:5.

(1) *lekichah* (לקיחה), or *lakach* (לקח),[168] and (2) *aseifah* (אסיפה/אספה), or *asaf* (אסף).[169]

In the New Covenant writings, there are also a few other words (other than *harpazō*), which allude to the concept of Rapture. They are: *Episunagōgē* (*ep-ee-soon-ag-o-gay*),[170] *apairō ah'ee-ro*,[171] *airō-ah'ee-ro*,[172] *epairō- ep-ahee'-ro*,[173] *paralambanō* (*par-al-am-ban'-o*),[174]

---

[168] H3947 (Strong). A primitive root; *to take* (in the widest variety of applications): *accept, bring, buy, carry away, drawn, fetch, get, enfold , X many, mingle, place, receive (-ing), reserve, seize, send for, take (away, -ing, up), use, win.*

[169] H622 (Strong). A primitive root; *to gather* for any purpose; hence to *receive, take away,* that is, remove (destroy, leave behind, put up, restore, etc.): *assemble, bring, consume, destroy, fetch, gather (in, together, up again), X generally, get (him), lose, put all together, receive, recover [another from leprosy], (be) rewarded, X surely, take (away, into, up), X utterly, withdraw.*

[170] G1996 (Strong)—a complete *collection*; specifically, a Christian *meeting* (for worship): *assembling (gathering) together.*

[171] G575 (Strong)—to *lift off,* that is, remove: *take (away).*

[172] G142 (Strong). A primary verb; *to lift; by implication to take up or away*; figuratively to *raise* (the voice), *keep in suspense* (the mind); specifically, to *sail* away (that is, *weigh anchor*); by Hebraism (compare [H5375]) to *expiate* sin: *away with, bear (up), carry, lift up, loose, make to doubt, put away, remove, take (away, up).*

[173] G522 (Strong), ἀπαίρω. From G575 and G142—to *lift off,* that is, remove: *take (away).*

[174] G3880 (Strong), παραλαμβάνω, paralambanō, *par-al-am-ban'.* From G3844 **and** G2983; to *receive near,* that is, *associate* oneself *with* (in any familiar or intimate act or relation); by analogy, to *assume* an office; figuratively, to *lear.*

ginomai (ghin'-om-ahee)[175] and *sullegō (sool-leg'-o)*.[176] These Greek words are also connected to the concept of a person, a group or even a nation, being *taken* (or "transferred") from one place, situation or condition to another. Let us now delve into a few examples where the conceptual demonstration of Rapture is shown.

Rapture — By Means of Separation

Gen. 2:23 — *And Adam said, this is now bone of my bones, and flesh of my flesh: she shall be called woman, because she was <u>taken out</u>* (in Hebrew, *lukachah* — לקחה) *of Man*. In other words, Eve was taken out, or separated from one place or position (Adam's body) into another one, a new one—her own independent body of flesh.

Gen. 3:19 — *By the sweat of your face you shall eat bread, till you return to the ground, for out of it you were <u>taken</u>* (in Hebrew, *lukachtah* — לקחת), *for dust you are, and unto dust you shall return.* Adam was an integral part of the ground, or soil, from which he was *taken*. In other words, he was separated from one position, or

---

[175] G1096 (Strong), Γίνομαι. A prolonged and middle form of a primary verb; to *cause to be* ("gen"-erate), that is, (reflexively) to *become* (*come into being*), used with great latitude (literally, figuratively, intensively, etc.): <u>arise be assembled</u>, be (come, -fall, -have self), be brought (to pass), (be) come (to pass), continue, be divided, be done, draw, be ended, fall, be finished, follow, be found, be fulfilled, + God forbid, grow, happen, have, be kept, be made, be married, be ordained to be, partake, pass, be performed, be published, require, seem, be showed, X soon as it was, sound, <u>be taken</u>, be turned, use, wax, will, would, be wrought.

[176] G4816 (Strong), συλλέγω. From G4862 **and** G3004, in its original sense; to <u>collect</u>: gather (together, up). See also G4863 (Strong), συνάγω, **sunagō**, soon-ag'-o. From G4862 **and** G71: to *lead together*, that is, to *collect* **or** *convene*; specifically, to *entertain* (hospitably): + accompany, <u>assemble</u> (selves, together), bestow, <u>come together, gather</u> (selves together, up, together), lead into, resort, take in.

condition, into another; and one day he will return to the place from where he came (due to his sin).

Ex. 14:11 — *Then they said to Moses, because there were no graves in Egypt, have you <u>taken us</u>* (in Hebrew, *lekachtanu* — לקחתנו) *away to die in the wilderness? Why have you so dealt with us, to carry us forth out of Egypt?* God, using Moses, *took* His Chosen People out of Egypt—once again, He repositioned them from one location to another—a new one (see also Deut. 4:20).

Isa. 24:22 — *They will be <u>gathered</u> together* (in Hebrew, *vusfu asefa* — ואספו אספה), *as prisoners are gathered in the pit, and will be shut up in the prison...* Again the concept of people being gathered (taken/separated/transferred) from one position or condition to another, appears.

Isa. 49:5 — *And now, the LORD says, who formed me from the womb to be his servant, to bring Jacob back to him, so that Israel is <u>gathered</u>* (in Hebrew, *ye'asef* — יאסף) *to Him....*

Matt. 13:40 — *Therefore, as the tares are <u>gathered</u>* (in Greek, *sullegō* — sool-leg'-o) *and burned in the fire, so it will be at the end of this age.*

Matt. 25:32 — *All the nations will be <u>gathered</u>* (in Greek, *sunagō* — soon-ag'-o) *before Him, and he will separate them one from another, as a shepherd divides His sheep from the goats.*

Matt. 24:40-41 — *Then two men will be in the field, one will be <u>taken</u>* (in Greek, *paralambanō* — par-al-am-ban'-o) *and the other left. Two women will be grinding at the mill; one will be <u>taken</u>* (in Greek, *paralambanō* — par-al-am-ban'-o) *and the other left.*

Jn. 20:2 — *Then she ran and came to Simon Peter and to the other disciple, whom Yeshua loved, and said to them, they have <u>taken away</u>*

(in Greek, *airō — ah'ee-ro*) *the Lord out of the tomb, and we know not where they have laid him.*

Rapture — By Means of Death

Gen. 49:29 — *Then he charged them, and said to them, I am to be <u>gathered</u>* (in Hebrew, *ne'esaf —* נאסף) *to my people. Bury me with my fathers in the cave that is in the field of Ephron the Hittite...*

Num. 20:24 — *Aaron shall be <u>gathered</u>* (in Hebrew, *ye'asef —* יאסף) *to his people: for he shall not enter the land which I have given to the children of Israel, because you rebelled against my word at the water of Meribah.*

Num. 27:13 — *And when you have seen it, you also shall be <u>gathered</u>* (in Hebrew, *vene'esafta —* ונאספת) *unto your people, as Aaron your brother was <u>gathered</u>* (in Hebrew, *ne'saf —* נאסף).

Num. 31:2 — *Take vengeance on the Midianites for children of Israel. Afterward, you shall be <u>gathered</u>* (in Hebrew, *te'asef —* תאסף) *to your people.*[177]

Isa. 57:1 — *The righteous perishes, and no man takes it to heart. Merciful men are <u>taken away</u>* (in Hebrew, *ne'esaf —* נאסף) *while no one considers that the righteous is <u>taken away</u>* (in Hebrew, *ne'esaf —* נאסף) *from evil.*

Job 1:21 — *And he said, naked I came from my mother's womb, and naked shall I return there. The LORD gave, and the LORD has <u>taken away</u>* (in Hebrew, *lakach —* לקח). *Blessed be the name of the LORD!*

---

[177] See also Deut. 32:50; 2 Kings 22:20; and 2 Ch. 34:28.

Rapture — By Means of Healing

2 Kings 5:3 — *She said to her mistress, 'I wish that my master was with the prophet who is in Samaria! Then he would <u>cure him</u> (in Hebrew, ye'esof oto — יאסף אתו) of his leprosy.'*

2 Kings 5:6 — *I have sent Naaman my servant to you that you may <u>cure him</u> (in Hebrew, ve'asafto — ואספתו) of his leprosy.*[178]

Rapture — By Means of Resurrection and/or a Changed and Glorified Body

Acts 1:9 — *Now when he had spoken these things, while they watched, he was <u>taken up</u> (in Greek, apairō — ap-ah'ee-ro) and a cloud received him out of their sight.*

2 Thes. 2:1 — *Now brethren, concerning the coming of our Lord Messiah Yeshua, and our <u>gathering</u> (in Greek, episunagōgē — ep-ee-soon-ag-o-gay') together to Him...*

2 Thes. 2:7 — *For the mystery of lawlessness is already at work, only he who now restrains will do so until he is <u>taken out</u> (in Greek, ginomai — ghin'-om-ahee) of the way.*[179]

We can see that the concept of *Rapture* (in the sense of being taken from one place or position to another) is scriptural and that it runs throughout the Old and New Covenant writings. We see it is not limited to only one eschatological event (i.e., the Rapture of followers of Yeshua up and out of this world), but also to individuals, a group of people and a nation who are transferred from one place, position

---

[178] See also 2 Kings 5, verses 7 and 11.

[179] As we progress, we are going to see that there is yet another way to translate this specific Greek word, which can change the entire understanding of this specific Biblical reference.

and/or condition to another - a new one, while still here on Earth. Likewise, it concerns individuals, a group of people, and nation, who are transferred from life in the flesh, here on Earth, to the next world by means of death. Lastly, a *Rapture* can refer to the sense of one's physical condition (in sickness) being changed, or transferred to a new condition, by means of healing or being cured.

Building the Foundations Part 2:
Four Main Views

Within Messiah's body, there are four main viewpoints regarding the timing of the last days' Rapture and our gathering unto Yeshua: (a) *the pre-Tribulation Rapture*—the belief that the Rapture will take place at any time prior to the great Tribulation; (b) *mid-Tribulation Rapture*—the belief that it will take place in the middle of the great Tribulation, i.e., in the middle of the seven last years; (c) *the post-Tribulation Rapture*—the belief that it will take place at Messiah's glorious return, i.e., at the very end of the great Tribulation; and, lastly, (d) *the pre-wrath Rapture*—the belief that it will take place at some point during the second half of the seven last years, just prior to God's outpouring of His wrath on this present world.

What follows are the main claims of the above four viewpoints. In this chapter, I will relate specifically to the main pre-Tribulation claims, as this is the view which concerns me the most. While doing so, you will see that my explanations also cover some of the other positions.

Main Claims of the Pre-Tribulation Viewpoint

- The Bible never claims that Yeshua's body will go through the Tribulation period.

- Yeshua's body had no part in the first sixty-nine weeks of Daniel, and it will have no part in the seventieth week as well. In other words, Daniel's seventy-week prophecy (Daniel 9:24-27) deals only with Old Testament Israel and thus, has nothing to do with Yeshua's body.

- While Yeshua's body is mentioned more than twenty times in the first three chapters of Revelation, there is no further mention of it from Rev. 4:2 all the way to 19:1. This is because John the Apostle, as a foreshadowing of Yeshua's body, is *taken out* or *Raptured,* in Rev. 4:1.

- Yeshua comes to meet His body in the Rapture (1 Thes. 4:16-17) and returns to Earth together with her in His Second Coming (1 Thes. 3:13). In other words, Yeshua's body goes up from the Earth in the Rapture and comes down to the Earth, together with Messiah in His Second Coming.

- The Anti-Messiah cannot be revealed until after the Rapture (2 Thes. 2:6-8). If Yeshua's bride goes through the Tribulation period, she will recognize the Anti-Messiah, since he will head the One World Government (Rev. 13:10), erect a statue of himself in the reconstructed Temple (Matt. 24:15), demand that people take his mark and number (Rev. 13:15-17), and kill the two witnesses (Rev. 11:7). All of this is not supported in Scripture.

- No one can know the day nor the hour of the Second Coming of Messiah (Matt. 24:15). But if Yeshua's body goes through the Tribulation period, some will know the day because it will be seven years from the signing of the seven-year covenant (Dan. 9:24-27) and 1,260 days from the day that the Anti-Messiah defiles the temple (Rev. 12:6).

- Yeshua's body must go to Heaven for the marriage of the Lamb (Rev. 19:7), before the Second Coming of Messiah at the end of the Tribulation period (Rev. 19:11-14).

- It is written that the Anti-Messiah will prevail against true believers during the Tribulation period (Rev. 13:7), but it also says that *the gates of hell won't prevail* against Yeshua's body (Matt. 16:18). So, it must be that there are two kinds of believers (or, "saints"): Old Testament ones—Israel, and New Testament ones - Yeshua's followers.

- The twenty-four elders are a representation of Yeshua's body. They are in heaven before the first of the seven seals of the scroll is broken.

- The pre-Tribulation Rapture is more consistent with God's grace, love, and mercy, as we were never appointed to God's wrath but to His everlasting grace and eternal life (1 Thes. 1:10, 5:9).

- Yeshua promised to come and remove His faithful ones and take them home to be with Him (Jn. 14:1-3).

- The Second Coming of Yeshua and the Rapture of His bride are separate events.

Main Claims of the Mid-Tribulation Viewpoint

- Reading about Daniel's seventieth week (Daniel 9:26-27), one needs to differentiate between the Anti-Messiah wrath, during the first three and a half years, and God's divine wrath, during the last three and a half years.

- Yeshua's body will go through the first three and a half years of Daniel's last week, and just before God starts to pour His wrath out on the Earth at the beginning of the second three and a half years, it will be caught up to heaven (some say, with the two witnesses of Rev. 11:12).

- Believers throughout history have gone through some very difficult trials and tribulations, even unto death (note the example of eleven of the first twelve disciples of Yeshua, as well as the persecuted believers - which included many martyrs), during the first three to four centuries CE, as well as the persecuted believers in China, Persia and other places in our own modern world. Thus, we should expect that this will repeat itself within the first three and a half years of Daniel's seventieth week.

Main Claims of the Post-Tribulation Viewpoint

- The Rapture occurs after the Tribulation—at Yeshua's Second Coming. Yeshua's Second Coming and the Rapture of Yeshua's body are not separate events.

- Yeshua's body will have to endure the entire seven-year Tribulation, as there is only one resurrection (called *the first resurrection*) before Yeshua's Second Coming.

- The Rapture occurs after the Sun and Moon have been darkened and after the heavens are shaken and the stars fall from heaven (Joel 4:15, Matt. 24:29).

- Yeshua comes with the sound of a trumpet at the end of the Tribulation (Matt. 24:29-31, 1 Cor. 15:51-53).

- Believers throughout history have gone through some very difficult trials and tribulations, even unto death (see above, mid-Tribulation claims).

Main Claims of the Pre-Wrath Viewpoint

- Daniel's seventy weeks prophecy is divided mainly into three sections: "Man's wrath," "Satan's/the Anti-Messiah's wrath" and, lastly, "God's wrath."

- The great Tribulation begins three and a half years after the Anti-Messiah *confirms a covenant* for one week, i.e., the seventieth and last week in the Daniel 9 prophecy.[180]

- Once the first three and a half year period ends, the Anti-Messiah will break that covenant, place *the abomination of desolation* inside the Temple in Jerusalem, declare himself to be *god* and rule over the Earth for the last three and a half years of this seventieth week.

- There is no way one can predict the exact timing of the Rapture, as it will take place sometime following the opening of the sixth seal (Rev. 6:12).

- God's wrath will be shortened (Matt. 24:29) by Yeshua's glorious Second Coming.

We can see clearly that all four of the above viewpoints are sincere beliefs (by those who hold to them), based solely on Scripture! None of those teaching them are trying to mislead Messiah's body! None of them possess some hidden agenda or have bad intentions... I'm truly convinced that all of them are well-intentioned, sincere and being taught by faithful followers of Yeshua. Nevertheless, no one can ignore the significant differences between their respective views! So, the question we should all ask at this point is: How is it that true,

---

[180] See a special portion dedicated to this well-known prophecy: "Daniel's Seventy Weeks" - following this chapter.

sincere followers of Yeshua, arrive at completely different conclusions while using the same book—the Bible?

Building the Foundations Part 3: Each of Us Needs Each Other So We Can See the Whole Picture

All of us have come to Yeshua from a different background, culture, and upbringing. Thus, we all look at life and circumstances through different lenses. God is a master artist and as such, He loves variations and different colors. As long as we - with all our different variations and colors - respect one another and try to have an open mind, humility, and true love toward one another, we can reach the much-needed unity in Yeshua, with an extra bonus, which is seeing what I call *the whole picture.*

None of us is able, nor called to change his or her own color or predisposition! After all, was it not given to us by our Maker? This entire book, which you are now reading, was naturally written through my own lens and color. I'm deeply rooted in God's Promised Land, where most of His Holy Word was written. Hebrew is my mother tongue, and I was brought up in what I call "the Middle Eastern Hebraic culture." And so, the only way I can discuss the timing of the Rapture is while using my own specific lenses.

The Middle Eastern Hebraic Mindset

I'm in the process of writing a five-book series, on portraits and foreshadowing of Yeshua throughout the five Books of Moses. I entitled it, *Moses Wrote About Me.* It is based on Yeshua's well-known words to the religious authorities of His time.[181] I am grateful to the Lord that in the Fall of 2020 I was able to complete the first book, which deals with the portraits and foreshadowing of Yeshua in the book of Genesis. There, in its introduction, I gave my own testimony and a very detailed explanation of this Middle Eastern Hebraic mindset. For those of you who have already read the book, the following are direct excerpts from it (with a different font and some modifications).[182]

There is a great necessity to understand the Scriptures in their historic and cultural contexts. It is an undeniable historical fact that Jews were the ones who wrote the *New Covenant* books. As a matter of fact, Jews not only wrote the books of the *New Covenant*, but also the vast majority of the entire Bible—both the Tanach and New Testament. Moreover, during the first few decades after Messiah's ascension, His body (the body of believers) was solely Jewish. Shortly after the death of the first apostles, His body became increasingly non-Jewish in its orientation and thus, lost its Jewish flavor and expression... As it became predominantly non-Jewish, the body started handling and interpreting God's Word outside of its original context, i.e.,

---

[181] See Jn. 5:46.

[182] See *Moses Wrote About Me*, pages 12-17. https://touryourroots.com/books-%26-articles. **Please note: All excerpts in this book are presented using <u>a different font</u>.** This is done to ease it on the reader, to better distinguish them from my present book wording.

disconnected or detached from its Hebraic/Jewish Middle Eastern mindset.

Without a doubt, Hebrew-speaking Jews who lived in the Middle East during the Tanach and New Covenant periods, understood and processed life, including God's Word, differently from Western, non-Jewish people. This remains true to this day. In order to better understand this book and the Hebraic/Jewish mindset I am using; I would like to offer a short explanation and give only a few examples that exemplify and emphasize the need to go back to study and apply God's Holy Word more properly than we have done during the past eighteen hundred years.

Logic and Mental Processing — Linear Versus Cyclical

The traditional Western mindset is heavily influenced by Greek culture. Greek thinking is expressed through words, ideas and logical definitions which often obscure the object of concern, removing it from its environment. To determine what an object is and why or how the object functions, a western thinker might compile a list of truths in an outline form, a1/b1/c1/c2/c3, placing them on a line (*linear thinking*). Historical events are put on a graphic line as well, following the idea that each of these events had actually been a new event. To the western thinker, it is the rational part that is important. Consequently, the rational part will often be abstracted from emotions so as not to hinder the logic of a matter. Using this Western thought process, one would say that something is true based on truth 1, truth 2 and truth 3. In the traditional Western mindset, truth is fixed, static and unchanging.

In contrast, the Hebraic/Jewish mindset is heavily influenced by Middle Eastern culture. Hebrew thinkers would express the truth in words, pictures, stories, or metaphors, which would keep the object of concern within its context and relationship to its environment. The effect of this is that the concept would not only provoke rational thinking but would also provoke imagery that could be physically seen, touched, tasted, smelled, and heard, with the aim of developing an emotional/spiritual link for the thinker. The Hebrew thinker might describe God as: *eagle's wings, honey, a rock, living water, a shepherd, bread, shade, a fortress, father,* and so on. Living water, for example, would provoke the image of *a river, stream,* or *rain.* A person can experience living water and know its benefits and effects. Hebraic/Middle Eastern logic is contextual and *cyclical* (or *spiral*) in nature. Events are constantly recurring and, thus, placed in a cycle, rather than on a graphic line.[183]

The Scriptures are filled with examples, but here I would like to present three very clear ones:

- King Solomon, who is described as the wisest man to have ever lived, said that all we see is actually a <u>repetition</u> of what has already taken place in the past, as well as what will actually take place in the future. He declared, *there is nothing new under the sun!*[184]

- Yeshua, Israel's Messiah, said, *I am the alpha and the omega— the beginning and the end.*[185] If you place these words on a line (i.e., read it via the Greek/Western *linear thinking*), it would mean that Yeshua once had a beginning and that, sometime in the future, He will also have an end. This conceptual understanding is in complete contradiction to Scripture, as God has neither a beginning nor an end; He is forever the living God. Alternatively, viewing this verse via the Hebraic/cyclical mindset, the beginning and the end meet one another (as with a

---

[183] See my suggested illustration regarding the cyclical manifestation of God in the Bible, on page 461 of my book titled *Moses Wrote About Me: Genesis.*

[184] Eccl. 1:9-10.

[185] Rev. 1:8.

ring, which is always round/cyclical) and, thus, are strongly connected, never actually having a beginning nor an end. In other words, <u>if you wish to understand the end/the future, first look at the beginning and the past, as they are very similar and strongly connected!</u>[186]

- It is sufficient to look at the stars on a beautifully clear night to understand the cyclical reality behind the One who created them. When looking at the sky, can we find one single star or planet which is triangular or square in shape? Are they not all circular?[187]

Numbers in the Middle Eastern Hebraic Mindset

To most Westerners, numbers are merely quantities. In contrast, to Middle Easterners, numbers often serve as symbols bearing spiritual significance. For example:

(As we already saw in chapter one of this book), the number 3 is often associated with double blessings or with resurrection. In the story of Creation, it was on the *third day* that God twice proclaimed, *and it was good.* The wedding at Cana was on the *third day.* Yeshua was resurrected on the *third day*, and lastly, Israel, as a nation, will be resurrected (from her spiritual death) on the *third day.*[188]

---

[186] See also Isa. 44:6-7, 46:9-10, 48:3.

[187] The reader will find it interesting to know that the Biblical words translated to English as *path/s* and *ways* actually read in the original Hebrew as *ma'agal* and/or *ma'agalim* — *circles* and/or *cycles* (see a few examples in Isa. 26:7; Ps. 17:5; and, particularly, Ps. 23:3. See also Prov. 1:9, 4:11; and many more).

[188] Gen. 1:9-13; Jn. 2:1; 1 Cor. 15:4; Hos. 6:2 (holding that *a thousand years in your sight are like a day,* see Ps. 90:4 and 2 Pet. 3:8).

The number 4 usually points to the entire world (*the four corners of the Earth, the four winds,* etc.). There are *four* gospels, which are directed to the entirety of humankind living on Earth.[189]

The number 6 is mostly connected with mankind. As the creation of humanity (Adam and Eve) happened on the *sixth* day, the number suggests weakness and fleshly deeds. It is no wonder that the number 666 is a multiplication of this very number.[190]

Most people agree that the number 7 is God's number, which symbolizes Him, as it is a number of completeness and perfection. For example, God the Creator created everything within *seven* days. He ordained the *Sabbath*, which is the *seventh* day of the week. Most of His (*seven*) Feasts are based on the number *seven*. There is the *Sabbatical Year*, and there is *the Year of Jubilee*, which is celebrated at the completion of *seven* Sabbatical Years. There are *seven* spirits before His throne, *seven* churches in the book of Revelation, and so on.[191] *Sheva* (Hebrew, *seven*) is also connected to *oath* and *swearing* (in Hebrew, the word is *sh'vuah*). This, by itself, speaks volumes about our great Creator, who is the only One who can keep His oaths and all the good promises He swore to the forefathers!

Numbers in Scripture are Not Always Mathematically Precise!

The following are a few examples, just as a little taste:

- According to 2 Sam. 5:4, David reigned in Israel for forty years. Yet, when elaborated upon in the next verse, it says that he reigned in Judah for *"seven years and six months,"* which brings his combined reign to a total of forty years and six

---

[189] Isa. 11:12, Ezek. 37:9.

[190] Gen. 1:27, 31; Rev. 13:18.

[191] Gen. 2:1-3; Lev. chapters 23, 25 and 27; Deut. 15 and 31:10; Rev. 1:12-13, 4:5.

months. It is clear then that the six months were included in, or, rounded off to forty years.

- Scripture tells us that David was the last son of Jesse. In one particular verse it states that he was the seventh son, and in another, the eighth (see 1 Sam. 16:10-12, 1 Ch. 2:15). Taking into consideration the symbolic meaning of numbers in the Hebrew Scriptures, could it be that there is no mathematical contradiction but rather the writer's desire to tell us about the significance of 7 (a godly number) and 8 (new beginnings, new hope, etc.), attributing them to the very same person, King David, who is the prototype or foreshadowing of *Messiah Son of David*?

- According to Gen. 46:27 and Deut. 10:22, the total number of the children of Israel, who went down to Egypt, was *seventy*. Yet in the book of Acts, they number seventy-five (7:14).[192]

- The Sabbatical (seventh) Year: Most of us know that Israel was commanded to have a *Sabbatical Year*, which was to take place *on the seventh year.* Nevertheless, a careful reading shows that in one place, it looks as if this might be the eighth year (*at the end of every seven years*... Deut. 15:1. Compare with verses 9-12).

- Gideon—exactly how many sons did he have? According to the book of Judges, he had seventy. Yet, it seems that Abimelech was not counted among them, even though he was also his son (see Judges 8:29-30 and 9:2, 5, 18, 23-24).

- How long did the famine in Elijah's time last? According to 1 Kings, it lasted for three years or even less (*in the third year —*

---

[192] *The Septuagint* (a third century B.CE Greek translation of the Torah) also mentions *seventy-five*, probably adding Joseph's family to the seventy.

see 1 Kings 18:1); yet, according to Yeshua and His faithful apostle, it lasted *three and a half years* (see Lk. 4:25 and James 5:17).

- Mathematically, on which day was Yeshua resurrected exactly? Was it on the *third day*? Was it on the *fourth*? In most references, Yeshua says He would rise *on the third day*, while in one other place He says that He must be *three days and three nights* in the tomb, which brings us to the fourth day (see Matt. 16:21, 17:23; Mk. 9:31; Lk. 9:22; compare with Matt. 12:40).[193]

- A very similar "mathematical contradiction" appears in 1 Sam. 30, about the *young man from Egypt*, who led David to the Amalekites' camp, after they had invaded Ziklag and took all the women and children captive. It says in verse 12: *For he had eaten no bread nor drunk water for three days and three nights.* Nevertheless, when David speaks to him in the following verse (13), the young Egyptian tells him, *because three days ago I fell sick...* In Hebrew it literally reads, *hayom sh'loshah*— Today is three (i.e., the third day).

It should then be no wonder that the Jewish sages, at times, understood numbers (including in Daniel 9, as we shall see later) symbolically, i.e., more than just literally.

---

[193] I'm well aware of different attempts by different commentators (especially my Messianic Jewish brothers and sisters) to reconcile this, whether by counting only parts of the day and night (a few hours) or in other ways. All I'm trying to say is that, at times, one cannot take numbers in Scripture too literally or precisely.

The Mindset and Background Behind the Pre-Tribulation Viewpoint

Above I have shared with you my Middle Eastern Hebraic lens, or the place from where I'm particularly coming. At this point, I will present you with the Greek Western lens behind one of the most accepted views regarding the timing of the Rapture—the pre-Tribulation point of view.

Theologians who hold to the pre-Tribulation Rapture base their beliefs mainly on four principles of Bible interpretation: (1) *Consistent literal interpretation*, (2) *Premillennialism*, (3) *Futurism*, and (4) *Distinguishing between Israel and the Church*. Pre-Tribulation proponents consider the above four principles not only as mere suppositions, but rather as important biblical doctrines from which the pre-Tribulation Rapture doctrine emerges! Allow me to elaborate:

1. **Consistent literal Interpretation:** This principle attempts to understand the Bible as plainly and naturally as possible, whether in relation to the Bible's historical context or the words' ordinary meaning, and the grammatical construction of the text. This method of Bible interpretation leans on the idea that properly understanding what God is saying is vital, and the emphasis on "literal" interpretation calls the reader not to "go beyond the facts," into the realm of elaboration or extrapolation. Language is understood to be inseparable from its contextual usage, both socially and culturally, and thus, Bible literacy requires insight into the customs, historical context and common perspectives that would morph into some form of linguistic expression.

Literal Interpretation understands that words or phrases in the Bible can be used plainly or figuratively, and that either could convey the same concept without detracting from its meaning. Figures of speech and metaphors would be understood as a demonstration of the shared and widely familiar linguistic artifacts of the society. Biblical language, whether conveyed plainly or figuratively, still refers to events that *literally* happened.

Some interpreters assume that a figure of speech, used to describe an event, implies the event was not literal and did not happen in history. Yet, in the early 20th century, David L. Cooper came up with the "Golden Rule of Interpretation," which is used by pastors and Bible scholars till today:

"When the plain sense of Scripture makes common sense, seek no other sense; therefore, take every word at its primary, ordinary, usual, literal meaning, unless the facts of the immediate context, studied in the light of related passages and axiomatic and fundamental truths, clearly indicate otherwise."

Following this view, pre-Tribulation Rapture proponents believe that Consistent literal Interpretation of the Bible as a whole, "logically leads to the pre-Tribulation position."

2. **Premillennialism:** Pre-Tribulationists adhere to *Premillennialism*, which teaches that the Second Coming of Messiah will happen before His thousand-year reign upon Earth, from Jerusalem (Revelation 19:11-20:6). Pre-Tribulation proponents consider Premillennialism foundational, this, in contrast to the Postmillennial or Amillennial views of Scripture.[194]

---

[194] **Postmillennialism** — A Christian End Times doctrine that holds that there won't be a millennial (1,000-year) reign of Messiah here on Earth; that rather, Yeshua established His Kingdom here on Earth already, through his preaching and redemptive work in the first century, and that he equips his Church with the gospel, empowers the Church by the Spirit and charges the Church with the Great

3. **Futurism:** Proponents of the pre-Tribulation Rapture adhere to biblical *Futurism*, which presumes that "virtually all the prophetic events of the Bible" will only happen during the <u>future</u>, at the Second Coming of Messiah, or during his millennial reign—and not in the present "Church Age." This view relies upon an expectation of a literal fulfilment of future events that prophecy promises will occur.

Interpreters' positions on fulfillment of Bible prophecy, as it relates to time, define four possible views: *Futurism* as described above. *Preterism*, suggesting that most, if not all, prophecy has already been fulfilled, mainly in relation to the destruction of Jerusalem in AD. 70.[195] *Historicism*, in relation to the present, sees extensive expression of the tribulations manifesting within the current Church Age, implying that prophecy is in the midst of its ultimate fulfillment during this present

---

Commission (Mt. 28:19) to disciple all nations. Postmillennialism expects that eventually the vast majority of people living will be saved. Increasing the success of the gospel message will gradually produce a time in history prior to Christ's return in which faith, righteousness, peace, and prosperity will prevail in the affairs of men and of nations. After an extensive era of such conditions, Yeshua the Messiah will return visibly, bodily, and gloriously, to end history with the general resurrection and the final judgment, after which the eternal order follows. **Amillennialism** — A Christian End Times doctrine that teaches that there will be no millennial reign of Messiah and His righteous ones on Earth. Amillennialists interpret the thousand years symbolically, to refer either to a temporary happiness, or rejoicing of souls in Heaven before the general resurrection, or to the infinite happiness and rejoicing of the righteous after the general resurrection. In other words: this view does not hold that Yeshua will physically reign on the Earth for exactly 1,000 years. They claim that the Millennium has already begun and is identical with the current Church Age. Amillennialism holds that while Christ's reign during the millennium is spiritual in nature, at the end of the Church Age, Messiah will return in final judgment and establish a permanent reign in the new Heaven and new Earth.

[195] See more on *Preterism* and *Futurism*, in "Daniel's 70 weeks" prophecy appendix, at the end of this chapter.

age. The fourth view, titled *Idealism*, adheres to a timelessness, that holds prophetic texts as "teaching great truths about God" with no relationship to any timeline of prophetic warnings and their effect on the decisions of Israel or others, or of prophetic promises and their ultimate fulfillment. This view does not see any explicit biblical timeline of prophetic events or allow for any preemptive understanding about future events, despite the prophets of Israel serving as important, well-trusted members of historical Israel, whose words did come to pass, according to the Bible.

4. Distinction Between Israel and the Church: Pre-Tribulationists also adhere to a final principle, which claims that God's "program" throughout history applies to two distinct peoples - Israel and the Church. This, according to various dispensations of time (what is known as *dispensationalism*). The pre-Tribulationist view on this distinction sets God's plan for Israel "on hold" until He completes His purposes for the Church, which culminate in His "rapturing His bride to heaven." Pre-Tribulation proponents offer their reason for this pre-Tribulation Rapture as removing the Church from the physical realm, so that God can "complete His purposes for Israel" by way of the "Seven-Year Tribulation" period. Per this position, Israel is to stand alone while undergoing this "Great Tribulation."

According to adherents of the pre-Tribulation Rapture, not only does God's Word contain distinct messages for the Church and Israel (despite offering "grace" to both), but "blurring the lines" between these distinct messages "destroys an important basis for the pre-Tribulation Rapture doctrine." As noted above, this view sets Israel as the sole target for great persecution, in a time described by Yeshua as *has not been from the beginning of the world until this time, no, nor ever shall be* (Matt. 24:21).

Reflections on the Pre-Tribulation View

While I understand and can accept most of the arguments in the first two principles of interpretation – Consistent *Literal Interpretation and Premillennialism*, when it comes to the third and fourth principles - *futurism* and *distinction between Israel and the Church,* my use of different lenses for attempting to understand God's Word, emerges. For example, I can identify with both the *Historicist* and the *Futurist* positions, as reading Scripture <u>using the "cyclical, Hebraic/Jewish lens,"</u> shows that prophecy can have more than just one fulfillment.

The fourth and last principle - *Distinction between Israel and the Church,* illustrates the biggest theological gap between me and the pre-Tribulation Rapture theologians. Are Israel and Yeshua's body really separate entities? To address this crucially important question, I need to take you once again to some (partially modified) excerpts from the introduction to my book, *Moses wrote about Me.*[196]

The New Covenant Versus the Old Covenant

The first mention in Scripture of the term *New Covenant* is in Jeremiah 31:31. In Hebrew, it reads *brit chadasha – ברית חדשה).* A covenant (*brit*) involves an act undertaken by two parties who agree on something specific. The word *brit* does not refer to the written agreement primarily, but rather to the act that seals the agreement, thus, giving it its authority.

By way of example, God's covenant with Abraham involved *the act* of killing animals and then dividing, or cutting, their bodies into pieces.[197]

---

[196] See, there, pages 26-49.

[197] See, Gen. 15:9-21.

The covenant at Mount Sinai involved *the act* of sacrificing oxen or bulls and, later, sealing the covenant with their blood.[198] The Hebrew verb used to describe the making of a covenant is *lichrot* (or, *Likhrot*) It speaks of *cutting*, and at that time, *entering into a covenant* almost always involved the shedding of blood.[199]

While many of us connect the words *Old Covenant* (or Old Testament – the Tanach) with a set of 39 books, the immediate biblical context shows something quite different. When the Bible uses the term *brit* (covenant) in connection with the Mount Sinai event, it relates to the *luchot* (or *lukhoht* - tablets) on which *Aseret haDvarim* (The Ten Words, or Commandments) were written,[200] and to *sefer haBrit* (The Book of the Covenant).[201] It never refers to the entirety of the Tanach writings!

When Yeshua talked about *the New Covenant*, He could not have been referring to the set of books to which we refer today as the *New Testament*, for the very simple reason that there were no New Testament writings arranged or canonized during His lifetime. Most of us know, all too well, to what He was referring as *the New Covenant*. It was *His blood*, which was going to be shed for many, for the remission of sin. He was speaking of the Golgotha experience that He

---

[198] See, Ex. 24:4-8.

[199] See Heb. 9:18, 22. The American reader may be reminded of the way Native Americans would make covenants between their different tribes and among themselves. Likewise, people from the Middle East or Africa are familiar, to this very day, with this description of a covenant.

[200] See, Ex. 34:28; Deut. 9:9, 11.

[201] *A book* (singular form), Ex. 24:7, 8. In both cases, the *tablets* and the *book* contain the description of the terms agreed upon between the two parties after (or some time before) they have *cut* and sealed, or stamped, the covenant (usually) with blood.

was going to endure. He was referring to *His body*, which was going to be *cut* and would bleed on that crucifixion tree.[202]

The parts of the Tanach known as *the Prophets* and *the Writings* were never referred to by biblical figures, as *a covenant* or a testament. Again—only the two Mosaic tablets and *the Book* were explicitly included in that covenant made on Mount Sinai.[203]

When Jeremiah delivered his famous prophecy, he never had "two sets of books" in mind (i.e., the Old and the New Testaments). He was simply differentiating between a new covenant that God was going to make with both Houses of Israel and an Old Covenant, which He had made in the past with the same body, Israel, at the foot of Mount Sinai (in Hebrew, this covenant would be called *Brit Sinai - ברית סיני*).[204]

Yeshua and the Old Covenant

Yeshua said that one should not think that He had come to *destroy* (or *abolish*) the Torah or the Prophets. He had come to fulfill them.[205]

Over the years, due to a lack of Hebraic and Jewish understanding of the terms *to fulfill* and *to destroy*, many thought that Yeshua, by *fulfilling* the Torah and the Prophets, exempted His followers from taking any responsibility in relating to or obeying them.[206]

---

[202] See, Matt. 26:28; Mk. 14:24.

[203] See this concept showing the direct connection between *brit* (covenant), the two stone *tablets* and *the book,* in other Biblical references, as well: Deut. 31:9, 25-26; Josh. 3:6, 8, 11; and 1 Kings 8:1, 6, 21.

[204] See, Jer. 31:31-34.

[205] See, Matt. 5:17."

[206] The issue of how followers of Yeshua should relate to and obey the Torah is discussed in both *Moses Wrote About Me*, especially in connection to the *Lech*

The terms *to fulfill* and *to destroy* are still in use within Orthodox Jewish circles, and they continue to bear the very same meaning they had two thousand years ago. *To fulfill* means to give the correct interpretation, while *to destroy* means to give an incorrect interpretation. Let us examine this statement with just two examples:

- *You have heard that it was said to those of old... But I say to you...*[207]

By the very use of *you have heard...* and *but I tell you*, Yeshua gives the correct interpretation of God's Holy Torah and the Prophets. Yeshua, indeed, *fulfills* them.[208]

- *But my servant Caleb, because he has a different spirit in him and <u>has followed Me fully</u>, I will bring him into the land where he went, and his descendants shall inherit it.*[209]

You likely remember the well-known story of the twelve men sent by Moses to spy out the Promised Land. Only two of the twelve had *a different spirit* in them—Joshua and Caleb. In Hebrew, the words *have followed Me fully* read *vayimaleh acharai. Vayimaleh* literally means *and he fulfilled.* This comes from the very same root from which the words *lemaleh* (to fulfill) and *maleh* (complete/filled up) are derived.

Indeed, there were two kinds of *interpretations* in that tragic story. On the one hand, Caleb, who had *a different spirit within him*, gave a

---

Lecha, Vayera, Chayey Sarah and *Miketz* Torah portions, and, in this book, as one of the appendixes closing the third chapter.

[207] See, Matt. 5:21, 27, 31, 33, 38.

[208] It is very interesting to note that here too , the definition of the Greek word translated as *fulfill* (G4137, πληρόω, *plēroō*) supports the correct Hebraic or Jewish meaning, i.e., *fulfilling* as giving the correct interpretation and *destroying* as misinterpreting.

[209] See, Num. 13–14 (especially 14:24).

correct interpretation of what he (and Joshua) saw while spying out the Promised Land. On the other hand, the other spies, who did not have the right (godly) spirit within them, gave a wrong interpretation to the very same things Caleb and Joshua had seen in the land; thus, the ten spies *abolished/destroyed* – misinterpreted – the situation!

Yeshua, exactly as Caleb and Joshua, came to provide us with the correct interpretation of His Torah and the words of His prophets. In contrast, the leaders of His day acted similarly to the ten spies, misinterpreting these things—thus, they did not and could not recognize Him as their long-awaited Messiah Redeemer.

The above explanations and examples are consistent with the context of Yeshua's entire message regarding the Torah and the Prophets. He said:

For assuredly, I say to you, till Heaven and Earth pass away, one jot or one tittle will by no means pass from the law till all is fulfilled. Whoever, therefore, breaks one of the least of these commandments, and teaches men so, shall be called least in the Kingdom of Heaven; but whoever does and teaches them, he shall be called great in the Kingdom of Heaven.[210]

First of all, heaven and Earth still exist today!

Secondly, according to Yeshua's own words, one's position in the Kingdom of God will be determined by how they relate to and apply the Torah and the Prophets in their life. Notice, I said one's position <u>in the Kingdom</u>—*not* outside of it! In other words, salvation itself (or the key to eternal life) is purely the free gift of God; nevertheless, one's position in eternity will be determined by how they relate to the words of God's Holy Torah and His Prophets.

---

[210] Matt. 5:18-19.

The First Century Believers and the Old Covenant

As stated earlier, the first body of believers did not have an orderly and canonized set of New Testament books. What did they have? They had the Torah, the Prophets, and the Writings (i.e., the *Tanach*). The first century followers of Messiah never looked down upon or neglected the first two-thirds of the Bible that we have today.

The New Covenant writings are filled with quotations from the Tanach. In fact, what we consider as being purely New Covenant teachings, beliefs, and doctrines, are <u>all</u> based upon, or directly quoted from the Tanach, especially from the first part which is referred to as the Torah.

Israel's Messiah, Yeshua, His disciples, and the large body of first century Jewish believers conducted their lives in obedience to the full counsel of God's Word, i.e., to what we know today as the Torah, the Prophets, and the Writings. Here are only a few examples:

- Yeshua visited the synagogues on the Sabbath. He never taught against the observance of the Sabbath. After all, was it not God who had commanded its observance?[211]

- Yeshua participated in God's Feasts (e.g., the Passover, the Feast of Tabernacles) and even the Feast of Dedication (known in Hebrew as *Chanukah,* or *Hanukkah*).[212]

- The disciples, after the death, burial, and resurrection of Yeshua, celebrated the Feasts and even kept their Jewish traditions (such as the traditional Jewish evening prayer at the Temple and others).[213]

---

[211] Matt. 12:9; Mk. 1:21, 3:1-2; Lk. 4:16.

[212] Lk. 2:41-42, 22:7-22; Jn. 7:14, 37, 39; Jn. 10:22.

[213] See, Acts 2:1, 3:1, 5:42, 10:14, 10:28.

- Many in the first century Jewish body of Messiah were *zealous for the Torah.*[214]

- Shaul the Apostle, himself, kept the Torah and even the Jewish traditions.[215]

But Didn't God Establish 'A New Thing' Through Yeshua?

Yes, He did. But we are all in great need of knowing and understanding the Biblical definition of this "new thing" that He established. *This new thing was, and still is, in effect, **only within the commonwealth of Israel** and never outside of it.* Let me elaborate.

The *brit chadasha* (New Covenant) was never promised to or made with anyone outside the nation of Israel. God promised it to His beloved Chosen Nation and to them alone![216]

The very first body of believers was solely an Israeli/Jewish body, at least until the days of Cornelius.[217] The first body of believers never understood the teachings of their Jewish Messiah as contradicting the previous teachings and instructions given by God, including His promises to their fathers.

(As we noted in chapter one), a key question the disciples asked Yeshua – the risen Yeshua, just before He ascended to heaven before

---

[214] See, Acts 21:20, 22:12.

[215] See, Acts 20:16, 21:24, 21:26, 22:17, 24:14, 24:18, 25:8, 28:17; and 1 Cor. 16:8.

[216] See, Jer. 31:31 — *the House of Judah and the House of Israel.*

[217] The Acts 10 narrative happened about ten to fifteen years after the ascension of Yeshua. There were two examples of non-Jews coming to faith in Israel's Messiah before Cornelius and his household—the new non-Jewish believers in Samaria (see Acts 8:4-25) and the Ethiopian eunuch (see Acts 8:26-39).

their very eyes, demonstrates and proves the above statements. That question was, *will you at this time restore the Kingdom to Israel?*[218]

Remember, these men had literally walked and lived with the Master for about three and a half years. They had witnessed all of the miracles He had performed and were with Him for forty days after that glorious *Yom Rishon* ("The First Day," Hebrew for Sunday, i.e., His resurrection day).

During that forty-day period, Yeshua had taught them about the Kingdom of God.[219] Did they totally miss His message concerning the "new thing" He had come to establish?

Notice that Yeshua did not rebuke them for asking what some people in the body today would consider, an immature, short-sighted question. He simply said that it was not for them to know the time that the Father *has set.* Set for what? Set for the return of His Son so that He could restore the kingdom to Israel and rule and reign from Jerusalem for a millennium.

Even today, it is not for us to know the exact time when God will restore the kingdom to Israel (or in other words, the time of Messiah's Second Coming). Nevertheless, all believers (Jews and non-Jews alike) need to recognize that Yeshua is going to come back to a specific geographic location on planet Earth. It won't be to America, Europe, or any location other than the Land of Israel, specifically, the City of Jerusalem. He will return to the exact place from where He ascended and returned to the Father almost two thousand years ago.[220]

When Yeshua came down to planet Earth the first time, indeed something new took place in Israel (both the nation and their Promised

---

[218] See, Acts 1:6.

[219] See, Acts 1:3.

[220] See, Zech. 14:4 and Acts 1:10-12.

Land). This new thing marked a fresh era in the life of God's ancient beloved people—the nation of Israel. From that point on, Israel's relationship with God would not be solely based on Torah-keeping, nor on what I call Torah performance, (righteousness based exclusively on obeying the covenant made at Mt. Sinai). Rather, it would be based on faith and full trust in what *their* Messiah had done for *them* in His atoning death on the crucifixion tree. In other words, their righteousness would not be based on mere external performance of the Torah, but rather on faith and full trust in the work of Messiah at Golgotha. This work would enable them to follow the Torah principles and laws as a direct result of their changed hearts and, in light of their Messiah's correct interpretation (*fulfillment*) of it. After all, does the Word not say that God would inscribe His Torah on their hearts?[221]

But Didn't Many in Israel Reject Their Own Messiah?

Yes, they did. On this occasion, as in many instances in their history, there was indeed *nothing new under the sun.*

Throughout our Jewish history, only a remnant of people has followed the Almighty. There have been a few exceptions to this general rule in Israel's past, such as during the times of the good kings (e.g., David, Hezekiah, Josiah), or when the people followed Joshua into the Promised Land. Unfortunately, even these exceptions did not last for long. Furthermore, prophecy clearly foretold that the Messiah would be rejected by His own people.[222]

This should not be a surprise. Let us remember that numbers never impress God in the same way that they impress the faithless. So, what

---

[221] See, Jer. 31:33. What exactly did God inscribe on our hearts? This question is discussed in greater detail at the very end of chapter 3, as well as in *Moses Wrote About Me: Genesis*, Appendix 1: "Shaul and the Torah," pages 427-452.

[222] See, Isa. 53 and others.

is it that really impresses the God of Abraham, Isaac, and Jacob? It has always been the men and women who belong to <u>a small remnant</u> who have trusted Him wholeheartedly - those who were willing to follow Him under any and all circumstances; those who walked in His footsteps, no matter what; those who considered themselves *a living sacrifice* on His holy altar as a daily life practice and those who always sought His kingdom before the things of this world. With these, God has always been impressed! This very *remnant* of people, both then and now, is an integral part of what Shaul described as *the Olive Tree* (see further discussion).[223]

Shaul (Paul) and the Nation of Israel

Shaul's epistle to the believers in Rome is one of the most important documents among all the New Covenant writings. It lays the foundation for doctrines such as *grace*, *faith* and *righteousness based on faith*. Actually, the first eight chapters of this epistle describe these doctrines in great detail, while the last chapters (12-16) deal mainly with the practical ramifications and expression of these doctrines in the lives of individuals who claim faith in Israel's Messiah.

At the very heart of this important epistle, Shaul pauses and dedicates three whole chapters (9-11) to address matters concerning Israel and her destiny. He does so in order to tackle an issue that has challenged both him and the majority of Yeshua's followers of that time. It had to do with the rejection of Messiah by many of their own flesh and blood—within the nation of Israel. At that time, many questions arose in the minds of Jewish believers, such as, "What will happen to our beloved nation now?" "What about all the promises God gave our forefathers?" But the question that bothered them the most was probably…

---

[223] See, Rom. 11:16-24.

Has God Cast Away His People Israel?[224]

This, indeed, is the million-dollar question that many believers to this day still ask themselves. Many in the body of Messiah, especially amongst Messianic Jews, agree that in these three chapters, especially chapter 11, Shaul proves beyond any shadow of a doubt, that God did *not* reject or cast away His ancient chosen people and that indeed, one day *all Israel shall be saved.*[225]

However, I think that many still fail to grasp other (no less important) hidden lessons in this crucial chapter—lessons which, if understood correctly, would help settle other controversial doctrines such as "replacement theology."

Back to Shaul. He answers his own million-dollar question in a manner that is difficult to misunderstand or misinterpret. He declares, *certainly not!*[226] What made him so confident that God had truly *not* cast away His beloved, ancient people?

Shaul went on to prove his point by presenting his audience (including us today) with two examples, probably following the biblical principle, *by two or three witnesses, everything shall be established.*[227]

1. He, Shaul, being an Israelite himself, is proof that God had *not* cast away His ancient people,[228] *and*

---

[224] See, Rom. 11:1.

[225] See, Rom. 11:26.

[226] See, Rom. 11:1.

[227] See, Deut. 19:15; Matt. 18:16.

[228] See, Rom. 11:2.

2. The seven thousand individuals who did not worship Baal in Elijah's time.[229]

Now, what in the world is the connection between Shaul, the seven thousand in Elijah's time and the question of whether or not Israel was cast away by God? Let us use Shaul's own words:

Even so then, <u>at this present time</u>, there is <u>a remnant</u> according to the election of grace.[230]

Here is the crucial point we need to grasp and hold fast to: <u>In every given generation</u>, there was (and still is) <u>a remnant</u> that *does not bow their knee to Baal!* In other words, since Israel was chosen to be God's beloved nation, there has existed in every generation *a remnant* who has walked with God and followed Him wholeheartedly, while the rest (i.e., the vast majority) have turned their backs on Him and followed other (pagan) gods. <u>In every generation</u>, there have been those who did not bow their knee to any kind of god or demon; there have been those who feared the Lord and called upon His name. <u>In every generation</u>, there have been those who let the Spirit of God lead them daily. Thus, these faithful Israelites, the remnant, were considered spiritual (Spirit-led) people. Notice that "spiritual" does not, in any way, mean that they were a kind of winged creature, flying around, praising God all day long. Spiritual simply means that they have followed the leading of God's Spirit. These Spirit-led people, <u>the remnant</u>, bring us back to Shaul's analogy of…

---

[229] See, Rom. 11:2-4.

[230] See, Rom. 11:5.

The Olive Tree

Who or what, according to Shaul, did *the Olive Tree* represent? Why did he use this analogy to begin with?[231]

First, we must understand that *the Olive Tree*, as Shaul uses it in Romans 11, is <u>not</u> a description of every individual in Israel! When carefully looking at what the Bible describes as the Olive Tree, we can see the following:

- The Olive Tree was a descriptive name for the city of Jerusalem.[232]

- The Olive Tree and its fruit were associated with God's righteous ones.[233]

- The priests and (some of) the kings were an integral part of these righteous ones. What made them righteous? The olive anointing oil by which they were consecrated to their calling.

Based on these three assessments, among other things, we can say that *the Olive Tree* speaks of <u>blessings</u>, of <u>Jerusalem</u>—the city God chose to place His name upon, of <u>God's anointing</u> and of <u>His righteous people</u>. These terms can easily be associated with <u>the remnant</u> we discussed previously, a <u>remnant</u> which has existed <u>in every generation within the nation of Israel</u>.

---

[231] See, Rom. 11:13-26. For a detailed description of an olive tree and its unique characteristics, please read *Moses Wrote About Me: Genesis*, pages 38-42.

[232] See, Jer. 11:16; notice the context, especially verses 6, 9, 12-13, 15 and 17.

[233] See, Ps. 52:8, 128:3-4; Zech. 4:3, 11-14. The Olive Tree symbolized those who were righteous in God's eyes.

They Are Not All Israel Who Are of Israel[234]

It is well-known that ever since Israel was called by God to be His chosen one among the nations, *not* every individual Israelite has followed that holy calling. Not every Israelite has obeyed His voice and His commandments. Not every individual within the nation of Israel has allowed God's Spirit to lead him or her on a daily basis.

Yes, every person who is born into the nation of Israel (to Jewish parents) is indeed an Israelite. Nevertheless, there are two kinds of Israelites: those who are "according to the natural" alone (bloodline Israelites), and those who are according to *both* "the natural" (bloodline Israelites) and "the spirit" (i.e., "Spirit-led"—true followers of God's Spirit). It is always the *remnant* that is defined as being both natural and Spirit-led Israel!

The Remnant Always Functions Within the Larger Body

Now to a very important historical and biblical fact. The faithful ones of Israel (those who are Spirit-led, as well as being Israelites through their bloodline) have always functioned *within* the larger body, i.e., the whole nation of Israel. For example, these faithful ones (the *remnant* or *the Olive Tree*) have lived in the Promised Land, worked the land, and lived their lives among, and as an integral part of, the rest of the nation of Israel. Yes, both the Spirit-led Israelites and the natural Israelites have walked side by side in the same Promised Land, such that there has hardly been any external difference between them (as far as clothing, culture, language, etc., are concerned).

Here are three examples from the history of Israel for these *two kinds of Israelites*:

1. When the children of Israel left Egypt, they comprised (mainly) twelve distinct tribes; nevertheless, they functioned as, and were

---

[234] See, Rom. 9:6.

considered, one body. When they arrived at the foot of Mount Sinai, the majority started worshipping a golden calf, while waiting for Moses to return. Only a small remnant followed Moses' call to follow the One true God and execute His judgment on the unfaithful ones. This small remnant was from the tribe of Levi.[235]

What the Bible clearly describes is that the tribe of Levi (and those who joined it) were led by, and obedient to God's Holy Spirit, while the others acted upon the desires of their nature/flesh and were thus, considered only natural Israelites (or *Israel according to the flesh*).[236]

Were these Spirit-led people (the Levites) completely separated from the rest of Israel that day? No! They still traveled and did everything together with the other children of Israel. They lived and functioned side by side with the rest of Israel; nevertheless, they were indeed the *Israel of God.*[237]

2. When Moses sent twelve men (each representing a specific tribe) to spy out the Promised Land, they went as representatives of one body - the nation of Israel. Even so, only two of them, Joshua and Caleb, walked *by faith and not by sight*, based on trust in what God was more than able to do with the fearsome giants they had seen with their natural eyes.[238] The other ten spies presented their conclusions based on what their natural eyes alone had viewed.

So, once again we can see that there are some who *walk in the Spirit* (choosing to follow the leading of God's Spirit), while others *walk in the flesh* (choosing to follow what their natural eyes see). However,

---

[235] See, Ex. 32:1-6, 26-28.

[236] Actually, because of this, only the tribe of Levi was allowed in God's presence (see Num. 1:47-51, 3:5-12).

[237] Review Rom. 9:6 and Gal. 6:16.

[238] In accordance with His promises (see Num. 13:28-33, 14:1-10, 14:20-24).

they are still with one another, walking side by side within the single body called the nation of Israel.

3. Going back to Elijah's time, have you ever noticed that he was not aware of the existence of the other *seven thousand* faithful who lived during his time? He thought he was the only devoted Israelite left. That *remnant* of seven thousand had been there all that time, living side by side with him as well as the rest of Israel, but they had no special outward look or distinguishing robes or religious title to identify themselves. They were mixed in and living side by side with everyone else. Elijah and the seven thousand were that *remnant* who followed God's Spirit and thus were indeed the *Israel of God.*

To conclude, *the Olive Tree* referred specifically to the Spirit-led Israeli *remnant*. Understanding this crucially important point will help us better understand Shaul's very important statements in Romans 11:

- *And if <u>some</u> of the branches were <u>broken off</u>, and you, being a wild olive tree, were grafted in among them and with them partake of the root and fatness of the olive tree...*

- *You will say then, the branches were <u>broken off</u>, that I might be grafted in. Well, because of unbelief they were broken off, and you stand by faith. Be not arrogant, but fear...*

- *And they also, <u>if they abide not still in unbelief, shall be grafted in</u>; for <u>God is able to graft them in again</u>. For if you were cut out of the olive tree which is wild by nature, and were grafted contrary to nature into a good olive tree, <u>how much more shall these, who are the natural branches, be grafted into their own Olive Tree?</u>*[239]

---

[239] See, Rom. 11:17, 19-20, 23-24.

We see again that *the Olive Tree,* in Romans 11, does <u>not</u> refer to the entire nation of Israel nor to each and every individual in Israel. It does <u>not</u> speak of Israelites who walk according to the flesh and are thus the broken branches. It speaks only of the righteous <u>amongst Israel</u> – *the remnant* – who follow the leading of His Spirit.

Biblical terms, such as *the Olive Tree, the seven thousand, the remnant according to election,* the *Israel of God,* and *Messianic Jews* (Jews who believe in and accept their Messiah and thus, follow the leading of His Spirit) are all synonymous terms describing Messiah's bride. This beloved bride is the one who is chosen, the elect, or *called out* by Him <u>in every generation</u> as the faithful remnant who abides in Him.

God has not cast His people away, *certainly not! The Olive Tree is indeed Israel.* Nevertheless, it refers to <u>Spirit-led Israel</u>. It speaks of the *Israel of God,* meaning those faithful ones who are connected to the roots of the Olive Tree.[240]

In Shaul's time, *the Olive Tree* described those Israelites who acknowledged Yeshua as their Messiah and followed Him wholeheartedly. At that time, they were called *yehudim notzrim* (a Hebrew term which means Jews who follow the man from Nazareth). Today, *notzri* refers to anyone who is neither a Jew nor a Muslim and who claims to belong to the Christian faith (a term which has become synonymous with the religion called "Christianity," and thus has lost, in my opinion, its first century Jewish flavor).

---

[240] In my opinion, the roots of the Olive Tree are God, His Word, and the faithful forefathers—Abraham, Isaac and Jacob. I'm aware that there are those who see the Olive Tree as Yeshua, Himself. I have no problem with that, as long as we also know that one cannot separate Yeshua from His people Israel. The best way to understand this statement is by carefully reading Isa. 49:1-6, where the parallel between Israel (God's *servant*) and her Messiah (also called God's *Servant*) is clearly portrayed.

Again, please note that the first century Spirit-led Israelites (today's Spirit-led Messianic Jews) were still living among their beloved people—the nation of Israel. *They did not see themselves as 'a separate entity' nor as a new nation or religious system!* <u>Those first century Messianic Jews were part and parcel of the nation of Israel</u>, exactly as it was in the days of Moses, the twelve spies and Elijah.

Israel according to the flesh (i.e., those Israelites who did not accept Yeshua as their Messiah), was indeed *put aside* (or *broken off*) from their own Olive Tree due to their unbelief, but only temporarily.[241]

Until the glorious return of Messiah, the King of the Jews (referred to as His Second Coming), God's calling and promises concerning Israel are unchangeable. Indeed, <u>*all* Israel shall be saved</u>.[242] And until then, both natural and Spirit-led Israelites must live side by side within one single framework called Israel, exactly according to the Biblical pattern described above.

One of the most terrible mistakes made by those who hold to any of the various types of replacement theology, is their claim that they are now the new Israel, while the old (or natural) Israel is no longer of any interest to God.[243]

How is it that believers arrive at such wrong conclusions regarding Israel? They completely misunderstand Shaul's analogy of *the Olive Tree* in Romans 11. They miss the clear Biblical pattern, according to

---

[241] See, Rom. 11:15, 17, 19, 21, 23

[242] See, Rom. 11:26, 29

[243] Notice, that the term "Spiritual Israel" is <u>not</u> found anywhere in Scripture. Nevertheless, while considering related Scriptures, one is able to see that within the Nation of Israel, there are and there always were both "Spirit-led Israelites" and "Israelites according to the flesh." My understanding of this concept of "Spirit-led Israelites" has nothing to do with anything or anyone that adheres to replacement theology!

which individual descendants of Abraham, Isaac and Jacob always have and always will function (living side by side) within a single body called Israel—whether or not they walk in the Spirit! They completely miss the vital connection between *the seven thousand, Shaul* (an Israelite, himself) and *the Olive Tree*, which is the *remnant called out* by God in every generation, a *remnant* that has existed always within the larger body called Israel.

In light of what has been covered thus far, we can better understand Shaul's grief concerning his non-believing fellow Israelites.[244] Actually, every follower of Yeshua should have this same kind of love and compassion for *Israel in the flesh* (non-believing Jews). Why? Simply because we are connected. Israel is the framework in and through which we (*the Olive Tree, the remnant*) are functioning. How can we hate our own framework (or home) or our own people?

Up until now, we have spoken of *the Olive Tree* as describing the Spirit-led remnant within the nation of Israel. "But what about gentile followers of Messiah?" one might ask. The following paragraphs will cover this very important gentile issue.

First *The Fullness of the Gentiles* and Only Then *All Israel Shall be Saved*

Is the concept of gentiles being grafted into *the Olive Tree* (the believing, Spirit-led Israelite remnant) only a New Covenant concept? Not at all!

A brief look at the biblical history of the nation of Israel shows beyond a shadow of a doubt, that since the nation of Israel was established by the Almighty, there have always been individuals from other nations,

---

[244] See, Rom. 9:1-2.

who were welcomed into His chosen sheepfold. Here are a few examples:

- Joseph married a gentile woman in Egypt, one of whose children was later fully adopted by his father Jacob (also called *Israel*).[245]

- Jethro gave Moses his daughter Zipporah in marriage, despite their ethnic and religious differences. They married and had two sons, Gershom, and Eliezer.[246]

- Rahab the harlot, together with her household, joined Israel after hiding the two spies sent by Joshua.[247]

- Boaz bought the estate from Naomi and married Ruth, the Moabitess. Ruth and Boaz became the parents of Obed, who became the father of Jesse, the father of David.[248]

It is very interesting to note that the apostle Shaul, while referring to the gentiles who are grafted into *the Olive Tree*, quotes directly from a well-known prophecy given by Jacob (Israel) to his grandsons— Joseph's two sons.[249]

---

[245] See, Gen. 41:45, 50-52; 48:1-20.

[246] See, Ex. 2:21-22

[247] See, Josh. 2:1-22, 6:22-25.

[248] The Book of Ruth. Both Rahab and Ruth are an integral part of Yeshua's genealogy (Mt. 1:5).

[249] See, Rom. 11:25; Gen. 48:8-20. Look especially at verse 19 — *"his* (Ephraim's) *seeds shall become the fullness of the Gentiles."*

Could it be that some of the gentiles who have been grafted into the Olive Tree since Yeshua's First Coming, have a biblical (and historical) connection to one or both of Joseph's sons?[250]

Meanwhile, as I understand it, until *all Israel shall be saved* actually takes place at Messiah's Second Coming, *the fullness of the gentiles* will continue to be in effect, since gentiles are still being invited to come into *the Olive Tree* of Israel. Once the last gentile has entered, the door for them will be closed and it will open wide to the Jews to come (back) in, and become a part of their own original tree.[251] As long as the majority of Israel has not accepted their Messiah (and, thus, are still put aside, cut off or broken off from their own Olive Tree), gentiles who accept the Good News are still being grafted into the olive tree of Israel.

These gentile followers of the Jewish Messiah can actually enjoy everything with which the nation of Israel was blessed and promised by God. They become equal and "first -class citizens" with Messianic Jews in their Olive Tree, exactly as Joseph's wife and children, Moses' wife and children, Rahab, Ruth, and others.

Conclusions Thus Far

The New Covenant was made (formed/*cut*) between God and the two houses, or kingdoms of Israel (the two houses/kingdoms formed at the split of the Kingdom of Israel, following King Solomon's reign). No

---

[250] For a detailed discussion on Jacob's blessings over the sons of Joseph and the historical ramifications of these blessings, read *Moses Wrote About Me: Genesis*, pages 397-417 and 453-460.

[251] See, Rom. 11:11-12, 15-16, 25-26.

other nation (or individual) is mentioned! As we all know, God does not change; especially with regard to His promises![252]

Gentile believers have been grafted into *the Olive Tree* of Israel – as individuals or families (*you and your household...*) – not as a different entity or nation! Gentiles are called into the *commonwealth of Israel!*[253]

Returning to the question I posed regarding the pre-Tribulation worldview; I would like to ask again: **Are the church and Israel separate entities?** Nowhere in Scripture do I see that God marries *two wives*! Nowhere in God's Holy Word do I see that He deals separately with two *bodies*.[254] It *is* true that He never forgot His promises to the nation of Israel and that, since Yeshua's First Coming, He has shown His great mercies to both *Spirit-led Israelites* (Jews and gentiles alike, as one body – Messiah's body – *the Olive Tree*) and to *natural Israelites* (non-believing Jews). Yet, Spirit-led Israelites must follow the first century *Olive Tree* example, seeing and considering themselves as being strongly connected to *Natural* Israel! The fact that the church, throughout history, diverged far away from her Jewish roots does not at all change the biblical truths concerning who she really is - A mixed body of both Jews and gentiles inside an Israelite Olive Tree and within the framework of *the Commonwealth of ISRAEL*!

---

[252] See Lev. 26:44-46; 1 Sam. 12:22; Jer. 31:35-40, 33:19-26; Ps. 94:14; Rom. 11:28-32.

[253] See, Eph. 2:11-17.

[254] I'm very aware of His dealing with the two houses of Israel – *the house of Judah and the house of Israel/Ephraim* – and even giving them different names (see, for example, Ezek. 23). Yet, they are always within what is desired by God to be one, united body called ISRAEL (see Ezek. 37:15-23; see also Jn. 10:16).

The Good News and the Cyclical Hebraic Mindset

Not only did God make a New Covenant exclusively with His Chosen Nation, Israel, but this New Covenant is directly connected with, and based upon, clear patterns that were established mainly in the Torah, which was given to Israel as well. The message of the good news (usually referred to as *the Gospel*), as presented in the New Covenant writings, is <u>not</u> "a new doctrine" but rather, strongly based on the Old Covenant writings. Allow me to elaborate.

Our Fathers Under Moses and the Good News Message

The clearest pattern upon which the story of our salvation is based, is described in the exodus of Israel out of Egypt. These are Shaul's own words:

*Moreover, brethren, I do not want you to be unaware that **all** our fathers were under the cloud, and all passed through the sea; <u>all were immersed into Moses in the cloud and in the sea</u>. All ate the same spiritual food; and all drank the same spiritual drink: <u>for they drank of that spiritual Rock that followed them: and that Rock was Messiah</u>. But with most of them God was not well pleased, for their bodies were scattered in the wilderness. Now these things became our examples, to the intent we should not lust after evil things, as they also lusted. And do not become idolaters, as were some of them; as it is written, the people sat down to eat and drink, and rose up to play. Nor let us commit sexual immorality, as some of them did, and in one day twenty-three thousand fell. Nor let us tempt Messiah, as some of them also tempted, and were destroyed by serpents. Nor murmur, as some of them also murmured, and were destroyed by the destroyer. Now all these things happened unto them as examples: and they were written* *for our admonition, upon whom the ends of the ages have come. Therefore, let him who thinks he stands take heed lest he fall.*[255]

The epistle to the Hebrews says something similar:

Therefore, since a promise remains of entering His rest, let us fear lest any of you seem to have come short of it. <u>For indeed **the good news was preached to us as well as to them**; but the word which they heard did not profit them, not being mixed with faith in those who heard it...</u> *For if Joshua had given them rest, then he would not afterward have spoken of another day. There remains therefore a rest for the people of God. For he who has entered his rest has himself also ceased from his works as God did from His!*[256]

From the above scriptures, we can clearly see how Shaul the Apostle (taking into consideration that he also wrote the book of Hebrews) makes a direct connection between the story of the great exodus of *our fathers* and our own personal story of salvation through Yeshua's atoning blood. Notice that he does not say "my fathers" as he clearly understands that gentiles, once having been grafted into the *Olive Tree* of the nation of Israel, even enjoy the Israelite heritage, i.e., being connected to the fathers of Israel during the time of Moses! Here are a few examples to further clarify this crucially important point:

- Our fathers were under Pharaoh's heavy bondage. Thus, Moses introduced them to the lamb of Passover as the only way out into freedom from their misery. The exact same thing happened for us—true followers of Israel's Messiah Redeemer: Once, we, too, were in "Egypt" (representing the world we live in) until someone introduced us to the lamb of

---

[255] See, 1 Cor. 10:1-12. See also Jude 5.

[256] See, Heb. 4:1-2, 8-10.

Passover, who is the Lamb of God – Yeshua, the only way into freedom out of Satan's grip of bondage!

- Our fathers were all *immersed into Moses and into the Cloud.* The exact same thing happened to us—true followers of Messiah: we were immersed into Yeshua in water. Our fathers received the Torah at Mount Sinai in the third month (during the Feast of Shavuot, i.e., Pentecost). We, the true followers of Yeshua, also received God's Holy Spirit at Shavuot.[257]

- Our fathers walked through the wilderness to the Promised Land. We, likewise, are walking through the wilderness of this world (sin, temptation, etc.) to our Promised Land.

And lastly,

- Only the new generation of our fathers finally crossed over the Jordan River to the other side, to God's Promised Land, under the leadership of Joshua the son of Nun. In the future, we, the true followers of Israel's Messiah, will also *cross the Jordan River* as *a new creation*, and enter our Promised Land!

So, we can see that everything taught in the New Covenant writings, concerning salvation through Israel's Messiah, is based on *the Tanach* and, in that sense, indeed *there is nothing new under the sun*!

Moreover, we can clearly see that *salvation is a process* and *not* a one-time event. The "wilderness walk" is inevitable and an integral stage that all true followers of Messiah Yeshua should and will go through.

---

[257] See Acts 2.

Only *the one who endures to the end* (i.e., crossing over the Jordan River) *will be saved!*[258]

In summarizing, we can see that there are actually three main stages to the story of our salvation through Messiah's atoning blood:

a. The application of <u>the blood of the Passover lamb</u> and <u>the crossing of the Red Sea</u> (immersion into Moses and the cloud).

b. The <u>wilderness walk</u> (to shape and mold us as *a new creation*, or, as some rightfully say, "to take Egypt out of us").

And lastly,

c. The <u>crossing of the Jordan River</u> into our Promised Land.

The Tabernacle, the Temple, and the Good News Message

The following is yet another pattern upon which the good news of our great salvation, portrayed in the New Covenant writings, is based.

Already from the very beginning, God greatly desired to dwell within us human beings to have intimate fellowship with us - the only ones He had created in His own image and likeness! Once He gave His Holy Torah to His Chosen Nation, the next thing He instructed Moses was:

And let them make me a sanctuary, <u>that I may dwell among them</u>![259] (emphasis added).

---

[258] See Matt. 24:13. Once we successfully have "crossed the wilderness," the very last stage every one of us must experience (following the example of our fathers) will be the crossing of the Jordan River into our "Promised Land"—this will be either by death or by transformation in the twinkling of an eye (see 1 Cor. 15:50-57).

[259] See Ex. 25:8.

Above, we saw that the gospel of salvation through Messiah's precious atoning blood, has three primary stages. All these stages can also be seen in what composed the three parts of the Tabernacle, and later the first and second Temples in Jerusalem:

a.   The Outer Court: Here were the Brazen Altar and the Laver. This court represented the first of the three stages of salvation, which we all need to go through in order to *endure to the end*—to make it to our Promised Land - God's Kingdom. There is the need to first apply the blood of the Passover lamb (represented by a pure sacrifice on the Bronze Altar) and to go through the Red Sea (via water immersion, represented by the Laver). The Laver also can be seen to represent the screen separating the outer court and the next (second) section of the Tabernacle.

b.   The Holy Place: Here were the Menorah, the Table of Show Bread, and the Altar of Incense. This Holy Place, with its three furnishings, represents the second stage of salvation – the Wilderness Walk – where our Lord and Savior sustains us with His own body/bread (represented by the Table of Showbread) and shines His Light (represented by the Menorah and reminding us of the pillar of fire in the wilderness), to direct us through our lifelong journey. Lastly, He leads us (as did the pillar of cloud) by way of the spiritual intercession that He offers on our behalf (represented by the Altar of Incense). Notice, that everything used in this second section of the Tabernacle has been crushed, pressed, and carefully purified (the olive oil that is used to light the Menorah, the grain used to make the Showbread loaves and lastly, the ingredients used for the Incense). Thus, this part of the Tabernacle also represents the crushing, shaping and molding processes we all need to pass through to "take Egypt out of us," and "die to self," so that the *new creation* can come out pure and ready for the next and final stage.

c. <u>The Holy of Holies</u>: In this last part of the Tabernacle, there was only one piece of furniture - The Ark of the Covenant. Only once a year could the High Priest of Israel come into this room, and that was on the Day of Atonement. This he could only do after having first atoned for himself and his family! He would then pass through a veil which separated the Holy Place from the Holy of Holies. This last veil can very well be a picture or representation of the Jordan River that separates between the wilderness (Holy Place) and the Promised Land (Holy of Holies). The New Covenant writings describe Yeshua as our High Priest in the Heavenly Tabernacle/Temple and His flesh/body as that very *veil!*[260] This last room represents the third and last stage in the process of our salvation—the entrance into our Promised Land, entering God's very presence (the Ark of the Covenant)—His heavenly throne room.

So far, we have discussed and established the following crucially important points: (1) there is a strong connection between the first century body of Yeshua (comprising *Spirit-led Israelites* and *grafted-in gentiles* in *the Olive Tree* <u>of Israel</u>) and the (natural, non-believing) nation of Israel; and (2) the story of our salvation through Israel's Messiah is based on and patterned after two main witnesses in the Biblical history of Israel: (a) the exodus out of Egypt, all the way to the crossing of the Jordan River into the Promised Land, and (b) the three parts, or sections of the Tabernacle—the Outer Court, the Holy Place and the Holy of Holies.

Now, after establishing the general Biblical context, or *the bigger picture*, we will go back to the main issue discussed in this chapter - the Rapture and its timing.

---

[260] See Heb. 2:17, 4:14, 5:1-10, 6:20, 8:9, 10:20-21. See also Lev. 16.

Israel and the Rapture

If Yeshua's body is strongly connected to Israel, God's ancient Chosen Nation, and if the good news message - the story of our own salvation through Israel's Messiah, has a strong connection both to the three stages that relate to the exodus out of Egypt and the three parts of the Tabernacle, then it would only be natural to continue this discussion by addressing the most important question: **Can we see any foreshadowing or any prototype of a 'Rapture' in the history of Israel as a nation;** and more specifically, **can we see a 'Rapture' in the two main patterns we have discussed above** (the exodus of our fathers and the Tabernacle)?

At the very beginning of this chapter, I dealt with both the literal and conceptual meanings of *Rapture* in Scripture. I said that it is not at all new. I demonstrated that there are multiple meanings for the concept of Rapture. As a short reminder, in God's holy word the concept of Rapture primarily refers to an individual, a group of people or even an entire nation being removed, or taken, from one place/situation/condition into another—a new one. This can be done by different means: separation, death, healing, resurrection, and transformation, such as into a glorified body in a twinkling of an eye.

I would like to suggest that when carefully looking at the history of the nation of Israel (*our fathers*), we can find one particularly clear example of "a Rapture." This Rapture has what I like to call a three-fold fulfillment.

The First Rapture is Physical

As discussed above, all *our fathers* were in Egypt (a picture of the world in which we are living). All were under the heavy yoke of

Pharaoh (a picture of Satan). As the yoke became more and more of a burden, they cried out to the Lord to save them from Pharaoh's strong grip. And so, God sent Moses and Aaron to save them and take them out of Egypt.

As an integral part of the process of taking them out of Egypt, God exercised certain severe judgments over Pharaoh, his people, their false gods, and his land. It is my understanding that these judgments (namely, *the ten plagues*), exercised over Egypt <u>prior</u> to the great exodus, are a picture, or a foreshadowing, of the severe judgments which God is going to inflict upon Satan and the different gods of this world (Egypt) just <u>prior</u> to Yeshua's glorious return.

There are two questions we should address at this juncture: (1) Did God take His Chosen Nation out of the land of Egypt at any point <u>before</u> inflicting His holy and just judgments upon Egypt? Did He take them out *seven years* before He afflicted the Egyptians with the ten plagues? Did He take them out *three and a half years* before? Not at all! (2) Did God's Chosen Nation suffer under these severe judgments? Again, not at all! A careful reading of Scripture shows that the Israelites were provided with a specific location - the land of *Goshen*, which was separated from the rest of the Egyptians but, nonetheless, was still <u>within the boundaries of Egypt</u>![261]

It is time to elaborate on the very last plague that God inflicted on Egypt—the death of every first born. As far as Pharaoh was concerned

---

[261] It is very interesting to note how Ps. 78:49 describes God's Severe Judgments upon Egypt prior to the Exodus of our fathers as *the fierceness of His anger, <u>wrath</u>* (in Hebrew, *charon* — חרון), *indignation and <u>trouble</u>* (from "Tribulation" — in Hebrew, *tz'arah* — צרה) and *a great trouble* (which can also be translated as *great Tribulation* (in Hebrew, *tz'arah g'dola* — צרה גדולה). See this same description as it relates to the great famine in Egypt in the days of Joseph, who is a clear picture of Yeshua, in both His First and Second comings (Acts 7:11).

(once again, Pharaoh as foreshadowing Satan), the tenth and last plague was the straw that broke the camel's back. Once it had taken place, Pharaoh could no longer keep God's Chosen Nation under his strong grip, and he almost immediately let them out of his land.

Two crucially important things are worth noting: (1) It was <u>the blood of the Passover lamb</u> that protected God's elect <u>while still in Goshen</u>, and (2) it was <u>at midnight</u> when the great outcry in Egypt was heard, granting freedom to our fathers![262]

So, when exactly were our forefathers Raptured — removed from, or *taken out* of Egypt? <u>It was at the very end</u>— the very last minute (after the last plague). And it was *at midnight*! Were our fathers afflicted with God's severe judgments? Scripture is pretty clear that at least from the fourth plague onward, they were not affected at all, nor were they affected by the final two.[263]

The Second Rapture is Spiritual

The above description of our fathers' Rapture in the physical realm, also took place in each of our lives in the spiritual realm. Allow me to elaborate.

Every born-again, or true follower of Israel's Messiah, has had to pass through their own exodus out of Egypt or *Passover experience*. Each one of us who is now an integral member of Israel's *Olive Tree*, was once a slave in Egypt. Each one of us was in heavy bondage inflicted by Pharaoh (i.e., under sin and under the god of this world). Each one

---

[262] See Ex. 12, especially verses 29-32, and compare with Yeshua's own words concerning His glorious return to His beloved in Matt. 25:6 — *And <u>at midnight</u> a cry was heard…*

[263] See Ex. 7:21; 8:6, 17, 22; 9:4-6, 25-26; and 10:22-23.

of us, once in our lives, heard the good news message of Messiah from someone, just as the Israelites heard it from Moses and Aaron. Each one of us heard about the urgent need for the blood of the consummate Passover Lamb – God's Lamb – Yeshua. Each one of us chose to apply this precious blood to the *doorposts and lintels* of our hearts and minds! Thus, each one of us has been delivered, or Raptured out of Egypt, in the spiritual realm!

Now, as it was with *our fathers* under Moses in the physical realm, so it was with our own spiritual *Passover experiences*. It did not take place years (*seven, three and a half*, etc.) before we were completely at <u>the end</u> of our human resources—broken and humbled before God, acknowledging that we could not do anything about our very lowly condition (as slaves to Pharaoh, sin etc.). Yes, as it was with *our fathers*, our spiritual Rapture out of Egypt did not take place at any time before we were at our <u>very end</u>, the end of all our natural resources as well as the end of the many gods we had served that were now consumed, finished, and judged by the Almighty. Only then, <u>at the very end</u> God miraculously intervened and saved us! He has spiritually Raptured (*taken*) us out of this darkened world (Egypt) and into *the Kingdom of His beloved Son* and made us *sit together in the heavenly places in Messiah Yeshua.*[264] As with our fathers, it was only *at midnight* – the darkest hour of our lives, at the very last minute that we asked Yeshua to take full control of our lives. And He graciously did!

Can we also apply the above two fulfillments to the next, third and last fulfillment of all? I think we can!

---

[264] See Eph. 2:6 and, Col. 1:13.

The Third Rapture is Both Spiritual and Physical

Based on the pattern established above, it is my understanding that the third and last Rapture will take place <u>at the very end</u> of what I described above as our salvation process (or journey).

Above, we saw that as followers of Yeshua, we cannot and should not be separated from non-believing Israel! As the first century body of Spirit-led Israelites walked side by side with the rest of their brethren (natural/ non-believing Israel), today's Spirit-led Israelites must return to the realization of their Jewish roots and once again consider themselves as an integral part of *the Commonwealth of Israel.*[265]

Both non-believing Israel and Yeshua's body – *the Olive Tree,* have one destiny—to be an integral part of the restoration of the Kingdom <u>to</u> <u>Israel!</u>[266] Both non-believing Israel and Yeshua's body need to arrive at the Jordan River, and cross it safely under the leadership of *Joshua* (a picture/ foreshadowing of *Yeshua*)! Both non-believing Israel and Yeshua's body must get to *the plains of Moab,* which are on the east bank of the Jordan River - opposite Jericho - which is the lowest place on Earth![267] Both are going to be protected by the Almighty until that glorious moment (Yeshua's Second Coming)!

When Will This Third and Final Rapture Take Place?

The apostle Shaul declared that *flesh and blood cannot inherit the Kingdom of God!*[268] Upon what was he basing his words? As a Jewish rabbi, there is no doubt it was on God's Holy Word! Yes, this Holy

---

[265] See Eph. 2:11-13.

[266] See Acts 1:6-7.

[267] See Num. 22:1; Deut. 32:49, 34:8; Josh. 1–2.

[268] 1 Cor. 15:50.

Word portrays patterns, foreshadowing and prototypes. The character of this Holy Word is *cyclical* rather than linear, and thus, it contains many narratives with multiple fulfillments, multiple repetitions, and multiple progressive revelations.

Note that it was only the *new generation* who crossed the Jordan River and entered God's Promised Land! It was not a group of old slaves with their slave mentality who entered the Promised Land. It was their children—being a foreshadowing, a picture, a pattern of the *new creation, the Israel of God!*

As flesh and blood cannot inherit God's Kingdom, there is a need for a change to take place just prior to the crossing of the Jordan River: a supernatural change only God can undertake Himself. Those who have already died will be raised with completely different, glorified bodies; and the ones still alive in this present body of flesh will be changed as *in the twinkling of an eye,* and, therefore, Raptured (removed or *taken*) to meet Yeshua in the sky. This third Rapture will occur *both* in the physical (with a changed body, a *glorified* one) and in the spiritual (with the new creation, newly generated spirit)![269] Indeed, *there is nothing new under the sun!*

Based on all of the above, the final/third Rapture will follow the exact same pattern set by the first two, i.e., occurring <u>at the very end</u>! If we speak about the pattern set in Egypt, it will take place <u>at the end</u> of the severe judgments of God on this world. If we speak about our own personal Passover experiences, it takes place <u>at the very end</u> of our fleshly resources —after all has been used up and we give up on our ability to save ourselves from Egypt, or from our enslavement to this world and all its sinful ways.

---

[269] See 1 Cor. 15:35-58.

Following the pattern of the twofold fulfillment described above, God knows all too well how to protect His beloved chosen ones here on this Earth, while at the same time inflicting His severe judgments upon those who reject His rulership over their lives. God knows where the different lands of *Goshen* are in this present world![270]

The Rapture cannot be artificially and un-Biblically detached from the history of the nation to which we are so strongly connected - Israel! In the same way that salvation is not a one-time "altar call" or "sinner's prayer," but rather a process we all need to endure and stick out to the very end. We cannot expect any kind of shortcuts, hoping to avoid, or be exempt from one of the three main phases of this salvation process![271]

Furthermore, the patterns, the foreshadowing and prototypes upon which our story of salvation is built – i.e., the three stages/phases above - involve walking through difficulties, persecutions and tribulations, all of which are under God's full control as He protects us

---

[270] See how He protects His chosen ones during hardships and different "tribulations" in other Biblical references, such as 1 Kings 18:4 and 13. See Yeshua's famous prayers on behalf of His chosen disciples (but not only them) in Jn. 17:15. See also Rev. 12:6.

[271] See Ex. 12; Num. 14 and 26:65; and Josh. 3–4. The three stages of the salvation story took place <u>at the end</u> of all human resources: (a) The applying of the Passover lamb's blood and the crossing of the Red Sea came at the very end of the people's human resources, i.e., at the very end of the final plague, and at the very end of their own resources standing before the Red Sea. (b) There were no shortcuts in the wilderness walk for the Israelites (and for us as well). The Israelites needed to walk all of the forty years, not any fewer—due to the sin of the spies, needless to say. And lastly: (c) Crossing the Jordan River involved God's miraculous intervention, as the Israelites could not do it by themselves or in their own (very limited) power!

and never tries us beyond our abilities![272] No wonder Yeshua, Shaul and the other apostles always encouraged true followers of Yeshua to hang on until the very end and to be encouraged and joyful, despite tribulations.[273]

---

[272] See 1 Cor. 10:13. See also Matt. 6:13.

[273] See Matt. 24:9; Jn. 16:3; Acts 14:22; Rom. 5:3, 8:35, 12:12; 2 Cor. 6:4; Heb. 10:33.

Noah, Lot, and the Rapture

Concerning the Rapture taking place <u>at the very end</u>, it is quite interesting that, when speaking of His Second Coming, Yeshua used <u>only two</u> biblical examples as patterns: Noah and Lot!

A careful reading of Scripture shows, beyond any shadow of a doubt, that both Noah (together with his family) and Lot (along with his wife and two daughters) were Raptured (removed or *taken*) out of their situation or condition (God's severe judgment upon all their surroundings) <u>*at the very end*</u>, only moments before He inflicted His judgments upon the sinful world during their times. God did not take them out of the trouble any time prior to that![274]

---

[274] See Gen. 6–7, especially 7:7, 11, 13 and 16! See Gen. 19:12-25, especially 19:16-17!

A Summary

Before I endeavor to answer some of the main claims of the pre-Tribulation view, I would like to give you a short summary of what has been discussed so far.

No doubt, the issue of the Rapture and more specifically, its timing, is one of the most controversial issues in Yeshua's present-day body. By now, I'm sure you have noticed that I have not dealt with the historical origins of the Pre-Tribulation doctrine at all. This subject is very much debated by different End-Time prophecy Bible teachers. All I would say about it is that whether the point of origin was J. N. Darby (at the beginning of the 19th Century CE), whose understanding of the Rapture was influenced by the vision of a 15-year-old girl, Margaret McDonald, or a specific 19th century believing group with which he was affiliated, or whether the origins go back to somewhere in the 4th or 5th century CE, my personal conviction is that <u>this argument is futile</u>, as it does not address this issue through its original first century lens![275] In other words, I have chosen to present the reader with what I call "the missing link," which in my understanding has been neglected

---

[275] For good articles regarding what I describe as "a futile debate" within Christianity, you can find studies of the Pre-Tribulation Rapture at Liberty University's Digital Commons-https://digitalcommons.liberty.edu/do/search/?q=pre-trib&start=0&context=234296&facet=; read a thesis by David Hebert, Oral Roberts University, on "The Rapture of the Church" — http://web.oru.edu/current_students/class_pages/grtheo/mmankins/DrHebert/M.A.%20Thesis/MA(Th)%20Thesis.CH-1a%20The%20Problem.pdf; or read "The Rapture Question" by Alan S. Bandy, The Gospel Coalition — https://www.thegospelcoalition.org/essay/the-Rapture-question/ — among many others.

by most End-Time prophecy teachers - i.e., to look at this specific subject through the Hebraic/Jewish Middle Eastern Lens!

I began by laying some foundational stones, such as the scriptural concept of *Rapture*. I stated that even though the specific term "Rapture" is not shown in the Greek manuscript of the New Covenant writings, it remains a scriptural concept, nonetheless.

I discussed what I call the Middle Eastern Hebraic mindset behind Scripture—for example, its cyclical characteristic (versus the Western Greek linear one) and the Middle Eastern Hebraic understanding of numbers.

I moved from there and presented the mindset and background behind the pre-Tribulation view. I expanded upon a few of the described foundational principles of this view, especially concerning the difference between Israel and Yeshua's body. I explained my understanding of *the Olive Tree* and its strong, undivided connection to the nation of Israel.

I shared my understanding of the patterns upon which the story of our salvation (or, more correctly, the process or stages/phases of our salvation) is based, including the exodus out of Egypt and the three parts of the Tabernacle and temples in Jerusalem. I connected these patterns to what I consider as the only possible timing of the Rapture.

According to the patterns set before us in God's Holy Word, God is going to gather us unto Himself <u>at the very end</u>, while simultaneously protecting us here on Earth while He inflicts His severe judgments upon this sinful world![276]

---

[276] This points to Rev. 6:10, where, as an integral part of God's protection, He orders his angels to *seal the servants of our God on their foreheads...* I know there will be some who will point me to the immediate context, which is the sealing of

Moreover: The biblical pattern clearly points out that the believer should *endure to the end*, and not to "seven" or "three and half years" before the end![277]

---

the 144,000 from the twelve tribes of Israel. Yet, according to the broader context of the Book of Revelation, everything has to do with Israel (see the gates and foundations of the New Jerusalem, who are none else than *the bride—the wife of the Lamb!* See 21:9-14). Again, I suggest going back and reading about the strong and undivided connection of *the Israel of God* (or "Spirit-led Israelites"- the *Olive Tree*), who are joined by gentile individuals and families from every nation in the world, to non-believing Israel!

[277] See for example: Matt. 10:22, 24:13, 1 Cor. 1:8, Rev. 2:26.

Assessment of Common Pre-Tribulation Claims

This is the time to go back to some of the pre-Tribulation claims and objections in order to address them in greater detail. Needless to say, I'm going to do it while considering the biblical context established above – namely, within their "Israeli- connection."[278]

Claim: Yeshua's body had no part in the first sixty-nine weeks of Daniel (Daniel 9:24-27), and it won't have any part in the seventieth week either. Daniel's seventy weeks' prophecy deals only with Old Testament Israel—not with Yeshua's body.

Above, I have made it clear that no one can artificially separate Yeshua's body and Old Testament Israel! Such a separation was not known to the first apostles nor to the multitude of disciples who followed Yeshua in the first century! They all saw themselves as an integral part of *the Olive Tree* of Israel. Moreover, they saw gentiles

---

[278] While dealing with some of the pre-Tribulation Rapture claims, as well as working on the appendix, at the end of this chapter – "Daniel's Seventy Weeks," my research led me to quite a few sites and books. Here I would like to give credit to, and highly recommend two resources that I found to be very helpful: (1) A book published in 2004, named, **"End Time Delusions," by Steve Wohlberg, head of the "white horse media"** (www.whitehorsemedia.com), and, (2) **"Logos Apostolic (online) Bible College."** A site that invites followers of Yeshua, from all over the world, and from all backgrounds, to freely study and use their online resources. I highly recommend visiting their "Bible Study Index" (https://www.logosapostolic.org/bible_study/studiesindex.htm), where you can find many good Bible studies, including word studies, articles and the like. **Disclaimer:** I do *not* agree with every point the above two resources present! Yet, I do wish to follow John the Apostle, who encouraged us to *not believe every spirit, but test the spirits, whether they are of God...* (1 John 4:1). Take whatever is good and reject whatever is not of God! This is operating with discernment.

who had joined them in the Olive Tree, as partakers within *the commonwealth of Israel!*

As it concerns Daniel's famous seventy weeks prophecy, I have dedicated an entire appendix to it, and I recommend that the reader carefully look it over.[279] Just to provide a small taste, I would like to draw your attention to the following: (a) Up until the 17-18th centuries CE, most Protestant Bible commentators did not draw a distinction between the sixty-ninth and the seventieth weeks but rather saw them as one continuous unit; (b) Many commentators saw Yeshua as the One who *confirms a covenant for the many;* and lastly, (c) This prophecy, as others in Scripture, has more than one fulfillment. In fact, for those with eyes to see, it is being fulfilled before our very eyes in our generation.

Claim: The Second Coming of Yeshua and the Rapture of His body are separate events. Yeshua comes to meet His body in the Rapture (1 Thes. 4:16-17) and returns to Earth with them during His Second Coming (1 Thes. 3:13). In other words, Yeshua's body goes up from the Earth in the Rapture, and it returns to the Earth during the Second Coming of Messiah.

I dare say that there is not even one clear scripture that supports the first two statements above. Rather, they are based on combining, or putting together different scriptures while, at times, taking them out of their immediate context. We shall clearly show this later. There are no scriptures to support the idea of three comings of Messiah: (1) the first , about two thousand years ago; (2) the second, when He comes to Rapture (or *take*) His body out of this world; and (3) the third and

---

[279] See at the end of this chapter.

last one, when He comes to restore the Kingdom to Israel for a period of one thousand years here on Earth.

Each one of the above claims must first be consistent with and based upon Messiah's own words! Yeshua spoke very clearly about the End Times as well as His glorious return, and this is recorded in a few places in Scripture. I would like to draw your attention to two well-known references:

Matt. 10: At the beginning of this chapter, Yeshua sends His disciples to preach the good news all over the land of Israel. Interestingly enough, in verse 16, there seems to be a kind of shift, as His instructions seem to apply not only to His time with His disciples back in the first century, but also to the future—to the very time He returns to establish His Kingdom here in the Promised Land (see specifically verses 21-23 and compare with Matt. 24:9-13). Notice, that there is no pre-Tribulation Rapture mentioned here! Quite the opposite: Yeshua's disciples (including those of us who, I believe, are living very close to His glorious return) are *no greater than the master/teacher!* (10:24) Whatever was done to Him will be done to His followers as well. In other words, as true followers of Messiah who walk in His footsteps, we should also expect persecution, even unto death! This has been a proven pattern, clearly and powerfully demonstrated in the first century, where most of Yeshua's close disciples and apostles, as well as many others, lost their lives while being severely persecuted for His Name's sake!

Matt. 24-25: In theological seminaries, Matt. 24 is known as "the Mount of Olivet Discourse." I would define this chapter as the clearest End-Time prophecy given straight from the mouth of the King of Kings.

Any kind of scriptural interpretation – including that given by Shaul and the other apostles – must <u>first</u> agree with and be based upon

Yeshua's own words! If it doesn't, then the interpretation has not come from God's Spirit but rather from the wishful thinking of men's own hearts' desires! So, let us now delve into some of Yeshua's descriptions of the End Times, in Matt. 24 & 25 as it describes the events preceding His glorious return:

*Immediately <u>after</u> the Tribulation of these days, the sun will be darkened, and the moon will not give its light; the stars will fall from Heaven, and the powers of the Heavens will be shaken. <u>Then</u> the sign of the Son of Man will appear in Heaven, and <u>then</u> all the tribes of the Earth will mourn, and they will see the Son of Man coming on the clouds of Heaven with power and great glory. **<u>And</u> He will send His angels <u>with a great sound of a trumpet</u>, and they will <u>gather together</u> <u>His elect from the four winds</u>, from one end of Heaven to the other*** (Matt. 24:29-31, emphases added. See also Mk. 13:24-27).

Note the order in which the events were arranged by Yeshua Himself:

a. His coming to gather the elect will be <u>after</u> the Tribulation has <u>ended</u>! Note that in the immediate context, *the Tribulation of those days* is that very *great Tribulation, such as has not been since the beginning of the world until this time, no, nor ever shall be!*[280]

b. The signs in the Heavens, including the sign of the Son of Man and His coming in the clouds with power and glory, are very similar to the description in the book of Revelation.[281]

c. The loud sound is of <u>the very last trumpet</u>.[282]

---

[280] See Matt. 24:21

[281] See Rev. 19:11-16

[282] See also 1 Cor. 15:52, 1 Thes. 4:16 and Rev. 11:15-19.

d. Only then, <u>after</u> the previous points (that we can call "precursors," or events which must take place <u>prior to the gathering of those holy/set apart</u>), the elect will be gathered to Him!

I cannot see anywhere in the above description that Yeshua separated the *gathering of the holy* (the Rapture) from His glorious Second Coming! A simple and basic reading of the above verses show beyond a shadow of a doubt, that only <u>one</u> great Second Coming (adjoined by a gathering of the saints), with a harsh sounding event is to be expected!

But what about 1 Thes. 3:13 and 4:15-17?

Let's see what the two Scripture references above really say: *For this we say to you by the word of the Lord, that we who are alive and remain <u>until the coming of the Lord</u> will by no means precede those who are asleep. For the Lord Himself will descend from Heaven <u>with a shout</u>, <u>with the voice of an archangel,</u> and <u>with the trumpet of God</u>. And the dead in Messiah will rise first . <u>Then we who are alive and remain shall be caught up together with them in the clouds to meet the Lord in the air</u>. And thus, we shall always be with the Lord. So that He may establish your hearts blameless in holiness before our God and Father <u>at the coming of our Lord Yeshua the Messiah with all His saints.</u>* (Or *holy ones*. 1 Thes. 3:13, 4:15-17; emphases added).

Note the following:

a. The events described in the above references clearly speak of *the coming of our Lord!*

b. It does not separate *the coming of the Lord* into two different events (we will see this later, when dealing with the references found in 2 Thes.).

c. It seems that from these two references, His coming won't be at all quiet, secret, or unnoticed. To the contrary: It will be a very noisy event, with (1) *a shout,* (2) *a voice of an archangel,* and (3) *the trumpet of God!* Pretty different than, for example, the description in the *Left Behind* series or movies featuring a pre-Tribulation Rapture, where a very "sudden and silent Rapture" occurs.

d. The phrase, *with all His saints/holy ones* does not necessarily mean with all of us—Yeshua's followers! I know this might come as a shock to some of us, but when assessing the broader context relating to Yeshua's Second Coming, one can clearly see that these *holy ones* are actually angels! Here are three clear examples for your careful review:

1. *When the Son of Man comes in His glory, and <u>all the holy angels with Him</u>, then He will sit on the throne of His glory* (Matt. 25:31, emphasis added).

2. *For whoever is ashamed of Me and My words in this adulterous and sinful generation, of him the Son of Man also will be ashamed when He comes in the glory of His Father <u>with the holy angels</u>* (Mk. 8:38, emphasis added).

3. *And to give you who are troubled rest with us when the Lord Yeshua is revealed from Heaven <u>with His mighty angels</u>...* (2 Thes. 1:7, emphasis added).

Claim: The Anti-Messiah cannot be revealed until after the Rapture (2 Thes. 2:6-8). The Holy Spirit is the restrainer who holds back the Anti-Messiah, and, as the Holy Spirit dwells in us — the Rapture must take place before the Anti-Messiah is

revealed on the stage of history. If Yeshua's body goes through the Tribulation period, it will know who Anti-Messiah is because he will head the One World Government (Rev. 13:10), erect a statue of himself in the rebuilt Temple (Matt. 24:15), demand that people take his mark and number (Rev. 13:15-17) and kill the two witnesses (Rev. 11:7), and all of this is not supported in Scripture.

"Not supported in Scripture?" Let us carefully assess this last statement.

2 Thes. 2:1-8 is one of the key scriptures used by our precious brothers and sisters who hold to the pre-Tribulation Rapture view. Let us see what it really says. We shall start with the first five verses and then move on to verses 6-8:

Now, brethren, concerning <u>the coming of our Lord Yeshua the Messiah</u> <u>and</u> <u>our gathering together to Him</u>, we ask you, not to be soon shaken in mind or troubled, either by spirit or by word or by letter, as if from us, as though <u>the day of Messiah had come</u>. Let no one deceive you by any means; for (that Day will not come[283]) <u>unless the falling away</u> <u>comes first</u>, <u>and the man of sin is revealed</u>, <u>the son of perdition</u>, <u>who</u> <u>opposes and exalts himself above all that is called God or that is</u> <u>worshipped, so that he sits as God in the Temple of God, showing</u> <u>himself that he is God</u>. Do you not remember that when I was still with you, I told you these things?" (2 Thes. 2:1-5, emphases added).

---

[283] Please note that the words, *that Day will not come* are <u>not</u> found in the original Greek manuscript! Those of us who read the NKJ English version, can clearly see that these words are *italicized*. Nevertheless, this fact actually strengthens my argument against the pre-Tribulation point of view, as without these specific words, the sentence reads: *Let no one deceive you by any means, <u>for unless the</u> <u>falling way comes **first**</u>, and the man of sin is revealed, the son of perdition.*

Note the following:

a. Shaul connects *our gathering together to Him* with *the coming of our Lord Yeshua the Messiah!* He does not see them as two separate events![284]

b. In complete contrast to what Pre-Tribulation brethren say, the order of things in 2 Thes. 2:1 is as follows: <u>First</u> comes the falling away (the great apostasy—see also Matt. 24:10); <u>Second</u> is the revealing of the Anti-Messiah, *the man of sin,* who *sits as God in the holy place of God* (translated as *the Temple of God*[285]—see also Dan. 9:27), and <u>only then</u> (i.e., following the two previous events) will Yeshua appear and put an end to all of it!

Let's continue with the three last verses:

And now <u>you know what is restraining, that he may be revealed in his own time</u>. For the mystery of lawlessness is already at work; only He who now restrains will do so until He is taken out of the way. And then the lawless one will be revealed, whom the Lord will consume with the breath of His mouth and destroy <u>with the brightness of His coming</u> (2 Thes. 2:6-8. Emphases added).

---

[284] See also 1 Cor. 1:7-8, where Shaul connects between *eagerly waiting for the revelation of our Lord Yeshua the Messiah and the day of our Lord Yeshua the Messiah* (see a similar idea in 2 Tim. 2:18). See 1 Cor. 15:23 and 52, where Shaul connects the resurrection of Yeshua's followers with the day of His (Second) Coming.

[285] G3485 **(Strong), naos,** *nah-os'.* From a primary word ναίω, naiō **(to** *dwell);* a *fane, shrine, temple: shrine, temple.* Compare G2411.

Who is this Restrainer, and what is he really taken out of?

The following points might be shocking to some of us, but nonetheless, they must be pointed out for the sake of a true and sincere seeking after God's truth. Since Yeshua's First Coming, there have been three main views concerning the identity of the *restrainer*:

a. Some influential Church Fathers[286] interpreted the restrainer as **the Roman Empire with Caesar at its head.** According to this view, Shaul didn't want "to call the baby by its name," out of fear this would lead to severe (Roman) repercussions on himself and the entire congregation of believers of his time. This was the very reason he *did* reveal the identity of the *restrainer* to those in Thessalonica while in person during one of his previous visits there (2 Thes. 2:5-6).

b. Some have interpreted the *restrainer* as **the preaching of the gospel itself.** They have based this on Romans 1:16-17, where the gospel is described as *the power of God* (see also 1 Thes. 1:5; 1 Cor. 1:18, 24; Heb. 4:12; Matt. 4:1-11). According to this view, the restrainer is the actual preaching of the gospel, which will cease just before the end of *this age* (due to severe persecutions. Matt. 24:14).

---

[286] See, for example, Tertullian (second to third centuries CE), Chrysostom, Jerome, and Augustine (fourth to fifth centuries CE). See also a few prominent Bible scholars and great men of God who fully agreed with the above church fathers— Edward Bishop Elliot (18th century CE), Dr. John Eldon Ladd (a very respectable Baptist theologian in Fuller Theological Seminary in the 1950s, who said: *this view, or a modification of it, best fits into the Pauline theology*). See Henry Grattan Guinness (19th century CE) and more. See also Daniel 2 and 7 which contain well-known prophecies about the *four kingdoms*—among which the last and worst was the Roman Empire, which severely persecuted Yeshua's body .

c. Some, including most modern-day pre-Tribulation brethren, have suggested that the restrainer is **the Holy Spirit, indwelling the body of Yeshua's followers**. According to this view, Yeshua said that the Holy Spirit would convict the world of sin, unrighteousness, and judgment (Jn. 16:8-11). When the Holy Spirit is removed from this Earth, it will lead to utter lawlessness which will naturally lead to the appearance of the Anti-Messiah on the world's stage.

I want to explain my take on this *restrainer*, by raising what I believe is a very challenging question: Is the translation we quoted above (2 Thes. 2:6-8) the only possible translation? The following is a literal translation of verse 7, taken from an interlinear Greek English New Testament:

For the mystery already operates, of lawlessness, only (there is) the (one) restraining just now until <u>out of (the) midst it comes</u>[287] (emphasis added).

Four Important Greek Words

The second part of verse 7, which is translated in the NKJ (as well as other translations) into no less than eight words – *until He is taken out of the way* – is based on only four Greek words: *heōs, genetai* (strongly connected to *ginomai*), *ek* and *mesos.*

---

[287] See *The Nestle Greek Text*, by Reverend Alfred Marshall, 1958. See also https://www.Scripture4all.org/OnlineInterlinear/NTpdf/2th2.pdf, where it literally reads as follows: THE (to – G3588) for (gar – G1063) CLOSE-KEEP secret (mustErion – G3466) ALREADY (EdE – G2235) IS-IN-ACTING is-operating (energeitai – G1754) OF-THE (tEs – G3588) UN-LAWness lawlessnes (anomias – G458) ONLY (monon – G3440) THE (to – G3588) one-DOWN-HAVING one-detaining (katechon – G2722) at-PRESENT (arti – G737) TILL (heos – G2193) OUT (ek – G1537) OF-MIDst (mesou – G3319) it-MA Y -BE-BECOMING may-be-becoming (genEtai – G1096).

While *heos*[288] and *ek* are translated correctly and are part of the proper context of the text, for some reason, the other two (*genetai* and *mesos*) are translated with no consistency in the same way that they are translated in the other scriptures where they appear, and with little connection to the immediate context. Let me elaborate.

Translating *heos* as *until* and *ek*[289] as *out of* fit the proper context of 2 Thes. 2:1-8 and agrees with other references where these words are shown throughout the New Covenant writings. Nevertheless, when considering *genetai* (or, *ginomai*) and *mesos*, there are much better ways to translate them than just *to be taken out of the way*.

Genetai (and *ginomai*[290]) occurs about 700 times in the New Covenant writings. Its basic meanings are *to come into existence, to be created, to be born* (or *to be produced*), *comes into being, comes to pass, to be*

---

[288] G2193 (Strong), ἕως, *heh'-oce*. Of uncertain affinity; a conjugation, preposition and adverb of continuance, *until* (of time and place): *even (until, unto)*, (as) far (as), *how long,* (un-) til (-l), (hither-, un-, up) *to, while.*

[289] G1537 (Strong), ἐκ, ἐξ, *ek, ex*. A primary preposition denoting *origin* (the point *whence* motion or action proceeds), *from, out* (of place, time or cause; literally or figuratively; direct or remote): *after, among, X are, at betwixt (-yond), by (the means of), exceedingly, (+ abundantly above), for (-th), from (among, forth, up), + grudgingly, + heartily, X Heavenly, X hereby, + very highly, in, . . . ly, (because, by reason) of, off (from), on, out among (from, of), over, since, X thenceforth, through, X unto, X vehemently, with (-out). Often used in composition, with the same general import; often of completion.*

[290] G1096 (Strong), Γίνομαι, **ginomai**, *ghin'-om-ahee*. A prolonged and middle form of a primary verb; to *cause to be* (**gen**-erate), that is, (reflexively) to become (come into being), used with great latitude (literally, figuratively, intensively, etc.): - *arise be assembled, be (come, -fall, -have self), be brought (to pass), (be) come (to pass), continue, be divided, be done, draw, be ended, fall, be finished, follow, be found, be fulfilled, + God forbid, grow, happen, have, be kept, be made, be married, be ordained to be, partake, pass, be performed, be published, require, seem, be showed, X soon as it was, sound, be taken, be turned, use, wax, will, would, be wrought.*

made, to be done, to become, may come to be and *to arise*. The last meaning (*to arise*) is the most frequent translation of this Greek word.[291]

Mesos[292] occurs about sixty times in the New Covenant writings. It is usually translated *midst, among* and *from among*.[293] Only in this one scripture, has it been translated as *way!*

If Shaul really wanted us to understand *mesos* as *way* in 2 Thes. 2:7, he could have used a better Greek word, *hodos* (ὁδός), which literally means, *a way, a road* and/or *a path*. And, indeed, *hodos* occurs about one hundred times in the New Covenant writings and is usually translated as *way, side way, journey, highway*, etc.[294]

Taking into consideration the above explanation of the different meanings of these four Greek words, the following is a very likely translation of this famous sentence in the second part of verse 7:

---

[291] See, for example, Matt. 8:24, 13:21; Mk. 4:17, 37; Lk. 6:48, 15:14; Jn. 3:25; Acts 6:1, 11:19, 19:23, 23:7 and 9-10. In every one of these cases the word *arose* could be replaced by *came into being* or *came to pass* without changing the meaning. The word *arises* could be replaced by *comes into being* or *comes to pass,* again, without changing the meaning. There is no thought of anything being *taken away* in any of these scriptures, and the verb *"ginomai"* should never be translated with any idea or thought of anything being *taken away,* unless it is clearly specified by other words, which, in this case, it is not. Other translations of this specific word include *be, come to pass, be made, be done, come, become* and the like.

[292] G3319 (Strong), μέσος, mesos, *mes'-os*. From G3326; *middle* (as adjective or [neuter] noun): - *among*, X *before them, between, + forth, mid [-day, -night], midst, way.*

[293] See, for example, Matt. 18:2, 20; Mk. 9:36; Lk. 2:46; Rev. 1:13, 2:1; and many more.

[294] G3598 (Strong), ὁδός, hodos. Apparently, a primary word; a *road*; by implication *progress* (the route, act, or distance); figuratively a *mode* or *means: journey, (high-) way.* See, for example, Matt. 13:4, 19; Mk. 11:8; and more.

ἕως (*heos*)   ἐκ (*ek*)   μέσου (*mesos*)   γένηται (*genetai*).

until	out of	midst	comes into being/arises

When I stumbled upon the different meanings of these four Greek words, I almost immediately asked: What is this *midst* and who exactly is he who *comes into being/arises out of* this *midst?* The following is what I sensed was from the Spirit, although <u>I might be wrong</u>, and I suggest that you, the reader, carefully assess and weigh all of this before the Lord!

Here is how I believe 2 Thes. 2:6-8 should read:

And now you know what is restraining (back then, <u>the Roman Authorities</u>. In our times, whatever political power there might be), *that he* (Anti-Messiah) *may be revealed in his own time. For the mystery of lawlessness is already acting (is operating) until he* (Anti-Messiah) *arises out/from our midst* (the Body of Messiah). *And then the lawless one* (Anti-Messiah) *will be revealed, whom the Lord will consume with the breath of His mouth and destroy with the brightness of His coming.*

Even though we have gotten so used to the idea that *He who restrains* is the Holy Spirit, I think we should truly consider the following questions: (1) Is God's Spirit <u>only</u> in Yeshua's body? And if it is, where will He be after we are Raptured from the Earth? What kind of *spirit* will then dwell in the "Tribulation believers?" From the most immediate context (see above), it clearly cannot be the Holy Spirit! Why? Simply because Shaul clearly states that *our gathering unto Him* will <u>not</u> be before the Anti-Messiah is <u>first</u> revealed! So, it must be something other than God's Spirit; (2) In Matt. 28:20, Yeshua says, *and lo, I am with you all the days <u>until the completion of the age</u>.* In Jn.

14:6, he says, *and I will ask the father and He will give you another helper, that He may remain with you <u>forever</u>, the Spirit of Truth...* (emphases added). In other words, Yeshua said that neither He nor His Spirit would leave us <u>before the end of the world</u>—at which time God will deal with the Anti-Messiah (see, for example, Rev. 19:11-21).

Note: In the above quotations, Shaul declares that *the mystery of lawlessness is already operating* (i.e., <u>in the first century</u>)! Should this surprise us? Not at all! Remember that John, Yeshua's beloved apostle, said that *<u>the spirit of Anti-Messiah</u> was already in operation <u>during his days</u>*! He said that there were some *Anti-Messiahs* who came *<u>from within us</u>, but were never from us...*[295] Moreover, some of Yeshua's parables clearly show that <u>not all who claim faith in Him are indeed true (saved) followers of Him</u>! In the general introduction, I mentioned, as an example, Yeshua's parables of *the wheat and tares*, and the *net filled with all types of fish*. We can add to the above examples His parable about the five foolish virgins.

Yes, since the very beginning (the first century), Yeshua's body has included fake believers, *false prophets*, *false teachers* as well as true, fully dedicated born-again followers! In other words, within the body of Yeshua – since His First coming – there have been some who have possessed the *spirit of Anti-Messiah* rather than His Holy Spirit![296]

The Identity of the Anti-Messiah According to Some Famous Church Leaders

In our modern-day world, to be politically correct, so as not to offend or hurt someone's feelings, is acceptable and very much encouraged by leaders, politicians and *even* some pastors and elders within

---

[295] See 1 Jn. 2:18-19, 22; 4:1-6; 2 Jn. 7.

[296] See Matt. 13:24-30, 47, 25:1-13; Jn. 6:70, 13:2; 2 Thes. 2:7.

Messiah's body. Yet, if we read expressions and declarations of some renowned church leaders within the last four or five centuries, we can see that they were not as worried about being politically correct. To the contrary, some of their statements would shock present-day leaders within Messiah's body. See Martin Luther (1483-1546), Thomas Cranmer (1489-1556), John Knox (1505-1572), Fox's *Book of Martyrs* (from 1563), John Calvin (1509-1564), Roger Williams (1603-1683), "The Westminster Confession of Faith" (1647), Cotton Mather (1663-1728), John Wesley (1703-1791), David Benedict (*A General History of the Baptist Denomination in America, 1813*) and others, who seriously thought and taught that the system or kingdom of the Anti-Messiah was <u>the Roman Catholic Church</u>, while its head, <u>the Pope</u>, is the Anti-Messiah himself![297]

The Son of Perdition — Judah Iscariot, and the Anti-Messiah

In 2 Thes. 2:3, Shaul warns, *let no one deceive you by any means; for (that day will not come) unless <u>the falling away comes first</u> and the man of sin is revealed, <u>the son of perdition</u>.* Interestingly enough, in the famous long prayer Yeshua offered to His Heavenly Father, He referred to *Judah Iscariot – one of His twelve closest disciples – as the son of perdition.* Here it is in His own words: *While I was with them (the twelve disciples), I was keeping them in Your Name, which You have given Me; and I guarded them and not one of them perished <u>but</u>*

---

[297] According to 1 Jn. 4:1-4 and others, one way to recognize the spirit of the Anti-Messiah is that it does not believe that *Messiah Yeshua came in the flesh.* I challenge the reader to assess one of the main dogmatic confessions within the Roman Catholic Church, with regard to the "sinless birth of... Miriam (Mary)!" Yes, this was not a typo! According to one of the pillars of Roman Catholic "Faith Statements," it was Yeshua's mother – <u>Not Yeshua Himself</u> (!) – who was born sinless, and thus, her flesh (the one that begot Messiah—her first born) was not like other human flesh! This is no less than blasphemy!

the son of perdition (Judah Iscariot, according to both the immediate and broader context), _so that the scripture would be fulfilled..._ (Jn. 17:12, emphasis added). Please notice: the only other reference in which this phrase (_son of perdition_) is used is found in 2 Thes. 2! Let me suggest that it is not merely a matter of coincidence...

The best example, or prototype (a foreshadowing or picture) of the Anti-Messiah _coming out of our midst_ (Yeshua's very body of believers) is Judah Iscariot! Judah was one of the twelve closest disciples of Yeshua. Yet, at the very end he was the one who betrayed Him, leading His capturers to Him and being the very tool used by the Almighty to put His only begotten Son on that Tree in Golgotha! Judah was in the inner circle (see Lk. 6:13-16). When Yeshua sent His twelve chosen ones to heal the sick, to cast out demons and preach the good news, He empowered them with His own Power and Spirit, and, Judah was one of them! Yes, Yeshua's power came upon him as well (Matt. 10:1-4). As you remember, Judah was also responsible for the finances—a responsibility given only to someone who is very close to the Master.

Outwardly, Judah Iscariot resembled a faithful servant and apostle of Yeshua, and he even used the right words when approaching Messiah – _my Master..._ Yet, the one who dwelt in him at the end, was none other than Satan himself (Lk. 22:3)! With Satan indwelling him, Judah gave the famous venomous _kiss_ to the Lord, a kiss that eventually led to Yeshua's death (Matt. 26:49)!

Claim: Yeshua's body is mentioned more than twenty times in the first three chapters of Revelation, but there is no mention of it between Rev. 4:1 and 19:1. This is yet one more proof that it is 'taken out' or 'Raptured' in Rev. 4:1, and that the Apostle

John is a picture or foreshadowing of Yeshua's body (following the pattern of Enoch and Elijah in the Old Testament).

The argument here is that the Apostle John, being called up to Heaven in Rev. 4:1 (*Come up here*) is clear proof that we, Yeshua's true followers, will indeed be Raptured out of this world just before all that the apostle is shown while in Heaven starts to take place. Here it is from Rev. 4:1-2:

After these things I looked, and behold, a door standing open in Heaven. And the first voice which I heard was <u>like a trumpet</u> speaking with me, saying, '<u>Come up here</u>, and I will show you things which must take place after this.' <u>Immediately I was in the Spirit; and behold, a throne was set in Heaven,</u> and One sat on the throne (emphases added).

First, have you noticed that Jews are also not mentioned (at least by name) after Rev. 3? Yet, deep into the book of Revelation, there are quite a few references of those who have *the testimony of Yeshua the Messiah* (Rev. 12:17, 20:4). I am acquainted with the argument that these are *the Tribulation saints* (i.e., "Old Testament saints"); nevertheless, as I have already established, there is no biblically based difference between Old Testament saints and New Testament saints! Both are an integral part of *the Olive Tree* of Israel throughout history![298]

---

[298] According to Matt. 8:11, many Gentiles *will sit down with Abraham, Isaac and Jacob in the Kingdom of Heaven...* Just to remind you, respected reader: Abraham, Isaac and Jacob are the fathers of a nation called *Israel!* Moreover: Yeshua sends His disciples, at least at the beginning of His ministry, *only to the lost sheep of Israel!* (See Matt. 10:5-6). As I have mentioned previously, the First century body of believers was comprised of only Jews, at least for a few decades before they were joined by non-Jews. So, in short, the whole story is about a God who makes

Second, note the following: The specific incident in John's life happened about 1,900 years ago, and it was a personal experience of the beloved apostle. According to ancient tradition, once the vision he received in Heaven ended, John descended back to Earth and later died a peaceful death.[299]

I would like to remind you that Yeshua, when speaking of End-Time events, used only two examples: **Noah** and **Lot** (see Lk. 17:26-36)! There is no scriptural evidence that John's personal ascension to Heaven was a picture, foreshadowing or a prototype of the pre-Tribulation Rapture. Is there anyone who would dare say that Yeshua was not aware of Enoch or Elijah's stories, when speaking of the End Times and His Second Coming?

As I mentioned before, if we wish to look for a scriptural pattern for the Rapture of Yeshua's body, we should never take it out of its broader context (what I called before, "the Israeli connection;" see the following). The only scriptural pattern is the exodus of *our fathers* out of Egypt (and, if you wish, also the three parts in the Tabernacle, as explained before). Over and over, there is no scriptural basis to claim

---

this *New Covenant* with His people Israel, while allowing others – Gentiles – as He did from the very beginning, to join with His Chosen Nation!

[299] Information regarding John's last days comes to us primarily from tradition. The *1913 Roman Catholic Encyclopedia*, in an article about his life, states that writers in the second and third Centuries CE accepted a widely held tradition that the apostle spent his last days in Ephesus. According to Roman Catholics, Justin Martyr also referred to John as an apostle of Yeshua who lived in Ephesus. St. Irenaeus, Eusebius, and others, again according to the *Roman Catholic Encyclopedia*, all agree that John left the isle of Patmos where he was banished for preaching the good news of Messiah (see Rev. 1:9). The last alive, of the twelve original disciples, John spent his remaining days in Ephesus until he died sometime around the close of the First century.

that John is a prototype or a foreshadowing of the pre-Tribulation Rapture!

With all due respect, I really think that this specific Rev. 4:1 argument is a stretch and is used only to support the preconceived idea regarding the supposed pre-Tribulation Rapture.

Moreover, claiming that the sound John the apostle heard, which was *like a trumpet*, is connected to *the last trumpet,* which is going to sound at the very end, is also no more than a stretch, trying once again to support a preconceived idea regarding the timing of the Rapture.

Claim: The twenty-four elders are a representation of Yeshua's body. They are in Heaven before the first of the seven seals of the scroll is broken.

As with the last one, I think that this argument is also a stretch. Is there any other scripture that supports this assumption? Not at all! As with the argument above, this is an attempt to fit any scripture possible into an already existing, or preconceived doctrine regarding the Pre-Tribulation Rapture.

Claim: No one can know the day or the hour of Messiah's Second Coming (Matt. 24:15). But if Yeshua's body goes through the Tribulation period, some will know the day, because it will be seven years from the signing of the seven-year covenant (Dan. 9:24-27) and 1,260 days from the day the Anti-Messiah defiles the Temple (Rev. 12:6).

This argument clearly demonstrates the departure of those who hold to a pre-Tribulation Rapture from their Hebraic/Middle Eastern (Jewish) roots. To remind you, despite the fact that most Western readers view numbers as merely quantities, to Middle Eastern readers, numbers often serve as symbols bearing spiritual significance.[300]

I'm very aware of the fact that the *three and a half year* period spoken of in both Daniel and Revelation is mentioned in different ways: *A time, times, and half a time* (Daniel 7:25, 12:7; Aramaic, *ad-idan v'Idanin uflag idan* -- עד | ועדנין | ופלג עד | עד), and *one thousand two hundred sixty days,* and *forty-two months* (Revelation 11:2, 12:14, 13:5). The question should be: Does it mean that *seven years* or *three and a half years* is to be understood in <u>a precise mathematical way</u>? If one remembers Yeshua's words, *No one knows **the day nor the hour**, not even the angels, nor the Son...* (Matt. 24:36), it stands to reason that the answer to my question is <u>no</u>. Of course, Yeshua also said, *when you see all these things, know it is near the door* (Matt. 24:33). Yes, we should know the times and seasons in which we are living. We should be able to recognize *the big picture* – in terms of those times – yet, at the same time, we should remember that we still cannot know (in a precise, mathematical, Greek manner), *the day* nor *the hour!*

It's important to understand that I am <u>not</u> claiming that numbers, such as *seven years* and *three and a half years*, could be stretched as if they had no limits! All I'm trying to convey is that *seven years* in Scripture can also be *seven years and six months* or *seven years and two days.* *Three and a half years* can also be *three and a half years and four days, or three hours...*

And so, to say that the Rapture must take place before the seven years starts, so that we cannot *calculate the day and the hour* is, once again, not only detached from the culture through which Scripture was given

---

[300] For a more detailed discussion, see Appendix 1: "Daniel's Seventy Weeks."

to us, but also demonstrates the attempt to fit certain scriptures into our already preconceived ideas and doctrines.

Claim: Yeshua's body must go to heaven for the marriage of the Lamb before the Second Coming of Messiah at the end of the Tribulation period (Rev. 19:11-14, 19:7).

If taken in the proper context, we can see that Rev. 19:7 does not clearly say that the *marriage* takes place in Heaven! It just says that *the marriage of the Lamb has come,* and that *she has made herself ready.* Actually, if taken in the broader context, we can see that <u>the marriage is at the very end of the Tribulation</u> and is directly connected to the following chapter, Rev. 20! Furthermore, the description of this marriage sounds very similar to another known scripture, Ezek. 39:17-20, when compared with Rev. 19:17-21.

Yes, indeed, there will be a marriage of the Lamb of God, and we are all welcome to be there, but only at its right timing—at the very end of the Tribulation!

Claim: It says that the Anti-Messiah will prevail against the believers during the Tribulation period (Rev. 13:7), but it also says that 'the gates of hell won't prevail against it' (Matt. 16:18). So, it must be that there are two kinds of believers: 'Old Testament saints —Israel,' and 'New Testament saints — Yeshua's very body.' Moreover, the Bible never says that Yeshua's body will go through the Tribulation period.

Above, we have already discussed the great error made by differentiating between Israel and Yeshua's body. We said that they are strongly connected, as had been in the first century, and that God has not changed His mind concerning His ancient beloved nation! Moreover, for at least the first few decades of the first century,

Yeshua's body was comprised solely of Israeli Jews! They did not see themselves as "New Testament saints" but rather as an integral part of the nation called Israel!

Exactly as it was at the beginning, so it will be at the end. Just as the first century believers experienced some very tough persecution, even unto death, so the present-day believers will go through persecution and tribulations (including the Great Tribulation), even unto death! Going through the great Tribulation will not at all mean that *the gates of hell have prevailed against the believers!* Otherwise, we would also have to say that they prevailed against the first century believers!

Present-day (End Time) believers will be delivered into our enemy's hands only for a relatively short period of time so that their faith can be tested. It's important to note that not all End-Time believers are going to suffer death and/or persecution! Some will be protected in whatever *Goshen* to which God will lead them, while others might be beheaded and so on.[301]

Believers throughout history have gone through some very difficult tribulations and trials, even unto death. For example, eleven of the twelve disciples of Yeshua were put to death; all the martyrs of the first three to four centuries CE; the persecuted in China, Persia, and other places in our own modern-day time! Do they consider themselves "defeated by the gates of hell?" Do they see themselves as "Old Testament saints?"

To say that "there are two kinds of saints," yet again demonstrates how disconnected some in Yeshua's body are from their authentic first century (Jewish/Israeli) roots! As I have frequently mentioned here,

---

[301] See Rev. 12:6. See also, the previous discussion regarding the Exodus from Egypt as a pattern for the Rapture.

God made *the New Covenant* with His Chosen Nation <u>Israel</u>—and no other nation or entity! Gentiles are grafted into *the Olive Tree* of <u>Israel</u>, and all those who are in that tree, are also part of *the remnant by election*, within the larger body of <u>Israel</u>!

Claim: The Pre-Tribulation Rapture is more consistent with God's grace, love, and mercy, as we were never called to God's wrath but to His everlasting grace and eternal life (1 Thes. 1:10, 5:9).

These statements are very true! God did not call (or appoint) us for wrath! Nevertheless, this does not mean that He takes us out of the world when inflicting His wrath or severe judgment upon it! The Biblical pattern clearly shows that as He protected His chosen ones – *our fathers* (Israel under Moses) who were still in Egypt - He also, at the same time, inflicted His wrath on the land and gods of Egypt. He is quite able to do the same during the great Tribulation! A loving God does not necessarily mean that He prevents His beloved ones from going through hardships, persecution, and tribulations even unto death, while taking some to a protected place in the wilderness and allowing (in accordance with His perfect will) others to be His holy martyrs! Whatever we shall experience in the great Tribulation, we should never forget that our reward is in His soon-coming Kingdom— not in the kingdom of this dark world in which we live! The more we are persecuted for His glorious holy name, the greater our reward will be!

Claim: Yeshua promised to come and remove His faithful ones and take them home to be with Him (Jn. 14:1-3).

No doubt He did! Yet, does this really point to a pre-Tribulation Rapture of His body? Is this at all in the context of "a great, silent Pre-Tribulation Rapture?" No, it's not! Why I am so sure about that? If His words in Jn. 14 did indeed refer to a pre-Tribulation Rapture, all of His faithful first century disciples, apostles and multitudes, who were true believers, completely missed it and would not even be worthy of being "Raptured before the Tribulation!" If it's true that these verses refer to an End-Time pre-Tribulation Rapture, where are all of the believers who have already preceded us? Are they not "home" with Him? Did He deceive them when promising He would come and take them to where He is? God forbid!

It is my understanding that Yeshua spoke of the natural (or unnatural) death each of His faithful disciples and followers throughout history since the time of His First Coming, and up to the end of this age, will experience! He truly will come and take everyone who dies in Him *home*. Indeed, each and every one of His children, since His First Coming, and until His Second Coming, has gone or will go to be with Him in His home—heaven!

A very similar idea of *taking you home to where I am,* in connection to natural or unnatural death, is clearly shown in the book of Hebrews. Abraham (and other faithful God-fearing people before and after him), did not look at an earthly city as their eternal home. They rather looked at the heavenly one (Jerusalem). In other words, they, as the first century believers, also awaited their (already prepared) home in heaven.[302]

---

[302] See Heb. 11:10, 13-16.

Assessment of Some Mid-Tribulation Claims

Claim: One needs to differentiate between the Anti-Messiah wrath (during the first three and a half years) and God's Divine wrath (during the last three and a half years) in Daniel's seventieth week. The entire body of Yeshua will go through the first three and a half years of the last week of Daniel's seventy weeks' prophecy (Daniel 9:24-27); and just before God starts to pour out His wrath on the Earth, at the beginning of the second three and a half years, they will be caught up to Heaven (Some say, with the two witnesses of Rev. 11:12).

I would like to respond to this specific claim with a few challenging questions:

- In the well-known Daniel 9 prophecy, where exactly does it say that the first *three and a half years* are "the Anti-Messiah wrath?" Furthermore, where exactly is the "Anti-Messiah" mentioned in that famous prophecy? At the end of this chapter (Appendix 1 - "Daniel's seventy weeks"), I'll share a few other possible interpretations regarding the identity of the one who *confirms a covenant with the many.* As previously stated, it might surprise you to know that up until the 17th or 18th Centuries CE, Bible scholars as well as church leaders, did not recognize an Anti-Messiah in that specific prophecy but rather Messiah Yeshua Himself! They believed that Yeshua is the One who confirms *a New Covenant* with all those who have believed and accepted Him as *the Lamb who takes away the sins of the world!*[303]

- Is there any scriptural basis for modern-day prophecy teachers splitting Daniel's first sixty-nine weeks from the seventieth and last week, while placing a two-thousand-year gap between them?

And lastly,

- Would someone please show me even one reference in God's entire Word that says that there will be "a seven-year Tribulation?"

Interestingly enough, when I read of the great Tribulation, it always refers to *three and a half year* period. A careful examination of Daniel 9:24-27 also shows that there is <u>only</u> *three and a half years* Tribulation![304]

Additionally, I have a hard time finding any scriptural basis for separating Daniel's sixty-ninth week from the seventieth and placing a two-thousand-year gap between the two. Even if we take it as "a given" that there is a 2,000-year gap between Daniel's first sixty-nine weeks and the seventieth and last week, there is not even one scripture that says that the first *three and a half years* of this seventieth and last week is characterized as some kind of "a wrath!"

If you do a thorough study of Daniel 9:27, you will see that it describes the first three and a half years as characterized by peace, tranquility and security, which are then suddenly interrupted at the end of the

---

[303] See Jn. 1:29. See also Matt. 26:28 — *the Blood of the Covenant, <u>for many</u>...* (emphasis added).

[304] See Dan. 9:27 and compare with Rev. 11:2-3, 12:6 and 12:14.

first half of this seventieth and last week! Again, up until the 17th or 18th centuries CE, Bible scholars and church leaders have understood Daniel's prophecy to be one undivided prophecy, which was completely fulfilled in Yeshua's First Coming![305]

Regarding the mid-Tribulation Rapture view, although it sounds very good and very encouraging, I strongly believe that it is not biblically based! There is no pattern or foreshadowing in Scripture showing that God's chosen ones are *taken* prior to, and/or in the middle of some great End-Time event.

---

[305] See, in Chapter II, Appendix 2, a discussion of "Respected Traditional Commentaries on Daniel 9:24-27." Also, see an example of how the early followers of Yeshua saw the timetable of Daniel's well-known prophecy, at: https://www.bible.ca/H-70-weeks-daniel.htm

Conclusions and a Call to Be Open-Minded

Beloved, I truly recommend reading Scripture as a whole, especially when contemplating the timing of Messiah's return. For some among us, this might require putting aside preconceived ideas which we have been taught, or those constructed by us based on a partial grasp of the message of Scripture.

Now that we have seen the ways various scriptures have been used to defend *different* positions regarding the timing of the Rapture, are we willing to put down even our strongest dogmas and allow the Lord to lead us according to His truth, even if these revelations might be accompanied by a new challenge to trust Him in and through what could end up being extremely frightening times?

Having taken time to consider that the Rapture *cannot* be artificially and un-biblically detached from the history and the nation of Israel; having recognized that salvation is *not* a one-time altar call, but rather a process requiring that we endure until the very end, are we willing to amend our perspective regarding God's timeline for the Messiah's return and our being gathered unto Him? I certainly hope and pray we are.

Chapter 2:

Appendices

Appendix 1:
Daniel's Seventy Weeks

Introduction

Daniel 9:24-27 is for sure one of the more controversial passages which has undergone a variety of interpretations. In the course of history, there have been many attempts to explain this well-known prophecy, and in this appendix, I will endeavor to present the main views, interpretations and commentaries concerning this specific prophecy. I have tried to present them in chronological order, beginning with the Jewish sages and moving on to the Roman Catholic view, the Protestant view, the Seventh Day Adventist view, all culminating with my own view. I have also added a few illustrations to help you visualize the different stated opinions.[306]

Daniel's ninth chapter is divided mainly into two parts: (1) Daniel's prayer, repentance, and supplication for his people, all after realizing that seventy years of exile are about to end (Dan. 9:2-19); and (2) God's response through His archangel Gabriel, which includes the well-known seventy weeks prophecy (Dan. 9:21-27). The two parts are strongly connected and cannot be arbitrarily separated. Alternatively stated, one cannot attempt to interpret the second part without first considering its immediate context in the first part.

Moreover, from the first section, we can clearly see that the nation and land of Israel are in the very center. The seventy weeks are *decreed* upon *your people* (Israel) and *your holy city* (Jerusalem). As with the timing of the Rapture, Daniel's seventy weeks must be

---

[306] See chapter 2 – appendix 3: illustrations.

interpreted within its "Israeli connection." In fact, since Israel - *God's first-born son*[307]- is the very tool or instrument God chose to use to save the entire world, she is indeed the center of all End Time prophecy!

Daniel 9 takes place *in the first year of Darius the son of Ahasuerus, of Median descent, who was made king over the Chaldeans* (9:1). According to the Jewish sages and most Bible commentators, this is the same *Darius* mentioned in chapter 6. Thus, the seventy weeks prophecy takes place during the second of four named kingdoms—the Medo-Persia kingdom (see the following. Also see Dan. 2:37-46).

A Short Summary of Related Historic Events

Daniel and his contemporaries were exiled during the first wave of the Babylonian Exile, **around 610-605-BCE**. The Babylonian Empire was replaced by the Medo-Persian Empire **around 539 BCE** (see Dan. 5). Cyrus, the Persian king, gave his famous decree concerning the rebuilding of God's Temple in Jerusalem **around 538-537 BCE** (see Ezra 1, based on Isa. 44:28, 45:1. See also 2 Chr. 36). A Jewish minority undertook the rebuilding of the Temple **around 537-536 BCE** (see Ezra 3). Their work was stopped and delayed for a few years by some of their opponents (see Ezra 4 & 5). The Temple was finally established in Jerusalem **around 516-515 BCE** (see Ezra 5:2, 6:15; Hag. 1:14). With King Artaxerxes' permission **around 457 BCE**, the walls of the city were finally completed. **Around 445 BCE** (see Ezra 7, Neh. 1, 2 & 6), the Greeks, under the leadership of Alexander the Great, defeated the Persians and established the Greek Empire. After Alexander the Great's death, **around 333-332 BCE**, his empire was divided amongst four leaders (see Dan. 7:6-7, 8:8 and chapter 11). **Around 170 BCE**, one

---

[307] See Ex. 4:22.

well-known Seleucid General, Antiochus Epiphanes the Fourth, made a covenant with some of the Jewish elites, a covenant that he broke after three and a half years. He placed a statue inside God's Temple in Jerusalem and began to persecute the Jews by imposing impossible restrictions upon them, all having to do with their observance of God's Torah (for example: they were not allowed to circumcise their boys, keep the Sabbath, and so on). This severe persecution finally led to the Maccabean Revolt, which lasted another three and a half years—up until sometime **around 164 BCE**. The Jews succeeded in driving out the Seleucids from Jerusalem. They cleansed the Temple from the desecration of Antiochus Epiphanes and rededicated it. Since then, Jews have celebrated the feast of Chanukah, which falls in the winter of each year. **Around 5-4 BCE**, Yeshua of Nazareth was born in Bethlehem. He started His three and a half year ministry sometime **around 26-27 CE**, which ended with His crucifixion, death, burial, and resurrection, **around the year 30 CE**. About forty years later, **in 70 CE,** the second Temple was destroyed by Titus the Roman, and most Jerusalemite Jews were, once again, exiled. Finally, the Roman Empire fell **around 476-477 CE.**

Seventy Weeks Are Determined...

This specific prophecy is not considered a sealed vision in comparison to other prophecies and visions Daniel, as well as other prophets, received.[308] This prophecy contains six objectives to be fulfilled within 70 weeks (of years):

1. *To finish the transgression.*

---

[308] Compare Dan. 9:22 — *I have now come forth to give you <u>insight with understanding</u>*—with 8:26-27, and 12:4, 9.

2. *To make an end of sins.*

3. *To make reconciliation for iniquity.*

4. *To bring in everlasting righteousness.*

5. *To seal up the vision and prophecy;* and

6. *To anoint the Most Holy.*

As we already mentioned, while dealing with numbers and their spiritual significance in the Hebraic/Middle Eastern culture/mindset, *six* represents humanity, as the first Adam was created on the sixth day. Thus, the six objectives have to do with <u>mankind's sin</u>, which started with the first Adam and his wife in the Garden of Eden. It is important to note here that in the New Covenant writings, Messiah Yeshua is described as the *second* or *last Adam*.[309]

Already now, we can see that the only One who is able to fulfill these six objectives is the Messiah of Israel Himself – the *second Adam*, because Yeshua is strongly connected to His nation Israel, and He is truly the only One who could fulfill all six objectives through His work on that tree at Golgotha! According to the New Covenant writings, the death of Yeshua is *the ultimate solution to sin* (the first three objectives). Yeshua makes those who are in Him *righteous* (the fourth objective). He is *the optimal fulfillment of prophecy* (the fifth objective). And lastly, He, as *Immanuel (God with us),* our heavenly High Priest, is the One who *sanctifies the Holy of Holies* (the sixth objective). More on this later.

Most scholars, commentators, and theologians throughout history, understood these seventy weeks to be weeks of years—i.e., the 490 days should be understood as 490 years. And indeed, these *weeks*

---

[309] See Rom. 5:14; 1 Cor. 15:45, 47; and 1 Cor. 15:22.

cannot be normal seven-day weeks, as it would be a very short time to accomplish all the above objectives, not to mention the following interpretations of this prophecy.[310]

Different Interpretations of Daniel's Seventy Weeks

In the following paragraphs, I present the four main commentaries on Daniel's seventy weeks prophecy. None of these views though, are etched in stone, even among the different theologians who hold them. Which is to say, within each of the following commentaries, there are slightly different understandings.

The Jewish View[311]

The Jewish sages did not take the number *70* as a literal (mathematically precise) number but rather as a symbolic one that represents God, completion, perfection, etc. Thus, they understood Daniel's seventy weeks to be a divine description of events in Jewish history, beginning with the seventy years of Babylonian Exile and ending with the destruction of the second Temple in Jerusalem in 70 CE.[312]

---

[310] In Hebrew, *weeks* is read as *shavueem* (masculine form) and not the normal *shavuot* (feminine ending form). See examples of *Shavuot*—seven-day weeks—in Ex. 34:22; Deut. 16:9 and 16; 2 Ch. 8:13. There might be one scriptural hint that points to a connection between "a week" and a seven-year period in Jacob's story (in Hebrew, *Sh'vuah* — see Gen. 29:18, 27). Moreover, these seventy weeks must be four hundred and ninety years; otherwise, the last week, the seventieth, would not correlate with other references in the book of Daniel (see there: 7:25; 8:14, 26; 11:31; 12:7; or 11–12).

[311] See chapter 2 – appendix 3: illustrations.

[312] According to the Jewish sages, Daniel did not know when to start his counting— from the renewed kingdom of Babylon (610 BCE)? From Jehoiakim's exile (610-605 BCE)? Maybe from Jehoiachin's (600 BCE)? From the time of Zedekiah and the

The First Seven Weeks: *From the going forth of the command* (in Hebrew, *min motzah davar*) was applied in two possible ways: (1) to God's Word through His prophet Jeremiah, around 588 BCE.[313] Jeremiah's prophecy concerning the seventy years of exile until *Messiah the Prince* brought them to King Cyrus, who issued the decree for the Jews to return and rebuild God's Temple; (2) Daniel's own words in the beginning of his supplications,[314] which leads to the time of Nehemiah or Ezra. There, according to them, we should find *Messiah the Prince*—which should have been Zerubbabel or Joshua the son of Tzadok, the high priest.

The Following 62 Weeks and the 70th Final Week: These 63 weeks were applied symbolically. The sages did not separate the 69th week from the 70th week. According to them, all 63 remaining weeks must have led to two crucially important events in Jewish history: (1) Antiochus the Fourth (Epiphanes), in whose time the high priest Chunio III was murdered,[315] or another Jewish leader of that time who they viewed as the *Messiah shall be cut off.* That murder led to severe persecution of the Jews which brought about the Maccabean Revolt. To this revolt they also connect (2) the severe persecution of the

---

destruction of the first Temple (587/6 BCE)? According to Zechariah, the seventy years were finished the second time with Darius (Zech. 1:12; Hag. 1:2, 2:20-23). According to historic calculation, there were seventy years and seven months between 587/6 and 515/6 BCE.

[313] See Jer. 25:1 (in Hebrew, *the word that was — hadavar asher haya...*) See also verses 25:10-11, and 29:10 (in Hebrew, for *I will come to you and fulfill my good word — vehakimoti aleichem et D'vari hatov*) and Ezra 1:1 (*that the word of the Lord, by the prophet Jeremiah might be fulfilled*).

[314] See 9:21 – Hebrew, *now while I was speaking;* Hebrew, *veod ani Medaber –* Daniel 9:23.

[315] See 2 Maccabi's 4:34.

Romans against the Jews, which led to the Great Revolt and included the destruction of the second Temple by Titus in 70 CE.

The Roman Catholic View[316]

Roman Catholic theologians have followed the Jewish sages' approach and have understood *70* to be a symbolic number. They also have applied most of the events described in Dan. 9:24-27 to a general description of two events in Jewish history: (a) Antiochus Epiphanes, his persecution of the Jews and the desecration of the Temple in Jerusalem, followed by the Maccabean Revolt and the rededication of the Temple (around 164 BCE); and (b) events in Yeshua's time, all the way through the destruction of the second Temple in 70 CE.

The First Seven Weeks: *From the going forth of the command* — most Catholic commentators saw this *command* as commencing from Jeremiah's prophecy (Jer. 25:11, 29:10) around 588 BCE. They interpreted the first *seven weeks* (forty-nine years) as the approximate amount of time that the exile in Babylon lasted. They saw *Messiah the Prince* as either Cyrus – *the anointed of the Lord* – who called for an end to the exile (Isa. 45:1), or the high priest Jeshua, who presided over the rebuilding of the altar of sacrifice after the exile (Ezra 3:2).

The Following 62 Weeks and the 70th and Final Week: *In the course of sixty-two weeks... rebuilt* was seen as a period of 434 years, roughly including the time between the rebuilding of Jerusalem after the exile, and the beginning of the Seleucid persecution. *An anointed one* was seen as Chunio the third (who was murdered around 171 BCE, see

---

[316] See the Revised Standard Version Roman Catholic Edition of Daniel 9 and a Roman Catholic perspective blog on Daniel 9 found at (http://blog.theotokos.co.za/?p=5171). See also chapter 2 – appendix 3: illustrations.

above), while *a leader* was Antiochus the Fourth (Epiphanes). The final week was seen as the time of Antiochus' persecution. According to this view, *he* is Antiochus himself; *the many* are the faithless Jews who allied themselves with the Seleucids,[317] and *half the week* is when the Temple was desecrated by Antiochus from 167 to 164 BCE; while *the abomination that causes desolation* is the pagan altar set up by Antiochus. They, as the Jewish sages, stretched the time to also include the destruction of the second Temple in 70 CE.

The Seventh Day Adventist View[318]

Seventh Day Adventists do not believe in a millennial kingdom with the leadership of Israel as a nation here on Earth, with Messiah as her King. Thus, Seventh Day Adventists do not acknowledge Israel's special place as having remained God's chosen people. Moreover, they connect Daniel 9:24-27 to Dan. 8 (especially verse 14) and group the 490 years with the 2,300 days (days of years, according to them), arriving at the year 1844 as marking the beginning of the final *heavenly judgment of God...*

The First Seven Weeks: *From the going forth of the command* is interpreted as the decree issued by Artaxerxes in 457 BCE, authorizing the restoration and rebuilding of Jerusalem (Ezra 4:7-23, 7:12-26). This decree allowed the Jews to govern Judah according to their own law

---

[317] 1 Maccabees. 1:11-11.

[318] See chapter 2 – appendix 3: illustrations. The Seventh Day Adventist Church is a Protestant Christian denomination which is distinguished mainly by its observance of the seventh day of the week as the Sabbath. It emphasizes the imminent Second Coming (the advent) of Yeshua. This denomination grew out of the Millerite movement in the United States during the mid-19th century, and it was formally established in 1863. See *https://ssnet.org/qrtrly/eng/02b/less05.html* and *https://www.adventistreview.org/the-70-weeks-made-simple*

(7:25,26). According to them, exactly 49 years later (seven prophetic days) the city was rebuilt (in 408 BCE).

The Following 62 Weeks and the 70th and Final Week: They see it as a time period that covers: (a) the anointing of Messiah Yeshua in the Jordan River by John in 27 CE; (b) His death in 31 CE (Seen as the middle of the seventieth week); (c) the severe Roman persecution on the first believers (beginning with Stephen's martyrdom in 34 CE), and then on the non-believing Jews, which ends in (d) the destruction of the second Temple in Jerusalem.[319]

---

[319] The following is a detailed explanation as found on one of their websites: "The first thing announced is the coming of the Messiah after 62 weeks plus 7 weeks (69 weeks). He will initiate His ministry at the end of the 69 weeks as *'the Anointed One'* (Mk. 1:9-11). According to Daniel 9:26, *'after the sixty-two weeks'* (plus the previous seven) *'the Anointed One'* will be killed, and no one will help Him. *This will take place during the last week of the 70 weeks—an obvious reference to Messiah's sacrificial death on the tree.* During the last week, *the Messiah will also 'confirm a covenant with many'* (verse 27). A better translation could be *'he will make a strong covenant.'* This is the new covenant firmly established through the blood of Messiah (Lk. 22:20), and includes Jews and gentiles who, through faith in Messiah, enjoy its benefits. *During the middle of the seventieth week, the sacrificial system of the Old Testament would end* (Dan. 9:27). Messiah's *sacrificial death brought to an end the Israelite sacrificial system* (Mk. 15:37-38; Heb. 10:8-10). The destruction of Jerusalem by the Roman armies is predicted in this prophecy, *even if it is not clearly stated that it will happen during the 70 weeks.* The destruction is decreed to take place in the future, but we are not told when (Dan. 9:26). The fate of the city was decreed by Yeshua during His ministry (Matt. 24:1-2) and took place about forty years later. Stephen died as a martyr in 34 A.D.—the date ending the 70-week prophecy, and from that point, the gospel went also to the gentile world" (emphases added).

The Popular Protestant View Within Recent Centuries[320]

Most modern-day Protestant prophecy teachers see the first week and the following sixty-two weeks as one unit.

The First Seven Weeks: *From the going forth of the command* is believed to have commenced with the letter written by King Artaxerxes around 458-7 BCE (Ezra 7:7-26). It leads them to the year 26-7 CE, when Yeshua would have begun His ministry. A few of them arrive at the year 29-30 CE, which points to Yeshua's entry into Jerusalem (see Lk. 19).

Between the 69th and 70th Weeks: A Pause of an Unknown Period of Time - The Time or Age (i.e., Dispensation) of the Church: According to this view, the first sixty-nine weeks in Daniel's prophecy is clearly separated from the seventieth and last week. The period in between is called "the Church Age," and/or *the times of the gentiles*. During this pause, Israel as a nation, is "set aside" and awaits God to fulfill Daniel's last, or seventieth, week. Just before He does, i.e., before the seventieth week starts, the church is Raptured, so she can take part in the heavenly *marriage of the Lamb*, which will last seven years (i.e., the seventieth week in Daniel's prophecy).

The Last Week: This week is all about the Anti-Messiah and the nation of Israel. It starts with the *confirming a covenant* with the Jews, which is being broken in the middle of that last week. He then lays heavy persecution on the Jews, which eventually leads to the battle of *Armageddon* (Rev. 16), bringing forth Yeshua's glorious return

---

[320] See Precept Austin's "Daniel Commentary" at https://www.preceptaustin.org/daniel_924. See chapter 2 – appendix 3: illustrations.

together with those who were Raptured, to *restore the Kingdom to Israel* for one thousand years (Acts 1:6, Rev. 20:1-6).

What we can clearly see so far is that Daniel's well-known prophecy is not as easy to understand as it seems! When looking at this prophecy with as objective a lens as possible (or open minds), we can see that the more commonly accepted interpretation held by those who believe in a pre-Tribulation Rapture, is <u>not</u> the only possible interpretation. There is indeed more than one legitimate (i.e., contextual, and linguistic) way to understand Daniel 9:24-27.

Different Presuppositions

In the following paragraphs, I would like to go back – now in greater detail – to our previous discussion about four views in Bible interpretation as related to time.

As I previously mentioned, the way one interprets Scripture, especially End Time prophecies, is connected to the "cultural lenses" he/she wears.

Since Yeshua's First Coming, there have been different theological takes or forms of interpretation within Yeshua's global body, especially when dealing with End Time prophecy. Here are, again, some of the main presuppositions upon which the different End Time interpretations are based.

Historicism: While attempting to interpret prophecies, *Historicism* considers past historical events, while connecting them with events throughout the history of humanity (i.e., those which are not necessarily described in Scripture). For example, *Historicism* sees the prophecies of Daniel as being fulfilled throughout history, extending from the past (biblical times) through to the present and into the future. Those holding to *Historicism* apply this method to ancient Israel, Romans, Catholics or the Papacy, and Islam, all the way to the End Times. An almost integral part of *Historicism* is **Literalism,** a method of interpretation described earlier in this book.

Preterism: *Preterism* interprets some (*partial Preterism*) or all (*full Preterism*) prophecies as events which have already been fulfilled. For example, preterists interpret Daniel's prophecies as referring to events that happened from the 7th century BCE until the first century CE and claim that, consequently, they will not be fulfilled again in the future! For example, in their view, prophecies in the Book of Revelation were already fulfilled in the first century CE. *Preterism* holds that the nation of Israel can find its continuation, or fulfillment, only in Yeshua's global body, especially since the destruction of Jerusalem and the second Temple in 70 CE.

Futurism: *Futurism* interprets portions of Daniel, Ezekiel and Revelation as events which will be fulfilled only in the future! According to this position, these future events will literally be fulfilled in a physical, apocalyptic and global context.

Dispensationalism: *Dispensationalists* have a close association with *Futurists*. They consider biblical history as divided by God into dispensations—defined periods or ages, in which God relates to distinct people, giving them special and distinct responsibilities. In other words, each period or age in God's calendar is different, accompanied by different goals to be executed. Dispensationalists believe that biblical history does not necessarily have a continuation but is instead divided with possible pauses in between.

I believe this is the place to elaborate some more on two of the four above presuppositions, *Preterism* and *Futurism*. They both are particularly connected to Daniel's Seventy Weeks Prophecy, and more specifically with the seventieth and final week.

The Birth of *Preterism* and *Futurism*

Up until the 14th-16th centuries (the Protestant Reformation), the Pope and his clergy were secure in their positions as God's appointed leaders of the international "Mother Church." However, when their positions and doctrines started to be challenged by the first Protestant leaders, they tried their very best to combat this "new apostate teaching," with severe persecution of anyone who didn't line up with Roman Catholic theology and dogmas. Many times it included even death at the stake![321] When they saw that severe persecution alone did not have a real effect, and to the contrary, more devoted Roman Catholics began to leave the mother church and join this new movement of "Roman Catholic protestors" (i.e., Protestants), the Pope and his clergy decided to fight this growing new movement in a completely different way—by presenting the only "correct" End Time theology. They called it "the Counter-Reformation." They started to present new interpretations of End Time prophecies, interpretations that would confront and contradict the Protestant interpretation, especially as it related to the identity of the Anti-Messiah and his system. Here is how it was applied practically.

In 1540, a devoted Spanish Roman Catholic named *Ignatius of Loyola* founded the Society of Jesus, which later became known as *the Jesuit Order.* It was (and still is) a very secretive and militant order.[322] Two

---

[321] See for example, John Huss, Jerome of Prague, and others. Refer to Fox's *Book of Martyrs.*

[322] This is not the place to discuss whether or not the Jesuits did some good as well. Historians still debate this. For sure, while some uphold their Christian devotion,

devoted Jesuits, named *Alcázar of Seville* and *Francisco Ribera of Salamanca,* were chosen to introduce new interpretations of well-known End Time prophecies to the world, especially those regarding the identity of *the man of sin, the little horn,* and *the beast.*

Alcázar was the first to present the world with *Preterism,* and Ribera was the first to present the world with *Futurism.* Note that both Preterism and Futurism had one goal in mind - to divert attention concerning the identity of the Anti-Messiah and his system or government, distancing itself from the Pope and the Vatican in Rome! Alcázar did that by diverting attention to the past, and Ribera did that by diverting attention to the future. Even though the differences between these two presuppositions seemed huge, the fact is that both achieved the same desired goal, *the man of sin, the little horn,* and *the beast* had nothing to do with Rome and the Pope!

Dispensationalism, which is connected to *Futurism,* as stated above, also originated in this old 16th century CE tense and bitter theological debate between two of the main denominations within Christianity—the New Reformation movement led by Martin Luther and the Counter-Reformation led by the Catholic Church! Until this 16th century theological debate, End Time prophecies were interpreted mainly through different variants of *Historicism.*[323]

---

much was written about their dark side as well, especially as it relates to the severe persecutions of early Protestants led by these Jesuits.

[323] This is not the place to discuss other theological presuppositions such as, "covenant theology," "critical scholarship" theology, "symbolic messianic" (which is actually a "contemporary evangelical") theology, and others. In this appendix, I'm trying to explain the main ways in which Daniel's seventy weeks prophecy was interpreted up until the 17th to 18th centuries.

Daniel's Seventieth Week, Messiah, and the Anti-Messiah Until the 17th-18th Centuries

As you could already see when I presented you with the four main views regarding Daniel's seventy weeks prophecy, while most modern-day End Time prophecy teachers connect this seventieth week to the Anti-Messiah and his relationship with the Jews, most Bible commentators of the Reformation, from around the 14th century CE, continuing with Martin Luther into the 16th century CE, and up until the 17th-18th centuries CE, understood this week as <u>referring to Messiah Yeshua Himself</u>! They saw His crucifixion on that tree at Golgotha (at the end of His three and a half year ministry), as the very fulfillment of *he shall bring an end to sacrifice and offering*. They understood the events described in that last (seventieth) week as a description of both Yeshua's crucifixion along with the persecution of His first followers after His death, as well as that which continued all the way to the destruction of the Temple by the Romans in 70 CE. You heard it right! Most Bible commentators up until the 17th-18th centuries CE, believed that Daniel's seventieth week had nothing to do with the Anti-Messiah and that (a) the Anti-Messiah system was nothing but the Roman Catholic or papal system; and (b) the Anti-Messiah was no one other than the Pope himself!

Back to the Middle Eastern Hebraic Lens

Earlier, we discussed the different lens through which Western theologians view or approach Scripture—especially End Time prophecies. As Daniel's famous prophecy was not given to us through a Western lens but rather, through a Middle Eastern Hebraic lens, it is important for us to return, once again, to some of the main characteristics of these original lenses.

Numbers

As mentioned previously, in Western cultures, numbers are merely perceived as quantities. In Middle Eastern cultures, numbers often serve as symbols bearing spiritual significance. As already discussed in the previous chapter, the number *3* is often associated with double blessings and/or with resurrection, the number *4* usually points to the whole world, the number *6* is connected to mankind while the number *7* is associated with God and perfection.

Through the Middle Eastern Hebraic lens, apparent mathematical contradictions, as they relate to the numbering of days and years, can be explained <u>conceptually</u> with no issue or risk to the reliability of the scriptures which contain them. The symbolic nature of numbers would enable the Jewish sages to find further layers of meaning within the biblical text (including Daniel 9).

Multiple and Progressive Fulfillments of Prophecies

To most Westerners it might sound completely inaccurate for one to suggest that Bible prophecies have more than one fulfillment. In general, prophets in the Bible first addressed their own generation, although their prophecies included predictions which related to future generations, as well! Here are a few examples to consider:

<u>Zechariah 14</u>

The main objectives to be fulfilled according to this prophecy:

a. God will gather *all the nations to battle against Jerusalem...* (14:1).

b. There would be chaos and hardships inside Jerusalem (14:2).

c. God Himself will fight against these nations, and *His feet will stand on the Mount of Olives...* (14:3-4).

d. The Mount of Olives will split in two and a river of *living waters shall flow from Jerusalem, half toward the eastern sea and half toward the western sea...* (14:13, 8).

e. *The Lord will be King over all the Earth...* (14:9).

There are those who think that this passage in Zech. 14 must be an End Time prophecy, as the three last objectives clearly point to Yeshua's glorious Second Coming and the millennial kingdom. This is true! Yet, a careful reading of the prophecy reveals that the first two objectives have already had at least two other fulfillments: (1) Before Zechariah's time,[324] when the Babylonian Empire besieged Jerusalem and eventually conquered it and destroyed the first Temple, sometime around 587-6 BCE, and (2) after Zechariah's time, when the Romans besieged the city, conquered it, and eventually destroyed the second Temple.[325]

---

[324] Zechariah was among the Jews who returned to Jerusalem from Babylonian captivity around 520 BCE. He prophesied together with Haggai and Malachi, trying to encourage his contemporaries to continue to build the second Temple, though amid hardships and in the face of enemies. In addition to his own scroll, he is mentioned in Ezra 5:1 and 6:14.

[325] Notice please that *all nations,* used here and in other scriptures, does <u>not</u> necessarily mean that all individuals, from every nation throughout the world, would be present at the given time of the fulfillment of this prophecy! A careful reading of the word *all* in Scripture reveals that it points to *all* that are present in each situation. *All* can be army units and/or delegations from all the nations; *all* can be individuals, families and groups of people who represent *all* the tribes of Israel, and so on. The two examples above, of *all nations* besieging and destroying Jerusalem, did involve all nations as they were counted back then. These great empires controlled vast areas, and thus, *all people* under their jurisdiction were involved in their conquests. See a few examples of the use of *all* in the Scriptures:

And so, we see that there are still three objectives to be fulfilled in the future. This does not mean that these will be the only objectives fulfilled, but (most likely) all five will be fulfilled at the same time. In other words, Jerusalem once again will be besieged, conquered, and destroyed; but this time, God Himself will fight against our enemies, and (Yeshua) will stand on the Mount of Olives, which will be split into two, etc.

Joel 2:8-32[326]

The main objectives to be fulfilled in this prophecy:

a. God's Spirit will be poured out upon *all flesh. Sons and daughters shall prophesy. Old men shall dream dreams. Young men shall see visions.* God's Spirit will be poured out also on *manservants* and *maidservants.*

b. There will be *wonders in the Heavens and on the Earth: blood and fire and pillars of smoke. The sun shall be turned into darkness, and the moon into blood, before the coming of the great and awesome day of the Lord.*

c. *Whoever calls on the name of the Lord shall be saved, for in Mount Zion and Jerusalem shall be deliverance.*

Judg. 6:33—here this certainly does not include women and children, and not even all the soldiers; 1 Sam. 17:24—from the immediate context, it is clear that *all Israel* did not mean every individual Israeli, but only those soldiers who were with King Shaul on the battlefield. The same is true regarding King Solomon at the dedication of the first Temple in Jerusalem (see 1 Kings 8:5, 14, 62).

[326] Bible scholars are not sure when Joel prophesied. Some say it was around the time of the first exile (of the ten tribes), in the eighth century BCE; some place him around the Babylonian exile; yet a few others say he prophesied much later, around the time of Ezra and Nehemiah.

From an initial look, it is clear that at least one fulfillment took place two thousand years ago during Shavuot (i.e., Pentecost. See Acts 2:14-21). The question is: will this specific prophecy, as other End Time prophecies, be fulfilled yet again in the future? The answer clearly is yes. Why? Simply because as we discussed in chapter one, the term *the Latter Days* (in Hebrew, *Acharit Hayamim* — אחרית הימים) speaks of a time period that started at Yeshua's First Coming, and ends with His Second Coming (See again, Heb. 1:1; 1 Pet. 1:20. Compare with Gen. 49:1; Num. 24:14; Deut. 4:30, 31:29; Isa. 2:2; Ezek. 38:16; Hos. 3:5; Micah 4:1; Dan. 10:14).

While it is a typical End Time prophecy, we can see that at least a few of its objectives were fulfilled in that well-known Shavuot event two thousand years ago (objectives "a" and "c"), while others have not been completely or ultimately fulfilled yet (see objective "b"). It is my understanding that all the objectives above will receive their final fulfillment at the end of this period of *the Latter Days* - at Yeshua's Second Coming.

Daniel 11:31 & 12:11:

The only objective to be fulfilled in this prophecy is the well-known *abomination that causes desolation.*

Daniel's prophecy (in the sixth century BCE) was also mentioned by Yeshua (see Matt. 24:15 and Mk. 13:14). Now, while most of us are familiar with the traditional interpretation of this *abomination* which applies it to the Anti-Messiah at the very end of the age, not too many of us are aware of the fact that this specific prophecy was already fulfilled twice: (1) just a few centuries following Daniel's time, when Antiochus the Fourth (Epiphanes) placed a statue in the Temple in Jerusalem, around 167 BCE; and (2) shortly after Yeshua's death, burial and resurrection—this time at the hand of Titus, the Roman general who destroyed the second Temple in 70 CE.[327]

Will this prophecy be fulfilled once again in the future, just before Yeshua returns? It might very well be! Yet, we must also consider that for almost two thousand years now, God has dwelt in <u>a spiritual Temple</u>—that is, in us, His true followers, the body of Messiah here on Earth![328] And so, it is my understanding and personal conviction that while it is good to keep our eyes on a physical (third) fulfillment of this well-known prophecy, we must first look and examine our own hearts, to see that there is no "abomination" that resides there, in God's very (spiritual) Temple!

Daniel Chapters 2, 7, 8 and 10-12:

Daniel describes four kingdoms: Babylon, Medo-Persia, Greece, and Rome, all of which are included in one image or statue (see Dan. 2:31-45). Later, Daniel is given much greater detail concerning two of these, especially as they relate to his people, Israel, and *the Latter Days* (see Dan. 7:1-27, 8:3-26 and chapters 10-12).

Here are the main objectives to be fulfilled in these chapters: the first two are described in chapters 2 and 7, and the others in chapters 8, and 10 through 12:

---

[327] Notice please that the Temple in Jerusalem is described as *the sanctuary fortress* (in Hebrew, *hamikdash hamaoz* — המקדש המעוז). This is probably because of God's very Presence which dwelt in the Temple in Jerusalem and which is often described as *my strength and power* (see 2 Sam. 22:33 — in Hebrew, *HaEl Ma-uzi* — האל מעוזי), *a strength to the poor* (see Isa. 25:4 — in Hebrew, *Maoz La'dal* — מעוז לדל); and *the strength of Israel* (as in Joel 4:16 — in Hebrew, *Maoz LeIsrael* — מעוז לישראל). See also Ps. 27:1, 28:8, 31:3, 31:5 and others. It goes to suggest that *the sanctuary fortress* is indeed the Temple in Jerusalem.

[328] See 1 Cor. 6:19; Eph. 2:22; 2 Pet. 2:5; Rev. 21:3.

a. Nebuchadnezzar, the head of this statue, is the king of the first kingdom—Babylon. His kingdom would be taken by *a lesser kingdom* – Medo-Persia – which would then be taken by Greece. The last and fourth, a most terrible kingdom, would be Rome.

b. In the days of the fourth kingdom (Rome), God's Kingdom will put an end to the four kingdoms and will be established forever and ever.

c. The four kingdoms are described, too, as *a lion with eagle's wings, a bear with three ribs in its mouth, one like a leopard with four wings,* and lastly, the fourth, *dreadful, and terrible, exceedingly strong … different from all the beasts that were before it.*

d. The third kingdom, or beast, who has *four wings on its back,* is also described as having *four heads* (see 7:6).

e. This third kingdom also has the infamous *little horn* that would cause many problems and hardships to God's nation, Israel (see 8:9-14, 19-26).

Interestingly enough, a very similar description of that *little horn* is also given in connection to the fourth kingdom, or beast (see 7:8-9, 11, 20-27).

It is quite easy to see that there was at least one fulfillment which involved all four kingdoms, or beasts -- Babylon, Medo-Persia, Greece, and Rome, were all in existence from the time of Daniel and continuing all the way through to the destruction of the Temple in Jerusalem by Rome in the year 70 CE (points "a" & "b"). We also know that God's Kingdom had already been established in the first century, although not to its optimal and maximum fulfillment; as that *stone, that was cut out without hands* and that became *a great mountain that filled the whole Earth* clearly speaks of Yeshua, whose Kingdom was established in the first century and since then, has truly been filling the whole Earth (point "b"). We also know from history that at least one person fits the *little horn* description -- Antiochus Epiphanes, from the second century BCE, of whom we have spoken more than once (point "d"). Lastly, we know that another *little horn* – Titus – caused many problems for God's people and eventually destroyed their (second) Temple in Jerusalem (point "e").

Once again, were the above fulfillments meant to be "one-time," sort of, "once-and-for-all" fulfillments? Should we expect at least one more fulfillment in our own time or soon after?

According to the above examples of prophecies which had more than one fulfillment, the answer should be a clear, yes. And indeed, it is my understanding that we can see the four beasts – united in one body, i.e., the statue (Dan. 2) – rising again in our own generation. Just as an example, did you know that one of the main symbols of Great Britain is a *Lion*? And what about Russia? Could she be the *Bear*? What about Germany of the last century with its third Reich and the *Leopard* as one of its symbols? Moreover, could Hitler fit *the little horn* description of that (third) beast or kingdom? And lastly, what about world organizations such as the United Nations, the European Union, the WEF (World Economic Forum), the WHO (World Health Organization) and the Vatican, collaborating as one united entity? Could they be a representation of the fourth and last beast—Rome? Could it be that what we have been awaiting in these very days is yet another (final) *little horn* – the Anti-Messiah – who is going to arise from this last and terrible beast? It is my opinion that the answer to the above questions is a resounding, yes.

Matt. 24:

Within His classic End Time prophecy context, Yeshua said, *Assuredly I say to you, <u>this generation</u> will by no means pass away till all these things take place!* (Emphasis added). Let us look at some of the main objectives that needed to be fulfilled within the immediate context:

a. Many will come in Yeshua's name and say, *I am the Messiah* (see verse 4. See also verse 11).

b. *Wars and rumors of war* (verse 6).

c. *Nation will rise against nation, and kingdom against kingdom...* (see verse 7).

d. There will be *famines, pestilences, and earthquakes...* (see verse 7).

e. As for Yeshua's followers, *you will be delivered up to Tribulation and they will kill you, and you will be hated for my namesake.* Moreover, *many will be offended, will betray one another, and will hate one another...* (see verses 9-10).

f. *The love of many will grow cold* (see verse 11).

g. The good news of God's Kingdom *will be preached in all the world... and then the end will come* (see verse 14).

h. An *abomination of desolation* (Dan. 11:31), which will be placed *in the Holy place,* will be a sign for many in Judea to *escape to the mountains,* as it will trigger *a great Tribulation, such as has not been since the beginning of the world until this time, nor ever shall be!* Unless these days are *shortened for the elect's sake,* no one would survive that Tribulation (see verses 15-22).

i. The coming of Yeshua – *the Son of Man* – will take place <u>only</u> <u>after</u> the culmination of certain things that must first be fulfilled: *The Sun will be darkened, and the moon will not give its light, the stars will fall from Heaven, and the powers of the heavens will be shaken!* His coming will be *as the lightning comes from the east and flashes to the west* (see verses 27-29).

j. At His coming, *all the tribes of the Earth will mourn; He will send His angels with a great sound of a trumpet and will gather together his elect from the four winds, from one end of Heaven to the other* (see verses 30-31).

And lastly,

k. As mentioned above, all the above points will be observed and experienced in a single *generation* (see verse 34).

Were all the above objectives fulfilled in Yeshua's own generation, or were they only partially fulfilled?

A simple study of history clearly shows that objectives "a" to "h" have already been fulfilled to some extent. *False prophets* and teachers had already been in existence during the first century (see 2 Pet. 2:1, 1 Jn. 4:1). There were also some *wars and rumors of wars* during Yeshua's ministry and certainly when the Great Jewish Revolt led to the destruction of Jerusalem and its Temple.

Famines, pestilence, and earthquakes had already occurred before Yeshua's generation and continued throughout time to our present day. The love of many, at least within Yeshua's first century body, had already grown cold; otherwise, why would the apostles have needed to encourage and emphasize the great need for the believers to love one another (see Rom. 12:10; 1 Pet. 2:17, 4:8; 1 John, Rev. 2:4)? Even the good news of the kingdom had been preached (at that time) to the then-known world (see Col. 1:23)! Lastly, the *abomination* or more correctly, *the complete desecration* – i.e., destruction of God's Temple took place in the year 70 CE!

Nevertheless, we can clearly see that objectives "i" through "k" had not yet been fully fulfilled. We know Yeshua's glorious Second Coming has not yet occurred! We know that, even though Yeshua's generation could have thought that the greatest Tribulation of all times had arrived during their own period, still, not all of them were killed or consumed during those hard times preceding the destruction of the second Temple; as well as the other tribulations and hardships that ended up being perpetrated upon God's people in the first century and continuing throughout their long years of exile (culminating in the Holocaust). Moreover, we know with assurance, that *the powers of the heavens* have not yet been *shaken!*

Since Yeshua spoke of *this generation,* it is pretty clear that He was indeed pointing to only *one generation*, which I believe points to <u>both</u> the first century, Yeshua's own generation, and *the last generation* which will exist at the time of His glorious Second Coming. I firmly believe that this last generation spoken of in Scripture is ours, and it *will, by no means, pass away until all these things take place!*

The last legitimate question we should all ask is: when Yeshua returns, will <u>all</u> the above objectives be fulfilled again? Will only the few that have not yet been fulfilled, finally be fulfilled? In my opinion, most, if not all the objectives will be fulfilled within this last generation.

After this lengthy explanation of the specific lens which I have used while attempting to interpret Daniel's seventy weeks prophecy, I would like to share my personal view with you.

Author's View

It is my opinion that to better understand this well-known prophecy, one first needs to understand the different meanings of a few Hebrew words and terms shown in this prophecy. The following are three examples:

1. ***The command*** — Dan. 9:25 reads, *know therefore and understand, that from the going forth of the command to restore and build Jerusalem, until Messiah the Prince, there shall be seven weeks...* In this specific verse, there are three Hebrew words to which I would like to draw your attention: *min motzah davar* (מן מצא דבר). These words are translated as *from the going forth of the command.* When reading it in Hebrew, it actually states, *from the coming out of the word.* In Deut. 8:3, we see a similar wording -- *motzah Pi Adonai* (מוצא פי ה'), which literally means, *[whatever] comes out of God's mouth.* The question that arises is, to what did the Archangel Gabriel refer when he said, *from the coming out of the word?* Which exact *word* was it, and specifically, from where did it come? In other words, who spoke that *word* and when? Was Gabriel referring to the word which came out of Jeremiah's mouth?[329] Was he referring to the word which came out of King Cyrus' mouth?[330] Was he referring to Daniel's own

---

[329] See Jer. 25:11-12, 29:10: *And this whole land shall be a desolation and an astonishment, and these nations shall serve the king of Babylon <u>seventy years</u>... I will punish the king of Babylon and that nation... For thus says the Lord, after <u>seventy years</u> are completed at Babylon, I will visit you...* Notice, the seventy years directly relate to *the <u>king</u> of Babylon* and, *at Babylon.*

[330] See Ezra 1:1-4 — *Thus says Cyrus King of Persia ... He has commanded me to build Him <u>a house at Jerusalem</u>...* Isa. 45 — *he shall build <u>My city</u>.* Thus, both *the Temple* and the city of *Jerusalem* are mentioned and related to king Cyrus.

words?[331] Was he referring to King Artaxerxes' words, given around 457 BCE, after years of delay in the building of the walls of Jerusalem?[332]

2. ***Messiah and Prince*** — In the Hebrew scriptures, Messiah (Hebrew, *Mashiach"* — משיח) and Prince (Hebrew, *Nagid* — נגיד) do not apply only to *the* Messiah—the One we believe to be Yeshua of Nazareth! *Messiah* is based on the Hebrew root *Mem, Shin, Chet (ה.ש.מ)*, which has to do with the use of the anointing oil (in Hebrew, *shemen hamishchah* (שמן המשחה), used for crowning kings and consecrating priests. Every king and priest in Israel was "a Messiah," as he was anointed with that consecrating ointment.[333] Similarly, *a prince* could describe a king, leader, commander, or even someone who is in charge of something in God's Temple.[334] Based on this

---

[331] See Dan. 9:21 — *Now while I was speaking* (in Hebrew, *medaber,* which is connected to *davar — word*). See also verse 23 — *At the beginning of your supplications, the command* (in Hebrew, *davar — word*) *went out...*

[332] See Ezra 7:11-26.

[333] Actually, not every king or priest in Israel, as King Cyrus was not an Israelite king — see Isa. 45:1. As we know, this anointing oil was a symbol of God's protection and guidance through His Holy Spirit (see Lev. 4:3). *Anointed* in Hebrew is *mashiach* (see 1 Sam. 24:7, 11), where King Shaul is called *mashiach Adonai—God's anointed one.* See also 2 Sam. 1:14, 16 and many others. See also Strong's H4886: A primitive root; to *rub* with oil, that is, to *anoint*; by implication to *consecrate*; also, to *paint: anoint, paint*; and H4899 — *anointed*; usually a *consecrated* person (as a king, priest or saint).

[334] See King Shaul in 1 Sam. 10:1; David in 2 Sam. 5:2, 6:21, 7:8; King Solomon in 1 Kings 1:35. See also Jer. 20:1; 1 Ch. 26:24; Neh. 11:11; and 1 Ch. 13:1. See this term as applied to Messiah Yeshua in Isa. 55:4 and many other places. See Strong H5057 and H5046: a *commander* (as occupying the *front*), civil, military, or religious; generally (abstract plural), *honorable* themes: *captain, chief, excellent thing, (chief) governor, leader, noble, prince, (chief) ruler.*

simple data, the questions we should ask are: who is this *Messiah, the Prince* in Dan. 9:25? Is he the same person mentioned in the following verse as the one being *cut off?*

3. ***The one who confirms a covenant with the many*** — Dan. 9:27 reads: *Then he shall confirm a covenant with many for one week* (Hebrew, *v'eegbir brit larabim shavua echad* — וְהִגְבִּיר בְּרִית לָרַבִּים שָׁבוּעַ אֶחָד). The Hebrew word for *confirm* in this specific verse, is *v'eegbir.* [335] It has to do with "strengthening" or "making something stronger," rather than just "confirming" it. And so, we should ask firstly: what exactly is this specific *covenant* that needed to be strengthened? Secondly: who is this one who makes this covenant stronger? As I mentioned previously, while most of us today believe "it must be the Anti-Messiah," up until recent centuries, most Bible commentators applied it to Messiah Yeshua Himself!

Israel is in the Very Center of Daniel's Prophecy

As I have previously said, Daniel's seventy weeks prophecy cannot and should not be separated from its immediate context—namely, Daniel's long prayer and supplication on behalf of his people, Israel. As I have already mentioned, Israel as a nation and a land (more specifically, Jerusalem and Judea) are in the very center of this well-known prophecy, and no one can ignore that!

---

[335] *V'eegbir* comes from the root *Ga-Va-R,* which has to do mainly with strength, making someone or something strong or powerful. Actually, the very name of the Archangel Gabriel in Dan. 9 is derived from this Hebrew root! See Strong H1396: *to be strong;* by implication to *prevail, act insolently: exceed, confirm, be great, be mighty, prevail, put to more [strength], strengthen, be stronger, be valiant.*

The Number 70 Cannot Be Taken Literally

It is my understanding that the number *70*, especially in this specific prophecy, cannot be taken literally. When attempting to take it literally and insert it into a mathematically precise chronological order, we quickly find ourselves with some inconsistencies, and this is true concerning all the main other views I have presented to you above! Let me try and prove this important point to you by using the views we have previously examined:

a. Placing the starting point around 588 BCE (Jeremiah's prophecy), the seventy weeks should have ended – if taken literally – around 98 BCE! Those who hold to this starting point are correct only regarding the first week, as it points to Cyrus who can be understood as *Messiah the Prince* (see above). The rest of the weeks (sixty-nine) are contrived in order to use real historic events so that they adapt and fulfill the other objectives of the prophecy.

b. Placing the starting point around 538 BCE (Daniel's own words) – if taken literally – the seventy weeks should have ended around 48 BCE. Even though the first week, according to this starting point, might fit into historic events such as the times of Ezra, Nehemiah, Joshua or Unio (Chunio) the high priest, here, one also needs to manipulate the amount of the remaining weeks, so that they comply with and fulfill the other objectives of the prophecy.

c. Placing the starting point around 457 BCE (King Artaxerxes), they should have ended – if taken literally – around 33 CE! This would have actually been the only view that would have fit most of the Daniel 9:24-27 objectives! Yet, here also there is a need to stretch and manipulate the numbers to literally match everything (see the Protestant and the Seventh-Day Adventists' views above). Why? Simply because while it is true that Yeshua was anointed by the Holy Spirit (John's baptism, see Matt. 3), and/or that Yeshua's crucifixion took place around 30 CE, there is still a great need to play with the numbers to literally make them fit with the destruction of Jerusalem and the second Temple, since these events took place approximately 40 years later!

As we can see, not even one of the views or commentaries we have presented in this appendix, can actually and literally employ the number *70*. It is simply mission impossible! No wonder the Jewish sages (and some of the Roman Catholic theologians following their example) chose not to take the numbers in this well-known prophecy too literally. They stretched and manipulated it in order to correspond with respective interpretations.

As I have previously displayed, in the Middle Eastern Jewish/Hebraic mindset (or, lens), numbers are not only mere quantities. They do have symbolic and spiritual significance! In this specific context of the Daniel 9:24-27 prophecy, we can see that the number 7 – God's Number – is very central throughout the prophecy, thus reminding us that He is the One who is in full control—with a particular focus on the destiny of His beloved Chosen Nation - Israel![336]

---

[336] There two good examples of the symbolic and spiritual meanings of the number 7 in Scripture, especially when considering Messiah's own words concerning that *generation that will not pass...* (1) The length of *a generation* is usually *seventy* years, or eighty (see Ps. 90:10). (2) In the gospel of Matthew 18:22, where Simon Cephas (better known as Peter) asked Yeshua, *Lord, how often shall my brother sin against me, and I forgive him? Up to seven times?* Please notice Yeshua's answer: *I do not say to you up to seven times, but up to seventy times seven!* (Emphasis added). Yeshua – an Israeli-born Jew – did not expect His faithful disciple to start counting and be mathematically precise when calculating the sins of his brother

Messiah Yeshua and Daniel 9:24

As mentioned above, Israel as a nation and a land, and - Yeshua – her Messiah – are in the very center of this well-known prophecy. Here are, once again, the six objectives according to Daniel 9:24:

1. *Finishing transgression*

2. *Making an end of sins*

3. *Making reconciliation for iniquity*

4. *Bringing in everlasting righteousness*

5. *Sealing up vision and prophecy*

6. *Anointing the Most Holy*

According to the New Covenant writings, the death of Yeshua was the ultimate solution to sin (objectives 1 through 3). Yeshua causes those who are *in Him* to be righteous (objective 4). He is the optimal fulfillment of prophecy (objective 5). Lastly, He, as *Immanuel* (God with us), and our very heavenly High Priest, is the One who sanctifies or *anoints the Most Holy* in the heavenlies (objective 6).

Messiah Yeshua and Daniel 9:26-27

As we have already established, up until the 17th-18th centuries CE, most Bible commentators had not distinguished the sixty-ninth week from the seventieth! Most agreed that verse 27 was actually an elaboration (a kind of explanation) of verse 26, as it was placed within the immediate context of the seventieth week. Thus, most believed

---

against him and his forgiveness thereof all the way until he reached the number 77! Again, we see that Yeshua rather pointed to an endless number and a perfect number, God's number!

that the one who *confirms a covenant with many for one week,* is none other than Yeshua Himself!

I do think that this is very possible since the New Covenant writings would seem to support it. In Matt. 26:28, Yeshua says, *this is my Blood of the New Covenant, which is shed for many for the remission of sins.* Heb. 9:28 teaches us that *Messiah was offered once to bear the sins of many.*[337] (emphasis added).

With His own precious blood, Yeshua sealed *a New Covenant* with His Chosen People, Israel.[338] While doing it, He *confirmed* (*made stronger*) God's first covenant that was given on Mount Sinai. Note, that although this *New Covenant* brought about some changes, especially in relation to the external way of keeping the Old (Mt. Sinai) Covenant, it did not *abolish* its very heart (principles)! Rather, the New Covenant *confirmed* the Old Covenant's truthfulness, righteousness, goodness, and holiness! Thus, the New Covenant *strengthened* God's holy and just Torah, by way of providing it with its correct, perfect and Spirit-filled interpretation![339]

Once it was understood that verses 26 and 27 were indeed connected (i.e., verse 27 elaborates on and explains verse 26), it led most Bible scholars and commentators to agree that Yeshua's earthly ministry, which lasted around three and a half years, perfectly fit the first half of that last seventieth week in Daniel's prophecy. Why? At the very

---

[337] See also Mk. 14:24; Rom. 5:16-19.

[338] See again Jer. 31:31: Only the *two houses of ISRAEL* are mentioned! As we stated previously, this is not to say that gentiles are not *welcome* to join together with *the Olive Tree* of ISRAEL!

[339] See Matt. 5:17–7:29. See also Rom. 3:31, 7:12; and Heb. 7:11-19. See also in "Building the Foundations Part 3" in Chapter two, the discussion on "The First century Believers and the Old Covenant."

end of this half a week, Yeshua was nailed to that tree at Golgotha as the ultimate sacrifice, which satisfied all of God's holy requirements in the Old Covenant, marking the *strengthening* and *confirmation* of it! Yeshua perfectly fit the description in Daniel 9:26-27, as His three and a half years of ministry ended right in the middle of Daniel's seventieth week, also marking the very end of the old sacrificial system at the Temple—as far as God was concerned. This Levitical Order now *ceased* so that the new *Malki-tzedek* (Melchizedek) Order would take effect![340]

It's important to remember that all six objectives in verse 24 had to do with Messiah Yeshua, and all were meant to be fulfilled within the timeframe of <u>seventy weeks</u>! Daniel 9:24 did not make any distinction between the first sixty-nine weeks and the seventieth! Please note that without the old earthly sacrificial system ceasing, the first three objectives of the prophecy could not have been fulfilled!

The Anti-Messiah and Daniel 9:26-27

Is the Anti-Messiah mentioned in Daniel 9:24-27? According to the accepted view of most of today's Protestants (as well as most Messianic Jewish believers), the answer is a resounding yes! Yet, a careful reading of the entire prophecy, free from any preconceived ideas or presuppositions, shows the two following facts:

a. Up until *Messiah shall be cut off* (verse 26), accepted by all of us to be Messiah Yeshua, there is no mention of any "Anti-Messiah."

b. Though the destruction of *the city and the sanctuary* (by Titus in 70 CE) immediately follows the verse stating, *Messiah shall*

---

[340] See Matt. 27:50-51. See also Heb. chapters 7–10.

be cut off, a simple study of history confirms that there were forty years between the two parts of this same verse. And so, we cannot with any certainty connect Messiah Yeshua with the deeds of the Anti-Messiah in a literal way.

Do the above points prove, beyond any shadow of a doubt, that the Anti-Messiah is not at all mentioned in Daniel 9? Could it be that even though the central figure of this prophecy is Israel's Messiah, the Anti-Messiah is mentioned "behind the scenes" as well? Is it a possibility that the very same biblical reference, which clearly points to Israel's Messiah, also points to the Anti-Messiah, yet in a more "hidden way?" Well, it really depends on whom you ask. If you ask someone who is detached from the Hebraic/Jewish Middle Eastern lens, the answer would be "certainly not!" Yet, if you ask someone who is fully connected to his/her Hebraic/Jewish Middle Eastern lens, you might be surprised to hear a big, yes!

This is, indeed, one example that demonstrates the beauty and the depth of the Hebraic/Jewish Middle Eastern culture. Together with all that I have previously said regarding the connection between verses 26 and 27, and accepting that *confirms a covenant,* most likely refers to Messiah Yeshua, there are some "hints hidden within the text" that <u>also</u> connect the Anti-Messiah to Daniel's seventy weeks prophecy. Allow me to elaborate.

Descriptions, such as *on the wing of abominations* and *desolate,* (verse 27) might very well be associated with *the abomination of desolation* mentioned in Dan. 11:31, especially when considering Yeshua's own words (see Dan. 11:31 and Matt. 24:15). As we have established, historically speaking, these descriptions point to two events within Jewish history: Antiochus Epiphanes' desecration of the Temple in the second century BCE (see above), and Titus - the Roman's desecration and destruction of the Temple in 70 CE. It is my understanding that both Antiochus and Titus are a sort of prototype or foreshadowing of the Anti-Messiah (see above: the similarities between the descriptions of *the little horn* within the two last kingdoms—Greece and Rome).

Anti-Messiah attempting to imitate Messiah Yeshua

One of the main characteristics of the Anti-Messiah is that he greatly desires to take God's throne. How does he go about achieving that ungodly goal? He tries his very best to <u>imitate</u> and <u>fake</u> God's goodness and likeness. One example of this is Satan (represented by the snake, or serpent) in the Garden of Eden. Note that he did not threaten Eve nor shout at her. He did not mistreat or dishonor her in any shape or form! He sounded like one who very much cared for her good, only wishing her the best, which would make him appear to be as God Himself (see Gen. 3:5: *and you will be like God, knowing good and evil...*). Another example of him trying to imitate and take God's very throne, is his attempt to have this world go through "the Great Reset" to usher in his satanic "New World Order" (see chapter one – "Covid 19 – the beginning of the end?").

Yes, the best description I can give for Satan, and thus, also his soon-coming representative, the Anti-Messiah, is that he is indeed "the best imitator of God."

Could it be that at the very end of what Scripture calls *the latter days*, Satan will try to fulfill Daniel's prophecy while presenting himself as "the ultimate solution to all of humanity's problems?" Could it be that he will indeed *confirm a covenant* with (some) of God's Chosen People and later reveal his true colors, following the pattern set by his ancient prototypes (Antiochus and Titus)? I think it is very possible, especially when reading this well-known prophecy through the Middle Eastern Hebraic lens.

Daniel's Seventy Weeks Has Multiple Progressive Fulfillments

It is my understanding that like many prophecies in the Bible, Daniel 9:24-27 has its own multiple progressive fulfillments. This would be especially true if we look at the prophecy within the broader context of the other End Time prophecies presented in Daniel. I speak especially concerning the *four kingdoms, or beasts* and their relationship to God's Chosen Nation.

Besides the six objectives mentioned in verse 24, there are others which need to be fulfilled within these seventy weeks (490 years). Let's look at all of them again:

a. *Finishing the transgression*

b. *Making an end of sins*

c. *Making reconciliation for iniquity*

d. *Bringing in everlasting righteousness*

e. *Sealing up vision and prophecy*

f. *Anointing the Most Holy*

g. *Messiah shall be cut off*

h. *The street shall be built again, and the wall, even in troublesome times.*[341]

i. *The people of the prince who is to come shall destroy the city and the sanctuary.*

---

[341] Note that while many commentators combine the first seven and the following sixty-two weeks, it is quite clear that in the original Hebrew, they are divided into two separate groupings.

j.   *There will be a 'war of desolation'.*

k.   *He shall confirm a covenant with many.*

l.   *In the middle of the week, he shall bring an end to sacrifice and offering.*

m. *On the wing of abominations shall be one who makes desolate,* and *the consummation ... is poured out of the desolate.*

If we see at least some of the numbers symbolically, and try to fit them into real historical events connected in some way or another to Jewish history, we can see the following:

Points "a" through "g" were fulfilled by Yeshua's First Coming two thousand years ago (see above). As far as foreshadowing, pictures and patterns that point to Messiah Yeshua, some biblical figures did serve as prototypes of Yeshua throughout Jewish history. People, such as Joshua the high priest in Nehemiah and Ezra's time, Zerubbabel, and Unio (Chunio), the high priest who was murdered in the second century BCE.

Moreover, we can see that some of the first six objectives are still being fulfilled to this very day within Yeshua's body. We are called to *finish transgressions and make an end of sins* in our own lives.[342] We are to be *ambassadors of reconciliation for iniquity.*[343] We are called to live righteously through His righteousness.[344] We are called to *anoint the most high* (both Yeshua our Messiah King, and us – His body – being holy unto Him).

---

[342] See Rom. 6:1-14; 1 Jn. 2:1, 3:6, 5:18.

[343] See 2 Cor. 5:18-19.

[344] See 1 Pet. 2:24; 2 Pet. 1:5; 1 Jn. 2:29, 3:7.

As far as points "h" through "m," Jewish history shows a few more of these multiple progressive fulfillments. Jerusalem was indeed built *in troublesome times,* more than just once - initially, when the first wave of Jews returned from the Babylonian Exile, [345] and later, in the days of the Maccabees, in the second century BCE. As we have seen previously, the *abomination of desolation* was fulfilled at least twice, by Antiochus Epiphanes, who also made *a covenant* with some of the Jewish elites of his time, breaking it *in the middle;* and, by Titus, who, three and a half years before destroying the Temple, also interrupted the sacrifices.

And so, we should not at all be surprised at the possibility that we might be the final generation just before Yeshua's glorious return, witnessing the very last fulfillment of Daniel's seventy weeks prophecy taking place. I personally believe that as Yeshua *confirmed a covenant with many* two thousand years ago by His atoning death on that tree at Golgotha, some of us – His true followers – will be martyred for His Holy Name's sake, in order to *confirm/strengthen* the truthfulness of the Gospel—His New Covenant <u>with Israel</u>. I do believe that He will give us all His power through the Holy Spirit to minister His truth and the gospel of the kingdom to people for *three and a half years.* I also am convinced that it will happen concurrently <u>to the revelation and acts of the Anti-Messiah</u>, who will first try to imitate Him, and then show his ugly, true colors, while persecuting us (Yeshua's true followers), some even unto a martyr's death! Sadly, I suspect the Anti-Messiah will cause the death of many of Messiah's true followers and destroy a good portion of Jerusalem.

To summarize, it is my opinion that all the objectives of Daniel 9:24-27 have multiple, progressive fulfillments. Many were fulfilled before

---

[345] See Ezra 4:5; Neh. 2, 4, 6.

Yeshua's First Coming. Some were fulfilled in Yeshua's time, two thousand years ago; and some will be fulfilled once again during the time of the last generation (likely our own).

May we all be found worthy of His specific calling on our lives during the coming days. Amen!

Appendix 2:
Respected Traditional Commentaries on Daniel 9:24-27 Up Until the 19th Century CE[346]

160 CE — Clement of Alexandria: From the captivity of Babylon, which took place during the time of Jeremiah the prophet, what had been spoken of by Daniel the prophet was fulfilled. Daniel 9:24-27 in the original manuscript says, *That the Temple, accordingly, was built in seven weeks, is evident; for it is written in Esdras. And, thus, <u>Messiah became King of the Jews, reigning in Jerusalem in the fulfillment of the seven weeks</u>.* And in the sixty and two weeks the whole of Judaea was quiet, and without wars. And Messiah our Lord, 'the Holy of Holies,' having come and fulfilled the vision as well as the prophecy, was anointed in His flesh by the Father's Holy Spirit. In those 'sixty-two weeks,' as the prophet said, and 'in the one week,' was He Lord? *<u>The half of the week</u> Nero... in the holy city Jerusalem placed the abomination; a*nd in the half of the week, he was taken away, and Otho, and Galba, and Vitellius *Vespasian rose to become the supreme power, and destroyed Jerusalem, desolating the holy place.* These are the facts,

---

[346] Note that (a) all quotations are as usually in a different font. (b) I certainly do not agree with every statement and interpretation by the Church Fathers or other respected theologians! I am only sharing *excerpts* to demonstrate that <u>there are other ways to interpret Daniel's famous prophecy and to show how far off these ancient interpretations were from the ones of the last 200–300 years</u>. (c) I am <u>not</u> *amillennialistic* in my theology! As I have said numerous times throughout this book, I believe that most Scripture conveys the "cyclical character" of the Middle Eastern Hebrew mindset. Accordingly, most prophecies have more than one fulfillment, and the different fulfillments are progressive—i.e., not all aspects of a prophecy are fulfilled each time; rather, they are fulfilled in stages, until the very last detail is completed in the last, complete fulfillment! Thus, there is yet one more fulfillment to expect within the Daniel 9:24-27 prophecy, a fulfillment I believe we have already seen as it has taken place over the last few centuries.

making it clear to whoever is able to understand, as the prophet said (*Stromata*, book 1, chapter 21).

220 CE — Sextus Julius Africanus: This passage touches on many marvelous things. At present however, I shall speak only to the things contained which impact the chronology, as well as associated matters. It is evident *that the passage speaks of the advent of Messiah, who was to manifest Himself after seventy weeks. For in the Savior's time, or from Him, are transgressions repealed and sins brought to an end*... For before the advent of the Savior these things had not yet occurred and were therefore, only awaited. And the beginning of the numbers, as it pertains to the seventy weeks which make up 490 years, the angel instructs us to take from the going forth of the commandment to answer and to build Jerusalem. This happened in the twentieth year of the reign of Artaxerxes king of Persia... *It is by calculating from Artaxerxes, up to the time of Messiah that the seventy weeks are comprised, according to the calculation of the Jews...*

225 CE — Origin: The weeks of years, which the prophet Daniel had also predicted, extending to the leadership of Messiah, have been fulfilled.

17th-18th Century CE — Matthew Henry, Bible commentator: Concerning the termination of them (*the 490 years/seventy weeks*); and here likewise interpreters are not agreed. *Some make them to end at the death of Messiah* and think the express words of this famous prophecy will warrant us to conclude that from this very hour when Gabriel spoke to Daniel, *at the time of the evening oblation, to the hour when Messiah died, which was towards evening too, it was exactly 490 years; and I am willing enough to be of that opinion*. But others think, because it is said that *in the midst of the weeks* (that is, the last of the seventy weeks) *he shall cause the sacrifice and the oblation to cease, they end three years and a half after the death of Messiah*, when the Jews having rejected the gospel, the apostles turned to the gentiles. *But those who* *make them to end precisely at the death of Messiah read it thus, 'He shall make strong the testament to the many; the last seven, or the last week, yea, half that seven, or half that week (namely, <u>the latter half, the three years and a half which Messiah spent in his public ministry), shall bring to an end sacrifice and oblation.</u>'* Others make these 490 years to end with the destruction of Jerusalem, about thirty-seven years after the death of Messiah, because these seventy weeks are said to be determined upon the people of the Jews and the holy city; and much is said here concerning the destruction of the city and the sanctuary. Concerning the division of them into seven weeks, and sixty-two weeks, and one week; and the reason of this is as hard to account for as anything else. *In the first seven weeks, or forty-nine years, the temple and city were built; <u>and in the last single week Messiah preached his gospel</u>, by which the Jewish economy was taken down, and the foundations were laid of the gospel city and temple*, which were to be built upon the ruins of the former.[347]

18th-19th Century CE — Adam Clarke, Britain: From the coming of our Lord, the *third period* is to be dated, viz., *'He shall confirm the covenant with many for one week,' that is seven years. <u>This confirmation of the covenant must take in the ministry of John the Baptist with that of our Lord</u>, comprehending the term of seven years, during the whole of which he might be well said to confirm or ratify the new covenant with mankind...* <u>These *seven years*, added to the *four hundred and eighty-three*, complete the *four hundred and ninety years*, or *seventy* prophetic weeks; *so that the whole of this prophecy, from the times and corresponding events, has been fulfilled to the very letter*.</u> Some imagine that the *half* of the last *seven years* is to be referred to the total destruction of the Jews by *Titus*, when the daily sacrifice for ever ceased to be offered; and that the intermediate space of *thirty-*

---

[347] See his whole interpretation at:
https://www.christianity.com/bible/commentary/mh/daniel/9

seven years, from our Lord's death till the destruction of the city, is passed over as being of no account in relation to the prophecy, and that it was on this account that the last seven years are *divided*. *But Dean Prideaux thinks that the whole refers to our Lord's preaching connected with that of the Baptist*. Vachetzi, *says he, signifies in the half part of the week; that is,* in the latter three years and a half in which he exercised himself in the public ministry, he caused, by the sacrifice of himself, all other sacrifices and oblations to cease, which were instituted to signify his.[348]

---

[348] See the full commentary at:
https://www.studylight.org/commentaries/eng/acc/daniel-9.html. See another 19th century perspective, a critical and explanatory commentary, titled "The 70th Week of Daniel: The total failure of Dispensational theology," with notes on Daniel 9:24-27 at: https://www.rivalnations.org/70th-week-of-daniel/.

Note that these old commentaries are made by "Amillennialists" who see everything through the Western, Greek (linear) lens! If they would be able to see through Middle Eastern Hebraic eyes, they would understand that there is more than one fulfillment of biblical prophecy! See Yeshua's own words, yet again, in Matt. 24:34: *Truly I say to you, this generation will not pass away until all these things take place. Heaven and Earth will pass away but my words will not pass away!* Now, if indeed He meant to speak only of His first century generation, then we have nothing to expect in our generation or the generations to come, as all has already been fulfilled! But the re-establishment of Israel, God's ancient chosen people in the 20th century, shows that there is still another final fulfillment to Daniel 9 as well as other prophecies throughout the Bible!

Appendix 3:
Illustrations

Book of Daniel – Timetable

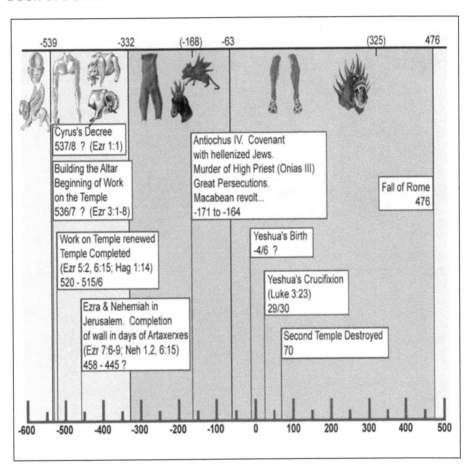

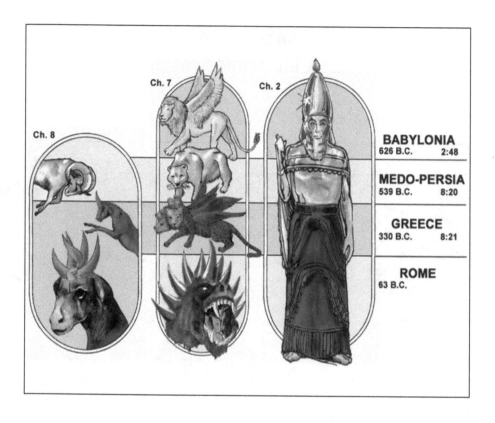

Ch. 8

Ch. 7

Ch. 2

BABYLONIA
626 B.C.   2:48

MEDO-PERSIA
539 B.C.   8:20

GREECE
330 B.C.   8:21

ROME
63 B.C.

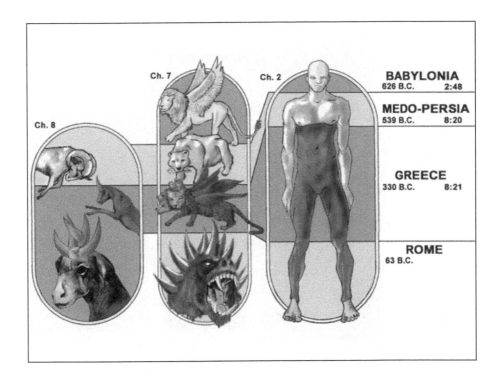

The Jewish Sages View

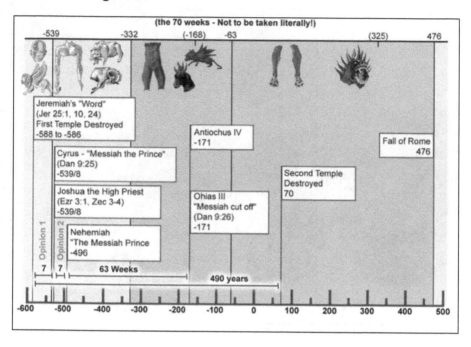

The Catholic View

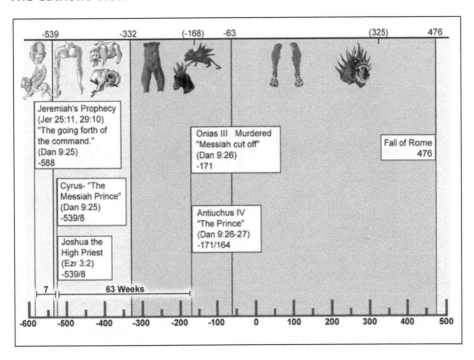

The Seventh Day Adventist View

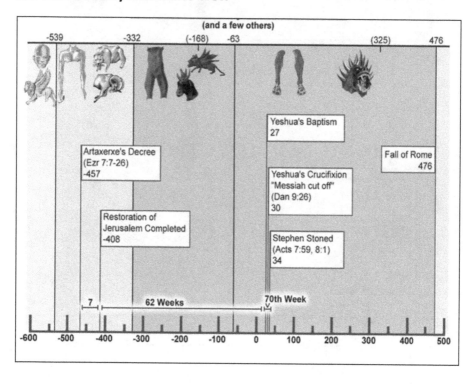

The Popular Protestant View

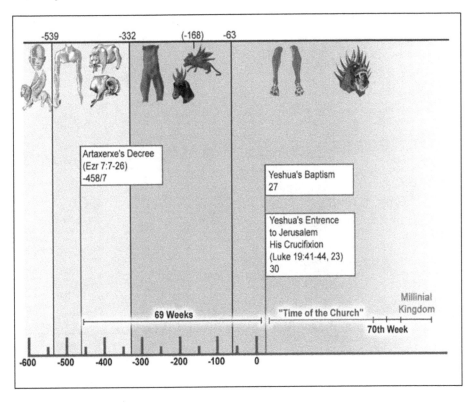

Alternative Views

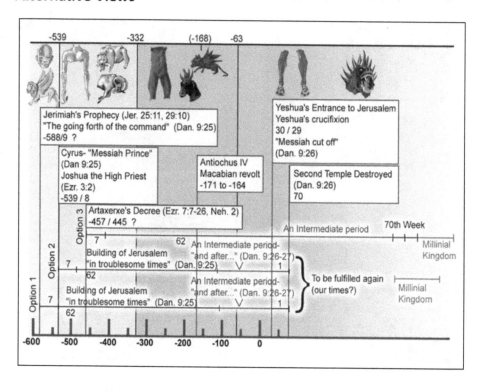

Chapter 3:

A Call to Get Back to the Model Used By Yeshua's Body In the First Century

Introduction

In the first chapter, we considered the Covid-19 crisis as "the beginning of the end," as it relates to the period Scripture calls *the latter days.* In the second chapter, we examined the doctrine of the pre-Tribulation Rapture and discovered that it might be an erroneous end time doctrine with a great potential of misleading many in Yeshua's modern-day body. Now, in this closing chapter, it is time to consider what scripture has to say about the way Yeshua's body functioned in the first century, or in other words, what "model" they used while at their congregational gatherings.

As I have said in the general introduction of this book, if we are indeed living at the very end of *the latter days,* and if we are truly going to (soon) face the rise of the Anti-Messiah's reign over this world, we should expect to pass through some very tough times, which will include severe persecutions! Under such harsh conditions, we certainly won't be able to continue to gather as His body in the way we have been accustomed to up until now.

As I said in the opening chapter, since the beginning of 2020, the world in which we are living has not been the same. As far as Yeshua's body is concerned, this Covid crisis has caused leaders within Yeshua's international body to have to adjust themselves to "a new normal." At least in the first year of this crisis, public gatherings were under new restrictions pertaining to the number of worshipers permitted, the institution of a green pass, mask mandates, and so on.

Interestingly enough, the first century followers of Yeshua were often under severe persecution and thus, forced to gather under many restrictions as well, especially as it related to their numbers (more on that later).

I do believe that God allowed this new Covid-19 crisis to happen for many reasons, one of which was to shake up Yeshua's body in order for true anointed leaders and shepherds to dig deeper into how the first century body really functioned, and to discover the biblical model that they used in their weekly gatherings.

Here I would like to stress one very important point: I do think that the present model used by Yeshua's international body has had its validity and importance! I do not wish to "throw out the baby with the bath water" as it relates to this present model! This model has had its time and season, and for more than one reason. I am persuaded that it existed for the last 16 centuries especially to serve the many gentiles joining into Yeshua's body, this, until *the times of the gentiles is ended.*[349] I do believe that that time period is about to end very soon, and thus, we should strive to get back to the first century model as soon as possible.

This is the time to remember: The main characteristic of the Hebraic/Middle Eastern culture, through which Scripture was written, is <u>cyclical</u> (*That which has been is what will be, that which is done is what will be done, and <u>there is nothing new under the sun,</u>*[350])! Thus, the beginning and the end are strongly connected with events repeatedly occurring! Therefore, it only makes sense that we need this closing chapter, if for nothing else, to better prepare and equip us to,

---

[349] See Lk, 21:24, Rom. 11:25. See also Act. 17:16-31; especially verse 30, where Shaul speaks of these *times of ignorance* that God overlooked… Look also at Yeshua's parable of the *wineskins*… (Matt. 9:14-17). I do believe the time has come for Yeshua to pour out His Holy Spirit in a new way, and for that He wishes His beloved body to get back to the first century *new wine skins*, as there is really *nothing new under the sun*, and the beginning and the end are strongly connected.

[350] See again, Ecc. 1:9. See also verse 10 and all the other references presented inside this book.

sooner than later, consider following the model that was used by our first century brothers and sisters.

The Middle Eastern Hebraic Roots of Yeshua's Body

To better understand the scriptural (first century) model, this chapter will mainly address the following: (1) the biblical definitions and descriptions of the body of believers and its true identity; (2) the first century model, i.e., how Yeshua's followers functioned in their weekly gatherings; and lastly, (3) the way we, living in our present place and time, can get back to that first century model.

The Hebrew Behind the Greek

In the New Covenant writings, there are primarily two Greek words which are associated with what English translations of the Bible describe as "Yeshua's body:"[351] (1) *Kuriakos* ("belonging to the Lord")[352] and (2) *Ecclesia* ("the called-out ones," or "to be called out").[353]

Kuriakos is used only twice in all of the New Covenant writings; however, in both references it does <u>not</u> speak of the body of Messiah itself. In one occurrence, it speaks of *the Lord's Supper*, and in the second, of *the Lord's Day*.[354] On the other hand, *Ecclesia,* in its

---

[351] Or "the church."

[352] G2960 (Strong), κυριακός, *koo-ree-ak-os.'*

[353] G1577 (Strong), ἐκκλησία, *ek-klay-see'-ah*: "a *calling out*"—that is (concretely), a popular *meeting*, especially a religious *congregation* (a Jewish *synagogue* or Christian *community* of members on Earth, or those holy/saints in heaven, or both); *assembly, church.*

[354] See 1 Cor. 11:20 and Rev. 1:10.

different variations, is used well over one hundred times, and it is <u>always</u> connected with the body of believers.[355]

It might surprise some of us, but the term *Ecclesia* and the idea behind it, are not rooted in the New Covenant writings. Its concept and description are deeply rooted in the Tanach.

As stated throughout this book, the vast majority of the Old and the New Covenant books were written by a Middle Eastern people, the Hebrews (Israelites, Jews). As you can see thus far, as an Israeli-born Jewish follower of Israel's Messiah, I constructed the whole book through my Middle Eastern Hebraic/Jewish lens.

So, let's start our journey by going back into the deep Hebraic/Jewish roots of the body of Messiah.

Called Out from the Very Beginning

As mentioned above, *Ecclesia* simply means *the called-out ones* (or *to be called out*). The questions we need to ask here are, *called out* from what? And, do we have any examples in the Tanach of others who were *called out*?

The following are just a few examples of individuals and groups that were *called out* by the Almighty, from the beginning of the history of the people of Israel – The only Nation through which God chose to accomplish His purposes:

- Abraham our father, *the father of our faith,* was *called out* of his own *country,* out of his own *family* and out of his own *father's house.* Yes, he was called out of his whole former life

---

[355] See just a few examples: Matt. 16:18; Acts 2:47, 9:31, 19:32, 19:41; Rom. 16:1; 1 Cor. 1:2; Eph. 5:29; Rev. 3:1, 7, 14.

in Ur and Haran, to the land that would be promised forever to him and his descendants—the land of Canaan, later to be known as the land of Israel. Why was he called out? - To eventually fulfill his calling of being a blessing to all nations.[356]

- Ruth the Moabitess was also *called* to leave everything behind and come *out* of Moab, so that she could join God's chosen people (Abraham's descendants) and fulfill her special calling and great privilege of being King David's great-grandmother and one of the four women mentioned in Yeshua's own genealogy![357]

- King David was *called out* from the role of tending his father's sheep, and into God's great calling upon him to be a shepherd over Israel, as their king and the father, or ancestor, of Israel's very Messiah—*Yeshua, Son of David*.[358]

- Each one of the prophets of old was *called out* to fulfill God's special mission for his or her life.[359]

- The people of Israel were *called out* of Egypt to be God's *kingdom of priests and a holy nation*.[360]

- Israel's Messiah was *called out* of Egypt, to take the position of King and High Priest.[361]

---

[356] See Gen. 12:1-3. See also Rom. 4:1, 16; Gal. 3:7 and many more.

[357] See Ruth 1:14-22, 4:10-22. See also Matt. 1:5-6.

[358] See 1 Sam. 16:11-13; 2 Sam. 2–7. See also Matt. 1:1, 15:22; Lk. 18:38 and more.

[359] See Isa. 6:8; Jer. 1:4.

[360] See Ex. 12-13, 19:6.

[361] See Matt. 2:14-15; Heb. 7:8.

And lastly,

- True followers of Israel's Messiah are *called out* to be *a kingdom of priests and a holy nation.*[362]

Hebrew Names of the *Called Out* and Their Deeper Meanings

The different callings and responsibilities of the Body of Messiah are reflected in the various descriptive names it has been given, starting within the Tanach, and moving through the New Covenant writings: *Kahal* ("Congregation"), *Adat Adonai* ("The Community of the Lord"), *Kalat HaMashiach* ("The Bride of Messiah") and *Avanim Chayot* ("the Temple of Living Stones"). Let us now elaborate on each one of them.

Kahal

The people of Israel who, as we were reminded above, were *called out* of Egypt, were described at times both as *Kahal* and as *Adah* of (or '*Adat*') *Adonai.*[363]

Kahal is based on the Hebrew root "Kuf, Hey, Lamed" (ק.ה.ל) and refers to a group of people gathering together, a congregation of people, and/or an assembly.[364] In modern-day Israel, Messianic Jewish gatherings that meet on the Sabbath day[365] are called *kehilot* (plural) or *kehilah* (singular), both based on this very same root.

---

[362] See 1 Pet. 2:9.

[363] See Num. 17:7, 20:12; Lev. 8:4.

[364] H6951 (Strong), Qahâl. From H6950: *assemblage* (usually concretely): *assembly, company, congregation, multitude.* See Ex. 16:3; Lev. 4:14, 21; Num. 10:7, 16:3; Jer. 31:7; Ezra 10:1; Neh. 13:1.

[365] See a discussion on the Sabbath as the day of worship, at the end of this chapter, in Appendix 1: "The Preferable Day of Gathering."

Now, the interesting thing is that when the Tanach was translated for the first time, from its original Hebrew into Greek, *Kahal* was translated as *Ecclesia*![366]

Adah

Adah (or *'edah'*) is based on the Hebrew root "Ayin, Daled, Hey" (ה.ד.ע), or "Ayin, Daled" (ד.ע), which has been translated as "congregation" or "assembly."[367] It is also connected to two other Hebrew words: *edut* ("witness" and "testimony")[368] and *adi* ("ornament," "jewel," "jewelry" and "precious stone").[369]

Speaking of the root "Ayin, Daled, Hey," it is interesting to note that there is yet another word in Scripture that is based upon this very same root—*eedeem* (or *idim*); only this time it is used in a very negative way: *bigdey idim* (*filthy rags*)![370] Thus, God's *called-out ones* – the body of Messiah – must be careful not to turn into a bunch of self-righteous people, i.e., adopting any kind of religious attitudes; otherwise, all her righteous deeds will be seen *as filthy rags*, and she will – God forbid – *wither and fade as the autumn leaves.*

---

[366] *Septuagint* — Greek translation of the *Tanach*, 3rd century BCE.

[367] H5712 (Strong), 'Edâh. Feminine of H5707 in the original sense of *fixture*; a stated *assemblage* (specifically a *concourse*, or generally, a *family* or *crowd*): *assembly, company, congregation, multitude, people, swarm.* Compare with H5713. See Lev. 8:5; Num. 1:16, 15:36.

[368] See Gen. 31:44, 52; Ex. 23:1; Isa. 43:12, 44:8. Or in Yeshua's words—we are all called to be *the salt* and *the light* of this world, Matt. 5:13-16.

[369] See Ex. 33:4-6, 38:25. See Isa. 61:10 for the connection between *Edah/Adi* (*assembly/jewel*) and *Kalah* (*bride*): *As a bride <u>adorns</u> herself with her <u>jewels</u>.*

[370] See Isa. 64:6.

Kalat HaMashiach (Messiah's Bride)

The term *Messiah's bride* is mentioned only once in Scripture. It is in the closing book of Revelation. There it relates to the heavenly Jerusalem, which will one day descend to Earth.[371]

The question that should be raised here is, why is this heavenly Jerusalem described as *Messiah's bride*? While many Bible scholars and theologians connect Rev. 21 with Scriptures such as Jn. 3:29 and Eph. 5:31-33, the truth is that the concept of God having a bride is deeply rooted in the Tanach, and more specifically in the context of His relationship with His chosen people, Israel! Allow me to elaborate briefly:

When reading the Tanach in Hebrew – its original language – one can easily see that,

(a) God always uses the feminine gender when speaking to the nation of Israel, as if she could be a woman, and not just a woman, but His own wife—His own bride.[372]

(b) when addressing the City of Jerusalem – the very heart of the Land He promised to Israel, His bride – and where His two temples (dwelling places) once stood, God, once again uses the feminine gender. Yes, in Hebrew it reads as if Jerusalem were a woman.

(c) from the immediate context, it is very clear that God is not addressing buildings made of stone and bricks—not even as it

---

[371] See Rev. 21:2. In my understanding, this specific reference in Revelation is connected to Isa. 62:1-5 and 65:18-19.

[372] See example: Isa. 54:5-8. See Ezek. 16 & 23. See also Hos. 2, especially verses 2, 14-16, 19-20.

relates to His dwelling place, the Temple. Rather, He addresses the people residing in and/or visiting this city—His people, His bride![373]

Thus, we can see a clear connection between God's Chosen Nation Israel, His bride, with an earthly Temple in an earthly capital Jerusalem, on the one hand; and the *Israel of God* – that remnant of the *olive tree* of Israel – connected with a heavenly Temple in a heavenly city, on the other hand.[374]

Bride in Hebrew is *kalah* (כלה).[375] Interestingly enough, *kalah* is connected to other Hebrew words like *lechalot* and *tachlit* ("to finish," "to put an end to," or "to bring something to an end").[376] It was on the sixth day, just before finishing His creation work and getting into His seventh day of rest (the *Sabbath*), that God created Adam and his wife Eve, who were the very last to be created. In modern-day Hebrew, one would say they were *"tachlit habriah"* (תכלית הבריאה) — "the end and the very purpose of all creation." We can say that they were the very climax—God's crown of creation.

---

[373] See examples: Isa. 40:1-2, 51:17, 52:1-2, 61:10, 62:5; Jer. 2:2, 13:27; Ezek. 16:2-3, 23:4.

[374] See Rom. 9–11. We discussed the strong and completely inseparable connection between Israel in the *Tanach* and *the Israel of God* in the New Covenant writings in much greater detail, in the previous chapter (chapter two).

[375] 3615 (Strong), kâlâh. A primitive root; to end, whether intransitively (to cease, be finished, perish) or transitively (to complete, prepare, consume): accomplish, cease, consume (away), determine, destroy (utterly), be (when . . . were) done, (be an) end (of), expire, (cause to) fail, faint, finish, fulfil, X fully, X have, leave (off), long, bring to pass, wholly reap, make clean riddance, spend, quite take away, waste.

[376] H8503 (Strong), taklîyth. From H3615: *completion*; by implication, an *extremity*: *end, perfect(-ion)*. See Gen. 2:1; Job 11:7, 26:10.

Note: It does not say that God got up from His (Sabbath) rest and continued to create new things in addition to what He had already created over the course of the previous six days. Once Adam and Eve were created, God *chilah* ("finished") His work![377] In other words, before Adam and Eve had sinned, God actually had called them (mankind) to enter – together with Him – into His Eternal Sabbath rest. Yes. Our original calling, or purpose, as God's body was to be with Him forever and ever, enjoying His eternal rest![378] Yet, we cannot fulfill this great calling without first *lechalot* ("putting an end") to our own ambitions—to our own flesh – or, in the New Covenant wording, we must first *die to self*![379]

A Temple Composed Avanim Chayot

According to the New Covenant writings, the body of believers is also Yeshua's (spiritual) Temple here on Earth. According to this description, each of us, as true followers of Yeshua, is *a living stone* with which this Temple has been built.[380]

As I have mentioned above, the concept of the *called-out* ones – Yeshua's body - is deeply rooted in the Tanach—the only scriptures which were known and read in the first century. What was the biblical basis, therefore, given by both Simon (Peter) and Shaul (Paul) for the above description of Yeshua's body?

Genesis 2:22 states the following, *and he took one of his ribs and closed up the flesh in its place. Then the rib, which the Lord God had*

---

[377] See Gen. 2:1.

[378] See also Heb. 3 & 4, where the writer connects between the very first Sabbath and entering the Promised Land.

[379] See Matt. 16:24-28 and Rom. 12:1-15.

[380] See 1 Pet. 2:4-6. See also Eph. 2:21-22.

taken from the man, He made into a woman and brought her to the man. The English phrase *He made into a woman* is a translation of only one Hebrew word: *va-yiven* ("and He built"). *Vayiven* comes from *ba-nah* ("built")[381] and *banai* ("builder"), which in modern-day Hebrew is usually connected to a mason—one whose profession is to build with stones (in Hebrew, *banai* and *eh-ven* – "stone" – are strongly connected).[382]

Based on the description above therefore, we can see that God, as a very skilled "builder with stones" *built* up a woman, Eve, for the first Adam. A wonderful revelation is that just as He did many centuries ago with Eve, so He has likewise been doing over the last two thousand years for the *second*, or *last Adam*—Yeshua.[383] He has been "building" a second wife (us!), and this time, for His only begotten Son. This "second woman," we, the body of believers, will one day be married to Yeshua! Yes, God *is building* us – Yeshua's bride (the Ecclesia) – just as He did with the first bride or wife, Eve. Thus, we are indeed *being built* as His Temple, *a temple of <u>living stones</u>!*

Here is what we have learned so far:

---

[381] H1129 (Strong), bânâh. A primitive root; to build (literally and figuratively): (begin to) build (-er), obtain children, make, repair, set (up), X surely.

[382] In the Hebrew language, the letters "b" and "v" often interchange (depending on the rabbinic vowels and punctuation system that was developed in the second century and through the tenth century CE). Also, many times, when the Hebrew uses "v" as the preferable pronunciation of the letter ב for the Hebrew reader, it changes into "b" in the English translation (see, for example, the name of the first-born daughter of King Shaul—1 Sam. 14:49. The Hebrew pronunciation of ב is "v" (Merav), while the English translation reads it as "b" (Merab).

[383] See Rom. 5:14-19; 1 Cor. 15:45-49.

- Both the idea and the different meanings of Yeshua's body (*the Ecclesia*) are deeply rooted in the Tanach, which itself is deeply rooted in the Middle Eastern Hebraic culture and mindset.

- The body by definition is a congregation, an assembly of *called-out* people—called out from wherever or whatever they were formerly, into a new calling, God's calling on their lives.

- The body is *called out* to be Yeshua's witnesses, Yeshua's testimony, here on Earth (in New Covenant wording, *you are the salt... you are the light*).

- The body is *called out* to be His ornament, His precious stone— His jewelry.

- The body is *called out* to be the *living stones*, with which His house – the spiritual Temple – is built (while He Himself is its cornerstone).[384]

- The body is *called out* to enter His eternal Sabbath rest.

- The body is *called out* to be His bride (*Kalah*). As such, she is called to discover her *tachlit* (her purpose, her calling in Messiah) and *lechalot* herself (to put an end to herself, to deny herself—*to die to self*), and to live for Him and Him alone!

- In the Greek translation of the Tanach, the nation of Israel was *called out* of Egypt and was at times called *God's ecclesia!*

Now, after explaining the Hebraic/Jewish Middle Eastern concept of the Body, it is time to dive deeper and examine how the first century model functioned and what it looked like.

---

[384] See Isa. 28:16; Ps. 118:22; Acts 4:11; Eph. 2:20.

First Century Model of Yeshua's Body

Reading New Covenant writings that relate to Yeshua's body in the first century and comparing them to what we see and perceive today as His body leads to one conclusion: The first century body and today's body look and function quite differently. Here are only three significant examples:

- Most gatherings of today's body are done in public (rented or purchased) buildings. This puts the community at times under heavy financial burden (high rent, mortgage and the like). Thus, leaders and shepherds often find themselves in need of developing a business plan, calling for special business meetings, and encouraging their members to give extra tithes and offerings... In the New Covenant writings however, we can clearly see that the model was instead, *family-style fellowships*, which were mostly held in private homes.[385]

- In most gatherings of the body today, only the shepherd, deacons, and worship team, which make up about ten to fifteen percent of the whole congregation, are <u>practically</u> active in the weekly gatherings. While this occurs, the rest – well over eighty-five percent! – sit passively, very much like an audience sitting in a movie theater (or at a big concert), taking in whatever they are receiving from the stage in front of them. The New Covenant writings, however, encourage <u>all</u> believers to participate in the weekly gatherings, stating that <u>all</u> true followers of Israel's Messiah have one or more spiritual gifts

---

[385] See examples: 1 Cor. 16:19; Col. 4:15; Phil. 1:2.

and thus, <u>all</u> can and are called to encourage and contribute to the edifying, or building up, of their local body![386]

- In many of the present-day groups, there are clear socio-economic differences between leaders/shepherds and the rest of the members. In the New Covenant writings however, we can see that the members of the first century body did not lack anything, as they all shared whatever they had with one another![387]

As we mentioned above, Yeshua's body of believers was *called out* to be the very <u>*living* stones</u> that constituted His <u>spiritual</u> House. Thus, the first thing we can see at this point, is that the biblical model does <u>not</u> point to any kind of physical buildings comprising stones and bricks. The first century model of the believers had nothing to do with the actual buildings in which they met during their weekly gatherings! This body of *living stones* was rather the believers themselves (the *called-out* ones; the *gathering/assembly*).

Now, naturally any gathering of people needs <u>a physical</u> place where they can meet. Thus, the next question should be, where did the first century believers meet? Where were these *living stones* gathered or assembled for fellowship and for the building up and edifying of one another? Where did they meet to worship and serve the God of Israel together through Yeshua, His only begotten Son?

---

[386] See examples: Rom. 12:4-5; 1 Cor. 12.

[387] See Acts 2:43-47, 4:32-35.

Places of Gathering

According to Scripture, the first century believers met <u>primarily</u> in three places:

- *The Upper Room:*

This description is based on two Greek words:

(1) *Huperōon,* which is mentioned eight different times throughout the New Covenant writings, and which is translated as "upper room," "chamber" or "room;"[388] and

(2) *Anōgēon,* which is translated as "above," "second floor," and "upstairs room."[389]

There are different opinions as to where exactly the first century upper room was located. As we will clearly see later, it could have been at any location and at any home owned by any individual who was part of this first century body of believers.

---

[388]G5253 (Strong), ὑπερῷον, *hoop-er-o'-on.* Neuter of a derivative of G5228; *a higher part of the house,* that is, *apartment* in the third story: *upper chamber (room).* See Acts 1:13, 9:37, 9:39 & 20:8—in this specific verse, it can probably be translated as *the third floor.* See also Acts 9:37, 9:39, 20:8 and 1:13.

[389] G508 (Strong), ἀνώγεοvanōgēon, *an-ogue'-eh-on.* From G507 and G1093: *above the ground,* that is, (properly) *the second floor* of a building; used for a dome or a balcony on the upper story: *upper room.* See Mk. 14:14-15; Lk. 22:12 and Mk. 14:15.

- ### The Temple & Local Synagogues:

The Greek word for "temple" is *Hieron.*[390] It is very interesting to note that Scripture says that they met there daily.[391] It seems that the first century believers did not consider themselves separated from the rest of their nation—the nation of Israel! To the contrary, they worshipped together with non-believing Israelites/Jews in their most important place of worship, at least until its destruction in 70 CE.[392]

Moreover, first century followers of Israel's Messiah did not find it strange, out of place and detached from a correct spiritual order to go and fellowship in synagogues filled with non-believers. A good example is Shaul of Tarsus, who followed the model of Yeshua Himself and visited synagogues while on his apostolic journeys.[393] In one New Covenant reference, it seems that at least some of the believers gathered in their own established synagogue.[394]

---

[390] G2411 (Strong), ἱερόν, *hee-er-on'*. Neuter of G2413: *a sacred place*, that is, *the entire precinct* (whereas G3485 denotes the central sanctuary itself) *of the Temple* (at Jerusalem or elsewhere): *temple*. See Acts 2:46, 5:12, 5:42.

[391] See Acts 3:1-3, 3:8-12.

[392] See Acts 5:20-21; 21:26-30; 22:17; 24:11-12, 17-18; 25:8. See also our discussion regarding the inseparable connection between Yeshua's body and the nation of Israel, in the previous chapter (chapter two).

[393] See Acts 13:5, 14-42, 44-45; 14:1-2; 17:1-3, 10-12, 17; 18:4

[394] G4864 (Strong), Συναγωγή, *soon-ag-o-gay'*. From (the reduplicated form of) G4863: an *assemblage* of persons; specifically, a Jewish "synagogue" (the meeting or the place); by analogy, a Christian *church: assembly, congregation, synagogue.* See Jam. 2:2 (the Greek word translated there as "*assembly*" is *sunagōge* (or *soon-ag-o-gay'*).

- ***Private Homes:***

The Greek word for "private home" is *Oikos*.[395]

By its nature, a private home (with its upper room) cannot hold or host multiple hundreds and certainly not thousands of believers.

Moreover, according to archeological discoveries here in the land of Israel, first century synagogues were mostly small and similarly could not accommodate multiple hundreds or thousands of believers or worshippers at the same time.

In conclusion, the first century believers met primarily in four places: the *upper room,* the *Temple, synagogues,* and *private homes.* How exactly did it work? What did it look like?

Seating Arrangements

As mentioned above, most modern-day believing congregants sit in organized pews, very similar to that of a theater. The congregants are quiet, submissive, and most importantly, *passive*! This way, they do their very best to absorb whatever the rabbi/leader/teacher conveys to them from the front stage/pulpit.

What were the seating arrangements in the first century fellowships? Can we really know? I believe that one doesn't need a Ph.D. to answer that. All we need to do is be open-minded enough to consider the First century Jewish context of the New Covenant writings.

---

[395] G3624 (Strong), οἶκος, *oy'-kos.* Of uncertain affinity; a *dwelling* (more or less extensive, literally, or figuratively); by implication a *family* (more or less related, literally or figuratively): *home, house (-hold), temple.* See Acts 2:2, 2:46, 5:42, 8:3, 20:20, 21:7-14; Rom. 16:5; 1 Cor. 16:19 and Col. 4:15; Phil. 1:2.

Visiting some famous first century archaeological sites here in God's Promised Land, such as the mountain fortress of *Masada* near the Dead Sea, the Jewish village of *Gamla* on the Golan Heights, and the recently discovered synagogue in the city of *Magdala* on the shores of the Sea of Galilee, a very clear picture can be seen.

In those days, synagogues had no pews at all! The seating areas were in the form of stone benches along the walls. It is interesting to note that all synagogues from the first through the four centuries CE had this very same architectural design.

It's fair to say that as far as seating arrangements went, first century synagogues very much resembled <u>living rooms in most private homes</u>! Yes, in first century synagogues, as well as in private homes, people did not sit in pews but rather, <u>facing one another</u>!

Keep in mind: The first century body of believers functioned as one big family. To this very day, normal functioning families throughout the globe do not sit in pews in their living rooms, kitchens or elsewhere in their homes. They naturally and rightly sit facing one another. Yes, normal, healthy families sit around their kitchen tables and when in their living rooms, generally sit in a manner where they can see one another and converse easily.

Let me stress this vitally important point once again: Back during the time of the first century synagogues, Jews fellowshipped, worshipped, read and studied God's holy Word (which included debating it), while facing one another, exactly as they would do when sharing a meal in their own private homes.

Order of Service

After having established the places and seating arrangements of the first century believers' weekly fellowships, it's time to delve deeper and see what their weekly fellowship looked like as well as what that included.

It is my opinion that we can gather considerable information concerning the first century fellowship from the teachings of one apostle in particular, Shaul of Tarsus. This great apostle and man of God, traveled throughout the (then-known) world, while visiting a great many of these home fellowships and synagogues, while also being familiar with the home fellowships and synagogues in Israel. His teachings shed much light on the issues into which we delve in this closing chapter.

Yet, before we deal with the first century order of service, let us describe the modern-day order of service with which we are so familiar.

As an Israeli, I can give examples based on the present-day Messianic Shabbat gatherings in Israel. Nevertheless, I dare say - based on my past teaching and ministering trips in many English-speaking countries - that *most* Israeli Messianic gatherings are no different from Protestant Sunday gatherings abroad...

There is a certain order of service, usually conducted by the leaders/elders at each gathering:

(a) A joint opening prayer/blessing over the service;

(b) A few announcements, limited in time;

(c) Worship for a limited time (i.e., music, songs and the like);[396]

(d) A few testimonies and/or praise reports, which are also limited in time (thus, only a few are welcome to give their testimonies or words of encouragement);

(e) Preaching/teaching, usually given by one of the congregational leaders. This is the main portion of the gathering and thus, is given most of the service time;

(f) A closing prayer (in Messianic congregations, this usually includes the *Aaronic Blessing*[397]).

Most of the weekly gatherings include what is known as "the two sacraments," i.e., water immersion (baptism) of new believers, [398] and the Lord's Supper (known today as *seudat ha-Adon* in Hebrew or, "communion" in English) for born-again members.

Many groups partake in the Lord's Supper only once a month (usually on the first weekend of each month). This is one example of how Messianic congregations are connected by the umbilical cord to Protestant Christianity, which itself is disconnected from its Middle Eastern Hebraic/Jewish roots. It is my understanding that this needs to change in order to be more biblically correct and, as a direct result, to be a better example and witness to our non-believing Jewish brethren.

---

[396] Worship that we are familiar with in our present-day body of believers is not entirely biblically grounded! For more about the Hebrew meaning and concept of *worship*, please see Appendix 4: "Worship" at the end of this closing chapter.

[397] See Num. 6:24-26.

[398] See Appendix 3: "Water Immersion in the first century" at the end of this closing chapter.

In conclusion, the above order of service in our modern-day believing groups is imported from abroad (mainly from the western Protestant Church tradition).[399] The problem I see with this is that it is detached from the first century, Middle Eastern Jewish/Hebraic biblical context. It is my hope that the explanation below will shed some light on this.

Now is the time to look at how things were run and what they looked like in the First century.

There is one very important (yet general) statement concerning the first century believers' gatherings and the things they involved. This statement followed the great and very significant Feast of Shavuot ("Pentecost"), during which God's Holy Spirit[400] fell upon Yeshua's followers:

And they continued steadfastly in <u>*the apostles' doctrine*</u>*, and* <u>*fellowship*</u>*, and in the* <u>*breaking of bread*</u>*, and in* <u>*prayers*</u>[401] (emphases added).

As we can see, <u>four activities</u> are mentioned in this verse. The following is an elaboration and explanation of each one of the four, while using other scriptures that shed considerable light on what the gatherings of the first century believers looked like.

---

[399] For my suggestion for a home fellowship order of service, see Appendix 6, at the end of this closing chapter.

[400] In Hebrew, *Ruach Hakodesh,* "the Spirit of Holiness" or "the Spirit of the Holy [One]."

[401] See Acts 2:42.

The Apostles' Doctrine

This above term is mentioned only in this particular scripture.[402] The question we should ask is, what was this *doctrine* that the apostles taught back in the first century?

Let's start with the Greek word translated here as *doctrine*. The word is *didache* (or *did-akh-ay,* which is based on another Greek word, *didaskalia*).[403] It can be translated as both "to learn" and "to teach." No wonder then that it was translated in different English versions of the Bible as *instruction, teaching* and/or *doctrine*.

What follows are all eight places where this word (*didache*) is mentioned throughout the New Covenant writings. As you see them altogether, you will clearly understand the true meaning behind the term *the apostles' doctrine*.

1. The very first time this term is mentioned follows the conclusion of what we know as the Sermon on the Mount. The multitudes who heard Yeshua's extraordinary teachings *"were astonished at His teaching/doctrine ('didache')."*[404]

2. Following Yeshua's response to those who questioned the resurrection of the dead, a topic of much debate among schools of thought at the time, they *were astonished at His teaching/doctrine (didache).*[405]

---

[402] See Acts 2:42.

[403] G1322 (Strong), Διδαχή, didachē, *did-akh-ay'*. From G1321: *instruction* (the act or the matter): *doctrine, hath been taught.*

[404] See Matt 7:28.

[405] See Matt. 22:33.

3.   Connected to Yeshua's teachings from the Torah, the Prophets, and related deeds while in the synagogue in Capernaum, they *were astonished at His teaching/doctrine (didache).*[406]

4.   Following Yeshua's teachings in the Temple in Jerusalem, they *were astonished at His teaching, or doctrine* (*didache*). [407]

5.   The fifth time relates to the teachings that the apostles spread throughout the Temple's courts: *You have filled Jerusalem with your doctrine.*[408]

6.   Here, *didache* relates to the teachings of Yeshua as presented by two apostles (Shaul and Barnabas) to *Sergius Paulus.*[409]

7.   This time is in the context of a teaching delivered by yet another (second-generation) apostle of Yeshua, Timothy.[410]

8.   The eighth and final time this specific Greek word is mentioned is connected to teachings of the apostles relating to *Immersions, the laying on of hands, the resurrection of the dead and eternal judgment.*[411]

Let us draw two main conclusions based upon the above eight appearances of the word *didache* (teaching, instruction, doctrine):

(A) Based on the first four references, all of Yeshua's teachings (*didache*) were good and correct interpretations of the teachings,

---

[406] See Mk. 1:22. See repeated also in Lk. 4:32.

[407] See Mk. 11:18.

[408] See Acts 5:28.

[409] See Acts 13:12.

[410] See 1 Tim. 4:1.

[411] See Heb. 6:2.

instructions and doctrines already presented in the Tanach – mainly in God's Holy Torah! After all, didn't Yeshua Himself say, *Do not think that I came to destroy the Law or the prophets; I did not come to destroy but to fulfill?*[412] As mentioned in the previous chapter (chapter two), the terms *to fulfill* and *to destroy* are still in use within Orthodox Jewish circles, and they still have the very same meaning they had more than two thousand years ago: *To fulfill* means to give the correct interpretation, while *to destroy* means to give an incorrect interpretation.

When teaching the Sermon on the Mount and the crowds in the synagogue at Capernaum, as well as those at the Temple in Jerusalem, Yeshua's teachings (*didache* or *doctrine*) were the actual fulfillment (i.e., the right or correct interpretations) of the *Tanach* doctrines![413]

(B) The last four references (5 through 8) deal with teachings delivered by the apostles and Timothy, both at the Temple in Jerusalem and (in synagogues) outside of God's Promised Land. What could the apostles teach in addition to what they had already learned from Yeshua, their great rabbi (teacher)?

Does it make any sense now, after His ascension back into heaven, that they would invent new doctrines or new teachings? Hadn't they

---

[412] See Matt. 5:17.

[413] In the Tanach, *"Torah"* or *"Law,"* has to do with instructions or teachings and not merely laws. In the New Covenant, it was translated (in Greek) as *"Nomos"*: G3551 (Strong), Νόμος, Nomos, *nom'-os*. From a primary word, νέμω, nemō (to *parcel* out, especially *food* or *grazing* to animals); *law* (through the idea of prescriptive *usage*), generally (*regulation*), specifically (of Moses [including the volume]; also, of the Gospel), or figuratively (a *principle*): *law*. In well over ninety percent of the references where it is mentioned, it has to do with the Law of Moses (see just a few examples: Lk. 2:22; Jn. 18:31, 19:7; Acts 13:39, 15:5; Heb. 10:28).

spent more than three years with the greatest Teacher ever? Hadn't Yeshua continued to teach them even after His glorious resurrection, for 40 more days?[414] Were they not all His *talmidim* (Hebrew for *disciples*)? Had he not given them the great commission to go and make *talmidim* of all nations?[415]

Given that all of Yeshua and His first century followers' *didache* (*teaching, doctrine*) was solely based on the Tanach (just a reminder that New Covenant writings had not yet been canonized back then), it is no wonder at all that a careful reading of the New Covenant writings shows that an integral part of the service, in the first century body, was the public reading of Scripture and its elaboration. This was based on the Jewish tradition of reading selected, consecutive portions of the Torah (the five books of Moses; in Hebrew: *Parashat Hashavua* — the portion of the week) and the Prophets (in Hebrew, *Haftarah*) every Sabbath.[416]

---

[414] See Acts 1:1-11.

[415] See Matt. 28:18-20. This verse can also be translated as: *"Go you, therefore, and teach all nations, baptizing them."* Interestingly, two Greek words are mentioned in this specific verse in connection with *teaching* and *disciples: didache* and *matheteuo (math-ayt-yoo'o)—to become a pupil, a disciple, instruct* and *teach*. Notice please, Yeshua does not commission us to go and "save all nations" (or individuals amongst the nations)! He rather wants us to make them disciples/talmidim! When considering the Hebrew language, it is interesting to note that *talmidim* is strongly connected to the other Hebrew words *lilmod, lemida, and limudim* – to *study/learn, studying/learning* and teachings/lessons/studies – again, showing the relationship between a *talmid/disciple/pupil/student* and his *teacher*, the one who teaches and passes his teachings on to him, so that he can then pass it on to others after him. No real *talmid* would teach anything which is not the very same teaching he has received from His Master teacher (in this case, Yeshua) or, at least based on everything his Master teacher has taught him!

[416] See Lk. 4:16-22; Acts 13:15, 27; Col. 4:16; 1 Thes. 5:27.

Fellowship

Another element mentioned as it relates to the first century gatherings was *fellowship*. The Greek word used for fellowship is *koinōnia* (*koy-nohn-ee'-ah*) and has to do with "partnership," "participation" or (social) "interaction," "communication," "communion," "distribution" and, of course, *fellowship*. It occurs twenty times in the New Covenant writings.[417] As we can see, the term *koinōnia* covers quite a broad spectrum of concepts. I would like to cover what I consider to be the most important amongst them in the following paragraphs.

One Body — Different Gifts

Between the years 1973 and 1980, I lived on a kibbutz.[418] When I first read the New Covenant's description of the first century body of believers, especially the way in which they had functioned, I could not ignore the similarities between their lifestyle and the one practiced in the kibbutz.

The kibbutz's original (socialistic) ideology encouraged its members to share almost everything they had, leaving them with almost zero personal possessions. The first century body of believers also shared everything they had, and (at least at the beginning) they did not consider anything as their own.[419] Furthermore, it seems as if they

---

[417] G2842 (Strong), Κοινωνία, *koinōnia*. From G2844.

[418] *Kibbutz* (Hebrew)—a communal farm, where, at the beginning of the 20th century, socialistic ideals were first implemented in Israel by Jewish pioneers.

[419] See Acts 2:44-45, 4:32. Besides the similarities with the kibbutz lifestyle, I also see great similarities between the first century believers' lifestyle and that of one of the contemporary Jewish groups called "the Essenes." The Essenes were a Jewish sect during the second Temple period that flourished from the second century BCE to the First century CE. They were mostly known for leaving

made a great impact on their surroundings. They were full of joy and enthusiasm and saw themselves as being responsible for one another.[420] At least in the beginning, they were accepted and appreciated by the non-believing Jews.[421]

Let us state a crucially important fact: The vast majority of Shaul's epistles were addressed to all believers, not only to the ones who were in leadership positions![422] Shaul was very clear in stating, again and again, that we – all of the followers of Israel's King and Savior – are *members* of *one body*.[423]

Moreover, he clearly stated that in this *one body*, each member has different callings and gifts. All are expected to be active in contributing from the treasures which God has deposited within them. Every member is important to the edification of this *one body*, and that would include even those members whom we tend to consider feeble, not so important or hidden away from sight.[424] According to this great

---

everything behind, for settling into a communal kind of lifestyle within the desert regions of Israel. They believed in piety, celibacy and the absence of personal property and money.

[420] See Acts 2:46, 4:32.

[421] See Acts 2:43-47. Many miracles, signs and wonders were done on behalf of the non-believing brethren (mostly, but not only, by the apostles). See Acts 3:1-10, 33; 5:12, 15-16; 6:8; 8:5-8, 13; 9:32-34, 40-42.

[422] See a few of the many examples: Rom. 1:6-8; 12:1 — *My brethren;* 12:3 — *To every man that is among you…;* 1 Cor. 1:2, 10-11; Gal. 1:2; Eph. 1:1. Moreover, Shaul did not limit his instructions to only the weekly services but directed them to the believers' daily life!

[423] See, for example, Rom. 12:4.

[424] See 1 Cor. 12:22-24.

rabbi, if the above is not applied or implemented, this *one body* cannot and will not function properly![425]

Relationships Between the Members of the Body

According to Shaul, every member is responsible for taking good care of the other members.[426]

When seeking counsel or just judgment, believers should do so within this one body, rather than look outside for non-believers' advice or judgments.[427]

Believers should not be afraid (or act politically correct) when dealing with issues such as sex, virginity, married and non-married members, eating, drinking, etc.[428]

Holiness is Required from Every Member of the Body

Shaul emphasized that holiness is required from <u>all</u> true followers of Yeshua![429] This is holiness that includes even rejecting or refusing to fellowship with people who continually live in sin nor wish to repent and change their ways.[430]

Moreover, it seems that back then even "a small sin" (such as "a white lie") was not acceptable and was dealt with severely, which led to

---

[425] See Rom. 12:6-8. According to 1 Cor. 11-14, *every believer* has one or more spiritual gifts and *callings* he/she should apply in the weekly gatherings (see 1 Cor. 12:4-11; look especially at verse 7. See also 12:12-21).

[426] See 1 Cor. 12:25-26.

[427] See 1 Cor. 6.

[428] See 1 Cor. 7, 8 and 10.

[429] See Eph. 5:27; 1 Thes. 3:13, 4:4, 4:7; Heb. 12:14.

[430] See 1 Cor. 5 and 6.

even more fear/reverence of God within the body.[431] One phrase that Shaul repeated twice in his epistles (in slightly different ways), was *deliver such a one unto Satan for the destruction of the flesh, that the spirit may be saved in the day of the Lord Yeshua.*[432] What exactly did this phrase mean? There are different ways to interpret it. According to my understanding, he spoke of excommunicating a brother or sister from the local home fellowship, in the hope that it would cause them to truly repent and then be restored back into the believing community.

Putting the Emphasis Where It Should Be Put

There are many religions and cults in the world today. Within the Protestant movement, there are more than thirty thousand different denominations (this has occurred only since the 16th century)! One big reason for this, in my opinion, is pride and selfishness on the part of some leaders within the body. Pride and selfishness are the opposite of having or possessing *love,* the kind of *love* Messiah has towards each one of us. I do believe that when we lack *Messiah's love* within, it will also cause us (especially leaders) to be unable to *rightly divide the word of truth.*[433]

Shaul emphasized again and again the unconditional and true kind of *love* that should exist in this *one body* of believers. This love, coupled with a humble attitude and spirit of meekness, should include the

---

[431] See Acts 5:1-11.

[432] See 1 Cor. 5:2; 1 Tim. 1:20.

[433] See 2 Tim. 2:14-15.

willingness to be hurt by other members in the body, something that is inevitable, rather than the impulse to be angry, fight back, etc.[434]

Doing Everything Within God's Order

When speaking of the First century fellowship as "one big family," one might consider or associate it with modern-day Israeli culture, which encompasses a great deal of "balagan."[435] And indeed, from Shaul's epistles it might sound as if the first century body did have a tendency towards some Israeli balagan.

Shaul tells us that while in our weekly gatherings, when fellowshipping with one another, *all things should be done decently and in order, as God is not the author of confusion but of peace!*[436] That's exactly where leaders come into the picture. While every member is indeed important and should participate and share the gifts and skills given to them, there is also a great need for leaders in every fellowship to maintain Godly order!

Scripture is clear: God, in His great wisdom and will, appointed some as *apostles,* some as *prophets,* some as *teachers, miracle workers, healers, helpers, and officials (leaders,* as some translations read), those who *speak in tongues,* those who *interpret tongues,* etc. Shaul is crystal clear that we are not all called to do the same thing while

---

[434] See Yeshua's words in Jn. 13:34. See also Rom. 12:3, 9, 10, 13, 15 and 16; 1 Cor. 6:7, 13:1-13; Gal. 5:22; Eph. 1:17-18, 3:16-19; 1 Jn. 4:8 — *for God is love!* (It seems that true love is the hardest thing to apply, simply because it involves a certain amount of *death to self!*)

[435] *balagan* (Hebrew idiom) — describing part of the modern-day Israeli culture that includes a mentality of disorder, messiness, chaos, etc.

[436] See 1 Cor. 14:26-40, especially verses 33 and 40.

fellowshipping together. We are *not* all leaders. We are *not* all teachers or all prophets and so on!

In every fellowship/group, there must be a leader to lead, a teacher to teach, a prophet to encourage (and if necessary, also to rebuke/reprove some), one with *a word of knowledge*, one with *the gift of service*, one who is gifted in writing songs, one who is gifted in singing, and so forth and so on...[437]

In the following paragraphs, I would like to further elaborate on the kind of true leadership needed in each of the (private home) fellowships of the body.

Shepherds, Elders and Teachers

As mentioned above, it is clear from Scripture that there are a few specific (spiritual) gifts and callings which have to do with leadership roles within the body.[438] It is my understanding that the callings and gifts of shepherds, elders and teachers are very similar.[439] Since the greatest leader of all is Yeshua Himself, and since He referred to Himself by saying, *I Am the Good Shepherd*,[440] I would like to deal mainly with the role of the shepherd within God's body.

---

[437] See 1 Cor. 14:1-33.

[438] See 1 Cor. 12:28; Eph. 4:11. In my understanding, being an *apostle* is not a *calling* or *a gift* that is usually exercised or expressed in the weekly gatherings. Rather, it has to do with establishing new fellowships in different places, visiting them periodically and overseeing them.

[439] See Acts 20:28 and 1 Pet. 5:1-4.

[440] See Jn. 10:11, 14.

As it pertains to all the doctrines and concepts within the New Covenant writings, so it is here also: The concept of *a shepherd* is very well-rooted in the Tanach. Let us examine now a few references.

The very first shepherd mentioned in Scripture was Abel. Other famous biblical figures who were also shepherds were Rachel, Jacob, Joseph and his brothers, Moses, and King David. Even the people of Israel were described as shepherds.[441]

The Hebrew word for *shepherd* is *ro'eh* (רועה). Its main meanings are "to tend a flock" (to "pasture it"), "to graze" and "grazing area or field." As Hebrew words are based on two to four root letters, it is very interesting to examine the root for *Ro'eh*: It is, *"Resh, Ayin, Hey"* (ר.ע.ה), and/or, just "Resh, Ayin" (ר.ע).[442] The following are a few other Hebrew words which are derived from this same root:

Re'ah and *Re'ut* (רע/רעות, "a friend"/"friendship"/"neighbor" and "lover").[443]

Ra and *Ra'ah* (רעה/רע, "bad"/"evil").[444]

---

[441] See Gen. 4:2, 29:9, 30:31, 37:2, 46:32-34, 47:3; Ex. 3:1; 1 Sam. 16:11, 17:34.

[442] H7462 (Strong), *râ'âh*. A primitive root: to *tend* a flock, that is, to *pasture* it; intransitively, to *graze* (literally or figuratively); generally, to *rule*; by extension, to *associate* with (as a friend): X break, companion, keep company with, devour, eat up, evil entreat, feed, use as a friend, make friendship with, herdsman, keep [sheep] (-er), pastor, + shearing house, shepherd, wander, waste.

[443] See Lev. 19:18; Judg. 14:20; 2 Sam. 15:37; Jer. 3:20; Prov. 27:10; Mt. 22:39.

[444] See Gen. 50:20; Ex. 10:10; Num. 14:27; Deut. 31:18, 29; 1 Sam. 16:14-15, 19:9, 25:21; and many more.

Ro'eh/Reut Ruach/Epher, Re'ah (רועה/רעות רוח/אפר, "to feed on the ashes/wind;" "neighbor" "friend").[445]

Here, we once again can see the beauty of the Hebrew language. Out of the same root, different words emerge with completely different meanings. Yes, *ro'eh* (a shepherd) is called to be *a good shepherd.* He is to *love* his flock, to *befriend* his flock, to treat it as if it were his own *neighbor* (*Re'ah*).

If the *shepherd* is not mindful enough to fulfill all of the above, he is then considered to be a *bad* shepherd, or "an evil one" (*Ra*). He can *abuse* his flock and think that nobody sees him and his evil actions. Consequently, that kind of shepherd is as one who is *feeding on the wind/ashes (Ro'eh/Reut Ruach/Epher).*

Notice that God is described in the Scriptures as the *shepherd of Israel.*[446] And, as previously mentioned, His Son, Yeshua, referred to Himself by saying, *I Am the Good Shepherd.*[447]

In Scripture, there is one story that sums up all that God and Yeshua expect from those called to be shepherds in His flock - Messiah's very body. It is recorded in Jn. 21. This beautiful narrative describes the third time that the resurrected Messiah appears to His disciples. In this incident, it occurs on the shores of the *Sea of Tiberias.* Yeshua calls Simon Cephas (Peter) to be a shepherd to His flock—His body. A careful reading of this story reveals the main characteristics of a good shepherd according to Yeshua, the greatest *Shepherd* of all.

---

[445] See Isa. 44:20; Jer. 31:10; Hos. 12:2; Mic. 7:14; Ecc. 1:14, 2:11; Lev. 19:13, 16, 18.

[446] See Gen. 48:15, 49:24; Isa. 40:11; Ezek. 34:12-15; Ps. 80:2.

[447] See Jn. 10:11, 14. See also Heb. 13:20; 1 Pet. 2:25. See also Zech. 11:16, 13:7; Ps. 23:1-3.

Initially, it seems as if Yeshua repeats Himself three times with the same words, or instructions, *Feed my lambs. Feed my sheep. Feed my sheep.*[448] Nevertheless, when digging deeper into the (Greek) words that the Apostle John quotes from Yeshua's mouth,[449] we can see the description and the role which is expected of a true shepherd.

The first time Simon confesses his love for his Master, Yeshua instructs or commands him to *bos'-ko* ("to pasture," "to graze"/"to feed"/"to keep") My *Ar-nee'-on* ("a lambkin"/"lamb"). In other words, Yeshua calls Simon to feed and protect <u>the little ones—the more sensitive, feeble, and vulnerable sheep</u>.

The second time Simon confesses his love for his Master, Yeshua instructs or commands him to *poy-mah'ee-no* ("to tend as a shepherd"/"to feed and to rule over") My *Prob'-at-on* ("a sheep"/"sheep[-fold]"). This time Yeshua calls Simon to rule or lead the entire sheepfold—<u>young and old alike</u>. Yeshua calls Simon to have a vision for his flock, to look to their future and thus, to provide them with the direction in which they should go.

The third and last time Simon confesses his love for his Master, Yeshua instructs or commands him to again *bos'-ko* ("to pasture," "to graze"/"to feed"/"to keep") My *Prob'-at-on* ("a sheep"/"sheep[-fold]"). Yeshua calls Simon to be a good shepherd, to feed and protect <u>the entire flock</u>.

---

[448] See Jn. 21:15-17.

[449] I do *not* think Israel's Messiah spoke Greek to His disciples. Nevertheless, and unfortunately, we do not have the original Hebrew (and partly Aramaic) manuscript of at least some of the New Covenant writings, which I believe are still "hidden" somewhere.

Needless to say, all that Yeshua asked of his disciple was to <u>imitate Him</u> and <u>take the example directly from Him</u>, *The Good Shepherd,* who feeds, protects and leads His entire flock—the little ones, the more sensitive, the feeble and the vulnerable; as they all make up His bride—His body!

Moreover, all of the above is directly connected to the level of a loving relationship a good shepherd has with His Master Shepherd, Yeshua! The more he loves the Master Shepherd, the more he will be like Him, a good shepherd. Here it is:

When Yeshua asks Simon three times, *Do you love me?*[450] The Greek uses two different words for *love: Agape* and *Phileo. Agape* is a very deep kind of love. While it comprises strong emotions, it also demands a complete submission of one's free will to an authority that is higher than him (which in this case is Yeshua—the Good Shepherd). *Agape* is a kind of love that expresses a complete loyalty and obedience to that higher authority.[451] *Phileo,* on the other hand, is more about very strong emotions toward an object of love, a kind of love that can be influenced or moved by changing circumstances of life.[452]

---

[450] See again Jn. 21:15-17.

[451] G25 (Strong), ἀγαπάω, *agapaō.* Perhaps from ἄγαν, *agan* (*much;* or compare [H5689]); to *love* (in a social or moral sense): *(be-) love (-ed).* Compare G5368. See, for example, Jn. 3:16; 1 Jn. 4:7-8.

[452] G5368 (Strong), Φιλέω, *phileō.* From G5384: to *be a friend to* (*fond of* [an individual or an object]); that is, *have affection* for (denoting *personal* attachment, as a matter of sentiment or feeling); while G25 is wider, embracing especially the judgment and the *deliberate* assent of the will as a matter of principle, duty and propriety: the two thus stand related very much as G2309 and G1014, or as G2372 and G3563, respectively; the former being chiefly of the *heart* and the latter of the *head*); specifically to *kiss* (as a mark of tenderness): *kiss, love.* See, for example, Matt. 6:5, 10:37; Jn. 5:20.

Yeshua twice addresses Simon with his question, using the word *agape.* The last time He addresses Simon, He uses the word *phileo.* Simon, on the other hand, uses only *phileo* to express his love towards his Master—all three times! The implication is this. While Yeshua, the only begotten Son of God, has <u>a perfect kind of love, *agape*</u>, which is steadfast and unchangeable, <u>Peter's love, *phileo*, is movable/unsteady</u> and dependent upon changing circumstances! Thus, Simon Peter, and everyone else who wishes to be a good shepherd, even in this present day, needs to be careful to be attuned to His Master's Spirit, to beseech the Master Shepherd for His mercies and grace, so that he is able to follow His Master's example of what it really means to be a good shepherd![453]

When shepherds follow the example of the Good Shepherd, it leads them to love their flock with the kind of love that the Master Shepherd has for them, i.e., to be willing to give up their lives for their sheep—the members of His body![454] Yes, what is expected from the leaders in Yeshua's body (apostles, shepherds, elders, teachers, deacons, etc.) is a higher calling than what is expected from the other members of the body! For example, they are expected to have much higher moral standards.[455] Real shepherds need to "calculate the costs" before taking on such a high position with such great responsibility in the body of Messiah!

With this consideration, we can better understand why the apostle warns us to, *obey your leaders and submit to them, for they keep*

---

[453] See Heb. 13:7-9, 17.

[454] See Jn. 13:34, 15:13.

[455] See 1 Tim. 3:2, 3:12; Tit. 1:6, 2:2.

watch over our souls, as those who will give an account ... and *the elders who rule well, are to be considered worthy of double honor!*[456]

On the one hand, the members of the body should take good care of the ones who are called to lead them. That also includes, <u>at times - when appropriate</u> - providing financial covering for leaders, such as apostles, shepherds, elders, teachers, and evangelists. Yet, on the other hand, those who are truly called by God to leadership positions should <u>not</u> take advantage of their high position within the Body and should do their very best <u>not</u> to be a burden to the other members![457] I do believe that this specific topic requires some additional attention.

One of the biggest evils mentioned in Scripture is the *love of money!*[458] We must be honest with ourselves and humbly admit that it is very tempting for some of us here in God's Promised Land, as well as in other places in the world, who believe we were called to some kind of leadership position, to imitate the way things are done in the non-believing world that surrounds us. Many of us are strongly tempted to open our own ministries, asking people to "partner with us" (i.e., to support us financially). Some well-intentioned believers, with or without noticing, have turned their ministries into a well-greased

---

[456] See Heb. 13:17; 1 Tim. 5:17. See also 1 Thes. 5:12-13.

[457] See 1 Cor. 9. As mentioned in the Introduction, in many modern-day congregations, there is a socio-economic difference between the shepherds and the rest of the congregants. Life in Israel is not easy, to say the least! Wars and rumors of wars, threats from within and from beyond our borders are "a given" on a daily basis. High taxes (especially upon the middle-class), high rental prices—not to mention the near impossibility of trying to purchase your own apartment or house, and so on. Add to all that the new Covid crisis, and you get the picture.

[458] See 1 Tim. 6:10. See related references: Ex. 23:8; Isa. 5:23; Prov. 11:28. Yeshua was very clear regarding people (leaders and non-leaders alike) who gather treasures here on Earth—thus, we *all* should pay careful attention to His words in Matt. 6:19-24, 19:16-30.

(worldly) business, and this should <u>not</u> be done—not here in God's Promised Land, nor elsewhere in the world! Those who feel called to leadership positions should first close the door behind themselves, go on their knees and ask HIM, the Great Leader and Shepherd, to open (financial) doors for them, without needing to sometimes employ manipulative tactics.[459]

People in leadership positions within the Body, should be very careful not to abuse their God-given gifts or skills or to use them in an evil way. As mentioned above (see the root letters of *ro'eh*/shepherd), a *shepherd* can be the opposite of what God expects him to be. He can actually be an evil *shepherd*, one who abuses the flock which God has put under his care. He can end up being the one who sucks the life out of his sheep for his own benefit and one who fails to operate in real love or compassion for his flock. Scripture has enough examples of evil *shepherds* whose evil deeds have been seen by God Almighty and who will therefore be rightly and justly judged on the dreadful day of judgment![460]

---

[459] One of the well-practiced ways of manipulating people to support leaders (whether knowingly or unknowingly) is by encouraging them to have more faith, and to give tithes and offerings even when they really cannot afford to do so... The Apostle clearly instructs us to give *according to what we have*, not according to what we do not have (see 2 Cor. 8:12-15 and 9:5-15). Note that tithing is mentioned only twice in the New Covenant writings - in Matt. 23:23 and, its equivalent, Lk. 11:42; and in Heb. 7:1-10, where the writer affirms that tithing is connected directly to the Temple services and the Levitical order, i.e., the Mount Sinai Covenant. Meanwhile, according to the Melchizedek order, i.e., the New Covenant, God does not limit you to giving the tithe alone, but rather to give according to your own ability. The key is to give whatever you give with a cheerful heart!

[460] See Jer. 10:21, 12:10, 23:1-7, 25:34-38; Ezek. 34; Zech. 10:2-3.

Breaking of Bread

The third point that Scripture reveals to us regarding the first century believers' gatherings, is that they were *breaking bread from house to house...*[461] What does *breaking bread* really mean when considering its Hebraic/Jewish Middle Eastern roots?

First, in Scripture, *bread* does not always speak of bread alone, but rather of meals that most times included bread.[462]

Second, why *breaking* and not simply "eating," "sharing," and so on? To answer this, we need to be acquainted with the Jewish tradition of blessing God for the food before partaking of it. Before sharing a meal together, Jews traditionally bless a piece of bread while breaking it.[463] A good example is the short ceremony called *kiddush*, which is done at the entrance of the Sabbath day (*Erev Shabbat* - Friday evening) in every observant Jewish home. This ceremony includes the blessings over the wine and the bread, which is broken into small pieces and then passed around to everyone around the Shabbat table. It is also done with the unleavened bread (Matza) at the *seder meal*, which marks the beginning of the Feast of Passover. Yeshua, the greatest Jew of all, did the very same thing on that Passover two thousand years ago, except that He gave it a much deeper meaning, which also led to what we know today as "the Lord's Supper" or "Communion."[464]

---

[461] See Acts 2:42, 46.

[462] See Gen. 18:5 (from the immediate context, we can see that Abraham did not serve the angels only bread); Gen. 31:54, 37:25, 41:54; Ex. 2:20; Deut. 8:9; Prov. 30:8; Matt. 6:11, 14:19; Mk. 7:5; Lk. 7:36; Acts 10:10; and more.

[463] Shaul followed this Jewish tradition of *breaking of bread*, as well (see Acts 20:7, 11; 27:35. See 1 Cor. 11:20-34).

[464] See Lk. 22:19-20. Unlike today's Christian (as well as Messianic) congregations, it seems that back in the first century, communion was an integral part of the

Prayer

The last point mentioned in Acts 2:42, is *prayer*. Indeed, joint public prayers were an integral part of the first century body of believers.[465] This fact should not at all surprise us, as collective prayers were and are still to this day, an integral part of the Jewish service in synagogues. Remember that, at least at the beginning, these synagogues were attended by Messianic Jews as well.[466] One good example for the centrality of prayer in Jewish life was the disciples' request to Yeshua to teach them *how to pray,* as they were accustomed to seeing other rabbis, such as John the Immerser, teach their own disciples how to pray.[467]

As we very well know, prayer was an integral part of the Master's life, and many times it was accompanied by fasting as well! When discussing the *apostle's doctrine,* we said that they taught others what they had themselves learned from their great Teacher and Master. So, it is no wonder they were interested in the preservation of prayer as an integral part of their weekly gatherings.[468]

---

festive meals which were shared by the believers when meeting for their weekly gatherings in one of the congregants' private homes. For more details, please see Appendix 2 at the end of this closing chapter.

[465] See 1 Cor. 11:3-16, 14:34-35.

[466] See, for example, Matt. 6:5; Mk. 11:25.

[467] See Lk. 11:1.

[468] See Matt. 6:17, 14:23; Mk. 2:18, 6:46; Lk. 2:37, 9:28, 22:44, 17:21; Acts 27:21.

A Call to Adopt the First Century Model

As I have said in both the opening general introduction to this book and the specific one at the beginning of this closing chapter, it has already been close to three years that the world in which we live has truly become a changed world. The forced changes, at least in the first year of this Covid crisis, should have challenged shepherds and leaders within Yeshua's Body to ask some crucially important questions such as, is God using this world crisis to call us to go back and adopt the model used by Yeshua's body in the first century? Are we willing to give up the goodies the present-day model has provided? Are we willing to take the time that is needed before Him, to weigh all that has been written thus far, and be ready to do whatever He tells us in order to follow whatever direction He instructs us to take?

The Covid Crisis and God's Calling for a Reset within His Own Body

As we discussed in the opening chapter, it is my understanding that our world is now in a reset mode. Those of us who are members of respectively large gatherings, could feel, at least during the first year of this pandemic, the dramatic changes that have been imposed by our authorities, including limitations on the number of attendees at each service, the instruction to wear masks while inside the congregational building, as well as sitting in capsules, separated by plastic (or any kind of) temporal walls, etc. At certain times, we have not even been allowed to gather in the congregational building and, consequently, have needed all kinds of electronic or digital ways in order to be able to communicate with one another.

Can it be that our Father in heaven is using current events to shake us – His body – and bring us back to the model that used to function so much more effectively in the first century? If the answer is yes, then it perfectly fits into what we already have said about the main characteristic of the Hebraic/Jewish Middle Eastern mindset, i.e., everything is indeed cyclical, and *that which has been is what will be; that which is done is what will be done; and, nothing is new under the sun.*[469] God is indeed calling us back to the path He originally intended for His body to take!

Home Gatherings

I am suggesting that God might be calling His Body to return to the first century model of *home fellowships*. However, having said that, I do think it is on the true humble leaders and shepherds in the body to encourage and lead this crucially important move.

Leaders and shepherds should consider, through prayer and fasting, who among their congregants is *called* and thus, suited to be a leader, teacher, elder and so on, in order to encourage them accordingly with their blessing to go ahead and open their own home fellowship.

The above does not at all mean that the respected original leaders have now retired... To the contrary! They should continue to lead their own respective home fellowship while overseeing the new home gatherings. Like Shaul, they should also take care of the different home fellowships that they have established. They should visit them at times, teach and encourage them and based on their wealth of experience, also give them good counsel.[470]

---

[469] See again, Ecc. 1:9, 2:15.

[470] See Acts 14:21-23, 15:36-41, 16:4-5, 18:23, 20:1-2, 17-38 and 21:7-9. See also 1 Tim. 1:3, 4:13; Tit. 1:5-6.

Community Living

As it was in the first century model, so it should also be in the present day. Just as home fellowships were not limited only to their weekly gatherings as they lived in their local communities, so present-day fellowships should also be in contact or in touch throughout the week, with the weekly gathering being the climax of this community-based type of lifestyle.

I believe home fellowships should strive to be open to non-believing neighbors in their surroundings. They should not become a restricted club; they should not live in a bubble; and they should certainly not scare people off with a sense of exaggerated religiosity.

I believe local home fellowships should be attuned to what's happening around them in the outside world, be aware of current news, and yes, even be involved, as long as it does not contradict their faith or convictions as it relates to local affairs of the community. I do believe all of us - followers of Yeshua - should be light, salt and a good testimony wherever we go and in whatever we do. We should love, help, and serve our non-believing neighbors and communities.[471]

Home Gatherings' Size and Name

It is my understanding that the modern-day phenomenon known as "mega churches" is incapable of fostering the main thing which God desired for His body of believers—i.e., personal relationships, which are the hallmark of a big healthy family. There can hardly be any deep relationships in a body of two hundred and fifty members—much less in a group numbering one thousand, ten thousand or more members. Furthermore, the revelation of sin in a public setting, so *the whole*

---

[471] See, for example, Acts 2:43-47, 3:32-37.

lump won't spoil,[472] is next to impossible in a huge group. Sin is easily hidden in a big crowd, compared to small, family-oriented local home fellowships. How in the world can a good, loving, and caring shepherd be acquainted with the problems of his flock among hundreds or even thousands? How can he pray for them, talk to them, give them good counsel, encourage them, and so on?

In addition, in my opinion it is very hard to remain humble and meek, as a shepherd in a huge congregation, especially as it helps one's social position (i.e., his salary). As I mentioned before, in most big congregations, there is also a difference between the poor (sometimes very poor) members and their wealthy (sometimes very wealthy) leaders. It is hard to believe that this would be acceptable to God's only begotten Son, who is our very head and the true *Good Shepherd.*[473]

Finally, my view is that it is difficult to share the good news with non-believers on a personal level in such an environment. This is the very reason why God commands us to *multiply and spread throughout the Earth;* so that we can be His ambassadors everywhere without remaining in our personal comfort zones.

Thus, it is my understanding that local home fellowships should be confined to no more than 15 to 35 people— in order to keep the

---

[472] See 1 Cor. 5:6-7; Gal. 5:9.

[473] See God's clear warning in Ezekiel 34, especially verses 3-4. I would like to stress the following: I'm very aware of the fact that there are many humble, true, and sincere followers of Messiah in these modern-day mega churches! I'm also very aware that many of their leaders are sincere God-fearing shepherds who do their very best to lead their huge congregations in the right direction while feeding them with His good food—His Word! Yet, I still don't see this phenomenon (of mega churches) in Scripture, and I still think we should strive to return to the first century model as it is God's perfect will for His Son's bride—the body of Messiah.

needed intimacy within their one big family. Once they reach 35 (or so), the leader of the specific home fellowship should prayerfully consider who amongst them are fitting future leaders and send them off with some people to start their own home fellowships (as described above).

Fellowships that have originated from the same mother fellowship can join together for big festive celebrations and fellowship whenever they decide to do so (once a month or once a year perhaps, or during the biblical feasts). This is completely at the discretion of the local leaders.

Further, I believe that leaders should not look for a specific name for their home fellowship, as this tradition is not Biblically based. In Scripture, the fellowships were named simply after and according to their physical/geographical locations.[474]

Everyone Should Participate

I believe these new local home fellowships should encourage <u>all</u> of their members to be as active as they possibly can in their weekly gatherings. <u>All</u> members of the body should seek His face and beseech Him in order to show and make clear to each one, what exactly their God-given spiritual gifts are, and how they should use them, especially within these weekly gatherings. <u>Every</u> member of these local home fellowships should strive to share their gifts with the others so that

---

[474] See how and to whom Shaul addresses his epistles (see Rom. 1:7; 1 Cor. 1:2 and so on). See Yeshua's seven letters to seven of Yeshua's bodies in Asia minor (Rev. 1:11).

each one is edified and together can grow to *the measure of the stature of the fullness of Messiah!*[475]

I believe these weekly gatherings should be held according to God's order. I also believe it is the responsibility of the leaders or shepherds to humbly lead the weekly gatherings as members give them their due respect.[476]

Further, I believe that the members should be encouraged by their leaders to give only out of a cheerful heart in order to cover potential needs, which might include financial ones of other members within the fellowship, in order to alleviate extreme socio-economic differences amongst them.

Children, Young Adults and Community Living

Finally, I believe, children, at least from a certain age, should have an integral part in the weekly fellowship and should be encouraged to stay with their parents, rather than attending Shabbat or Sunday school. Grown children and youth should be taking part in the service, perhaps by reading, praying or being part of the worship team and so on. For the babies and those who simply cannot participate, parents should bring something from home to occupy them, even in a corner of the private home where everyone is gathered.

---

[475] See Eph. 4:13.

[476] See 1 Tim. 5:17; Heb. 13:17.

The First Century Model — A Short Summary

In this closing chapter, I tried to show the differences which exist between the present-day model and the first century one. I did not touch on every aspect but chose to concentrate on the following issues:

I tried to establish the fact that both the concept and different definitions of the body (*Ecclesia*-the *called-out* ones) are deeply rooted in the Tanach (Old Testament writings), which themselves are deeply rooted in the Hebraic/Jewish Middle Eastern culture.

I showed that throughout the pages of the Tanach there are examples of individuals, people, and a nation, all of whom were *called out* by God. I mentioned renowned figures such as Abraham and David. I stated that the interesting biblical fact is that the nation of Israel, itself, was called *Ecclesia,* as she too was *called out* from Egypt to be God's unique and only Chosen Nation!

I went on to compare the present-day body model with that of the first century. This comparison included the places of gathering (rented or privately owned buildings as opposed to private home gatherings), the different order of service and more...

While dealing with the way the first century body of believers functioned and how it looked, I chose a single biblical reference and elaborated on it in great detail (Acts 2:42).

I suggested that it is God who is using this Covid crisis (and the others to follow) to call us to return and adopt His first century model. I humbly suggest that we acknowledge it and thus, also submit ourselves to it, if we really want to find ourselves *in Him*, doing His perfect will!

I encourage you, respected reader, to continue reading the following appendices, in which I deal with some crucially important issues pertaining to Yeshua's body: On which day of the week should we gather as a home fellowship? How should we partake in the Lord's Supper? How and when water immersion (Baptism) should take place? What is true worship? How should our weekly service look (Or, in other words: What kind of order of service should we adopt)? And, lastly, how should true followers of Messiah Yeshua relate to God's Torah, which was given to Moses on Mt. Sinai?

Chapter 3:

Appendices

Appendix 1:
The Preferable Day of Gathering

For almost two thousand years our forefathers in the Diaspora yearned and prayed that God would bring them back to their homeland. God answered their prayers, and according to His perfect sovereignty and timing, they are now back in their ancient Promised Land. We, the Israeli followers of Yeshua, are an integral part of this great modern-day story of redemption!

One of the most important concepts to Jews who live here in the Land (and in fact all over the world) – even those who call themselves "secular" – is the biblical day of rest and worship - the Sabbath. For modern-day Jews living in Israel (exactly as it was for first century Jews), the first day of the week – *Yom Rishon*/Sunday – is a workday which starts another weekly cycle. God-fearing Jews go to work on the first day of the week as they take God's commandment quite seriously: <u>Six</u> *days you shall work, and* <u>*on the seventh*</u> *you shall rest.*[477]

As all of us should know from a basic reading of Scripture, Yeshua never taught against the observance of the Sabbath! After all, wasn't God the One who commanded its observance? Yeshua regularly visited the synagogue on the Sabbath. The apostles and His other first century followers observed the Sabbath day as well![478]

---

[477] See Ex. 20:8-11; Lk. 23:56. I exclude some of the extreme ultra-Orthodox Jews who do not hold a day job or go to work for an income.

[478] See Matt. 12:9; Mk 1:21, 3:1-2; Lk. 4:16; Matt. 5:17-20, 24:20; Acts 13:14, 44, 15:21, 17:2.

Called to Enter His Eternal Sabbath Rest

The Hebrew word *Shabbat* (Sabbath) is derived from the root "Shin, B/Vet, Tav" (ש.ב.ת - to repose or desist from exertion, cease, put away, or make to rest). To the Hebrew speaker, it corresponds to the Hebrew word *lashevet* meaning "to sit." It is like saying that on the Sabbath day, after He finished His work of creation in the six previous days, God "sat down" on His heavenly throne and "rested."

Now, please note that it does not say anywhere in Scripture that God got up on the eighth day (the first day of the week or, as people call it today, Sunday) to continue creating. Moreover, while each of the six days of creation has a time frame (*and it was evening and it was morning*), the *Shabbat* does not have any time frame. Thus, the first biblical reference to the *Sabbath* actually pointed to <u>an eternal day of rest</u>!

Adam and Eve, who were created on the sixth day, were the crown of God's creation and held a unique position before Him. They were the last to be created, and everything which was created before them was actually created for them. All they needed to do was join in with their gracious and loving Creator, enter into His (seventh) day of rest and enjoy it together with Him <u>forever</u>!

Together with his wife, Eve, Adam was to rule over God's creation and to take care of it, but God never meant it to be a heavy burden on them. Adam and his wife were called to do all this while being in a position (or state of mind) of a <u>continual Sabbath rest</u>. This is the very rest each true follower of Israel's Messiah is called to enter after receiving Him into his or her life and choosing to follow Him.[479]

---

[479] See Heb. 3 & 4, especially 4:9.

The Sabbath as God's very private signature

The seventh day is one of the main signatures of God. It is *a sign* that points to the One and true Author and Creator of the entire universe. Honoring the seventh day as the day of rest is like declaring, "I serve the One True God, the Creator of Heaven and Earth." Honoring the seventh day (rather than any other day of the week) points to the God of Heaven and Earth, who created them all in six days and then rested on the seventh. Throughout Scripture (both the Tanach and the New Testament), God never commanded us to honor any other day of the week as His holy day of rest—only the seventh day. The Sabbath is indeed *a sign* between God and His faithful ones.[480]

It is my understanding that the original Jewish body of Messiah (joined later by non-Jewish believers) did <u>not</u> meet on the first day of the week—at least not according to the modern definition of it. In Christianity, most denominations chose Sunday as the "Day of the Lord" in accordance with the common belief that Yeshua was resurrected on a Sunday.

Saturday? Sunday?

In the Greek manuscript of the New Covenant writings, the phrase *first of the week* actually reads, *the first of the Sabbath!*[481] When understood in its biblical and Hebraic/Jewish context, *the first of the Sabbath* refers to the time that starts at the end of the Shabbat, or seventh day (Saturday), after sundown. Unlike the modern-day method of counting days, the Biblical days commence in the evening, and not at midnight or at 6 a.m. *And it was evening, and it was morning, marking the first day... And it was evening, and it was*

---

[480] See Ex. 31:13, 17.

[481] Greek: *"mia"* (μία — *one* or *first*) *"ton"* (ὁ, ἡ, τό — *to*) *"sabaton"* (σάββατον — *Sabbath*). See Jn. 20:1.

morning marking the second day and so on.[482] To this day, Jews all over the world, as they leave the synagogue on the evening after the Sabbath service (Saturday evening), greet each other with the words "Sh'eeyeh lecha Shavua tov" (Hebrew, may you have a good week). This is simply because they follow the biblical counting of the days in which the new week has already begun at the end of the Sabbath day.

It is my understanding that Yeshua was resurrected sometime after the traditional Jewish ritual service known as the *Havdalah.*[483] Please note that His <u>empty</u> tomb was visited before the break of day![484] If what I said above regarding the first day of the week being a normal working day is true, both for Jews who lived back then and for Jews today, then the first century believers more likely met at the close of the Sabbath day after sundown, sometime around the Havdalah ritual.[485]

Now, since it is accurate to say that there is an extension of freedom for true followers of Messiah to consider whatever day they deem to

---

[482] See Gen. 1:5, 8.

[483] *Havdalah* (Hebrew)—*separation*, distinguishing between weekdays and the Sabbath. An old Jewish tradition which involves special rituals and prayers and takes place at the closing of the Sabbath day (on Saturday evening).

[484] See Jn. 20:1.

[485] It may be shocking to some of us that the very first reference to Sunday as "the Christian day of worship," is derived from the second century (around 110 CE). It was Ignatius from Antioch who encouraged followers of Israel's Messiah <u>to forsake the Sabbath</u> for what he (mistakenly and unbiblically) called "The Lord's Day." He considered it a frightening thought to believe and speak of Yeshua while still observing Judaism or Jewish traditions.

be holy/separated, we should not judge any brother or sister who thinks differently from us![486]

Furthermore: It is also true that when reading within the context, it seems that first century believers *did* meet on the evening of Sunday, as well.[487] Yet, this *did not* replace the Sabbath Day as a holy day of rest unto the Lord, nor unto them!

It's important to understand that Sunday became known or connected to the biblical *Day of the Lord* in traditional Christian thought, but it was *never* biblically based![488] Please remember: When Yeshua came to Israel the first time, He had much to say about man-made traditions which did not adhere to biblical truths but rather, added to or subtracted from them.[489] I am convinced that this approach of Yeshua towards man-made traditions has never changed.

The Weekly Sabbath Day of Rest and the Two Other Sabbaths

The purpose of the scriptural Sabbath and Feasts is to serve as pictures and a foreshadowing pointing us to His prophetic calendar and to His only begotten Son, the Messiah of Israel.[490] If we choose to observe

---

[486] See Rom. 14:5-13; Col. 2:16.

[487] See Lk. 24:33-35; Jn. 20:19, 26; Acts 1:12-14, 2:1—the Feast of *Shavuot,* or Pentecost, was celebrated on the fiftieth day, after seven Sabbaths—which must fall on Sunday. Please note! According to the biblical counting of the days, Sunday evening, when the first followers met, is actually the beginning of the second day/Monday!

[488] *The Day of the Lord* (Hebrew, *Yom Adonai/YHVH*)—this phrase never pointed to the Sabbath or any other day of the week! It pointed rather to God's terrible Day of Judgment! See for example, Isa. 13:6; Joel 1:15, 3:4; Amos 5:18-20; Zeph. 1:14; Mal. 3:23; Acts 2:20.

[489] See Matt. 23; Mk. 7:1-13.

[490] See Col. 2:17.

unbiblical, man-made (sometimes, even pagan in origin) Sabbath and feasts, we assume a high risk of missing both the timing and the true identity of Messiah Yeshua, when He returns to restore the kingdom to Israel![491]

Besides pointing us to His prophetic calendar and to His only begotten Son, the Messiah of Israel, the Sabbath day is meant to remind us of two other Sabbaths: (1) the first one, immediately following the six days of creation, which was celebrated by God and His first created human beings - Adam and Eve (see above), and (2) the future "Sabbath:" The 7th millennial kingdom, where the whole Earth will enjoy conditions that existed on the first Sabbath, in the Garden of Eden. Please note: In both the first and the last Sabbath, neither sickness, nor demons, nor the like are mentioned! Thus, Yeshua performed most of His healing miracles (including casting demons out of people) on the seventh day of the week - the Sabbath! He did it following His own words: *I did not come to abolish... but to fulfill...* Indeed, Yeshua came to give the correct interpretation as pertaining to the Sabbath and one of its main purposes: Pointing us to the first Sabbath before the fall and causing us to look towards the optimal fulfillment during the last Sabbath - the millennial kingdom!

---

[491] See Act. 1:6.

Appendix 2:
The Lord's Supper in the First Century

In most present-day believers' gatherings, communion is taken during or towards the end of the service and includes two elements: bread and wine. Leaders encourage their congregants to examine their hearts and repent of any sin they have committed up to that moment of partaking of it. They also encourage, and at times clearly warn people who are "not yet saved," or immersed in water not to partake of the bread and wine. Why? Not being saved makes them *unworthy* of partaking in the Lord's Supper.

Generally speaking, modern-day communion is done in a more serious type of religious atmosphere. Everyone closes their eyes and asks God to forgive them for all the sins they have committed up to that point so that they can be worthy of sharing this "holy sacrament."

The question I would like to raise here is, does the above description of communion in God's modern-day body fit the biblical description? I'm afraid the answer is clearly *no*! Allow me to explain.

As already established, the weekly gatherings of the believers were most likely not in big (rented or owned) facilities but rather in private homes where the members functioned more as one big family. And as with most Jews (to this very day), an integral part of these family gatherings was the sharing together of a good, festive meal.

The very first communion, or *the Lord's Supper* (In Hebrew, Seudat haAdon – סעודת האדון) was established by Yeshua Himself, and it was within the context of the Passover meal that He and His disciples most likely held - (a shortened version of) what we know today as the first eve of the Passover "Seder meal." The specific items of bread and wine were an integral part of that abundant, festive meal that Yeshua shared with His close disciples.[492]

Later, when the disciples met together with the other followers of Messiah, they continued this Jewish, Middle Eastern cultural tradition and probably ended each of their weekly gatherings with a big, delicious meal.[493]

Now, for the first century believers, the meal was most likely prepared in advance by individuals who brought it to a specific private home, for all attending members to share and enjoy together (again, probably at the very end of the gathering). Since the body included people from all economic and social levels, a few verses seem to suggest that some members partook of the congregational meal (i.e., this *love feast*) before the appropriate time for which it was set.

Reading Shaul's instructions, as it pertained to the *worthy manner* in which every believer should partake of the Lord's supper, does not leave much room for incorrect interpretation: Eating from the bread (the meal/food, see above) and drinking the wine before the appropriate time without considering the others (the poor, who did not have the means to eat or drink in their own homes), was considered a grave sin, as they indeed had not *discern Messiah's body.*[494]

When read in the proper context and considering the broader Jewish Middle Eastern first century context, Shaul could not have been speaking of just any sin which may have been committed during the preceding week! When asking the members of the body to examine

---

[492] See Lk. 22:14-22.

[493] See Jude 12.

[494] See 1 Cor. 11:17-34.

themselves before partaking in the bread and wine, Shaul clearly was addressing the sin of *not considering the body of Messiah* at that specific *love feast* which they shared together at their weekly gatherings. In other words, Shaul did not ask the believers in Corinth to examine their hearts for all the sins they had committed during the previous week but rather to regard their specific sin of eating the bread and drinking the wine before its set time!

The restriction, placed by leaders and teachers on those who wish to partake of the Lord's Supper, which stresses that they must first be born again in order to be considered worthy, is, in my opinion, not biblically based, and, at the very least, taken out of context.

1 Cor. 11:27 reads: *Therefore, whoever eats this bread, or drinks this cup of the Lord, in an unworthy manner, will be guilty of the body and blood of the Lord.* The word for *unworthy* is *anaxiōs.*[495] It can literally be translated as *unworthy* or *in an unworthy manner.* When reading all of Shaul's instructions in the proper context, it's very clear to me that the second definition is the correct one. Again, those who selfishly partook of the meal before the big, celebratory *love feast* had started, had indeed done so *in an unworthy manner!*[496]

I encourage all home fellowships to share communion together. Yet, let us do it as <u>an integral part of the main meal</u> we share at each of our weekly gatherings! I do believe with all my heart, that in the first century home fellowships, those who took communion did so with great joy! It was a happy event, where all were commemorating Messiah's precious death for them. The event served to remind them

---

[495] G371 (Strong), ἀναξίως, *an-ax-ee'-oce.* Adverb from G370: *irreverently— unworthily.*

[496] Please read again: 1 Cor. 11:21-22 and then 11:27-34. Note, especially, verse 29.

that they gathered as saved and redeemed people who otherwise would not be able to enjoy such a nice, festive meal together.

Appendix 3:
Water Immersion in the First Century

The second of the two sacraments, among the traditional body of Believers, is water immersion.

Archaeologists have found great numbers of *mikvaot* (ritual baths) in Jerusalem and other places throughout Israel, dating back to Yeshua's time and even to earlier centuries.

In most present-day congregations, an unbiblically-based distinction is made between receiving the Lord into our hearts, i.e., becoming a follower of Yeshua, and immersion in water. In many gatherings, leaders today often require new believers to go through a specific course on water immersion (a two-week or even a year-long course) in order for them to have a better understanding of what it means.

In contrast to the above description, the first century body did <u>not</u> distinguish between the event of someone's heart conversion and the need to undergo water immersion.

The first century Jewish leaders in Yeshua's body understood the biblically based connection between repentance and water immersion. The main scripture by which Jewish interpretation connects repentance and water immersion is Lev. 16:4. It has to do with the priests' service in the Tabernacle (and later in the Temple in Jerusalem). Traditions go all the way back to the first Adam, who the sages say, stood in the river in the Garden of Eden asking God for His mercy, that neither he nor his wife Eve would be driven out of the garden.

In their teachings, the apostles Shaul and Simeon (Peter) connect *water immersion* (water baptism) with two events from the history of

Israel: the crossing of the Red Sea and the flood in Noah's days. According to Simon, Noah and his family were *saved through* (or by) *water.*[497]

Immersion in water, according to the plain description in Scripture, is not a matter of choice on the part of the follower of Yeshua. It is described as the spiritual circumcision every true follower of Yeshua must go through.[498] Immersion has to do with the separation of a true follower of Yeshua from this world (represented by Egypt, as far as it concerns the crossing of the Red Sea). In immersion, the true follower cuts (I.e., washes, cleanses) Egypt/ the world out of his life. By being united and identified with the death, burial and resurrection of Yeshua, the true follower buries his old nature (sinful mentality, slavery to sin, etc.) in the water and rises up as *a new man, a new creation.*[499] It is interesting to note that the water that saved the eight souls in Noah's ark was the same water used by the Almighty to execute His just judgment upon the sinful inhabitants of the ancient world. This very phenomenon is repeated at the crossing of the Red Sea; the waters of the Red Sea "saved" the Israelites that crossed it, while the pursuing Egyptians were severely judged while trying to cross it the same way.[500]

When carefully reading the detailed stories of conversion in the New Covenant writings, we see that they always involved water immersion. Yes, all detailed scriptural narratives of conversions (i.e., new believers joining the body) in the first century included two central components (neither of which, by the way, included "a sinner's prayer" or "an altar call") – (1) repentance; and (2) water immersion. Here they are:

---

[497] See 1 Cor. 10:1-2, 1 Pet. 3:20-21.

[498] See Col. 2:11-13.

[499] See Rom. 6:3-5, 2 Cor. 5:17.

[500] See Ex. 14.

- The first three thousand at the Feast of Shavuot (Pentecost. Acts 2:37-43)

- The Samaritans who heard the good news through Philip's ministry (Acts. 8:12)

- Simon the sorcerer (Acts 8:13)

- The Ethiopian eunuch (Acts 8:36-39)

- Shaul (Paul) himself (Acts 9:17-19)

- Cornelius, along with his household (Acts 10:47-48)

- Lydia (Acts. 16:14-15)

- The prison guard in Philippi (Acts 16:31-33)

- Crispus and the others in Corinth (Acts 18:8)

I encourage leaders in present-day home fellowships to adopt the Jewish/scriptural way above and have spiritual newborns go through immersion immediately following their repentance and the submission of their lives unto Yeshua. This does not mean they should not first receive a thorough explanation of the meaning and symbolic act which they are about to undergo as they enter the water. Yet, this thorough explanation should not be separated by a long-time span from their actual wish to follow Yeshua as their Messiah Redeemer!

Appendix 4:
Worship

In the present-day gatherings of believers, "worship" is an integral part of the fellowship. What does it look like, and how does it operate? We have a few musicians, usually on an elevated stage in front of us, singing songs of praise to the God of Israel and His only begotten Son, Yeshua the Messiah; while some of the congregants stand, lift their hands, and worship.

On a personal level, I must admit that this specific time in the service is my favorite part! I love singing to the Lord. I love the holy atmosphere it brings in, the sense of His presence with us, His bride— I love it! In this appendix, I hope to present you with the broader biblical description and meaning of true worship.

Worship in the Hebrew Language

In Scripture, there are primarily three Hebrew words that describe and define the English word worship: *hishtachvayah* (השתחוויה), *avoda* (עבודה) and *halel* (הלל).[501] As we shall see, each of these three Hebrew words is mentioned within a context (or connotation) of Master-to-Servant/Slave relationships. In other words, true worship of God is the demonstration of total submission, love, appreciation and adoration of a servant/slave towards his master!

---

[501] The word for praise in Hebrew (הלל) is often spelled in English as *hallel*. I intentionally spell this word with only one "L" (*halel*), so it matches the Hebrew root *Hey, Lamed, Lamed* (ה.ל.ל) and other words which are derived from this very root.

Now, let us delve into the deeper meanings of each of the biblical Hebrew words that describe worship:

Hish-tach'vayah

This word is based on the Hebrew root "Shin, Chet, Hey" (ש.ח.ה).[502] It is very interesting to note the first three times it is mentioned in Scripture:

- Our father Abraham *lifted up his eyes and looked, and lo, three men stood by him: and when he saw them, he ran to meet them from the tent door, and <u>bowed</u> himself toward the ground ('va-yish-tachu artzah' ארצה וישתחו*).[503]

- *Va-yish-tachu* is mentioned again, this time, when his nephew, Lot, <u>bowed</u> down before the two angels.[504]

- Later, Abraham is tested in his most difficult trial ever. He is called to sacrifice Isaac, his son, on Mt. Moriah. Just before they arrive at the place, he leaves his servants at a certain place and tells them, *stay here with the donkey, the lad and I will go yonder and <u>worship</u>. (ve-nish'ta-cha-veh) and come again to you.*[505]

The following are a few other interesting contexts in which this Hebrew root "Shin, Chet, Hey" is mentioned:

---

[502] H7812 (Strong), *shâchâh*. A primitive root; to *depress*, that is, *prostrate* (especially reflexively in homage to royalty or God): *bow (self) down, crouch, fall down (flat), humbly beseech, do (make) obeisance, do reverence, make to stoop, worship.*

[503] See Gen. 18:2.

[504] See Gen. 19:1.

[505] See Gen. 22:5.

- When the Israelites hear the good news brought by Moses regarding their coming redemption out of Egypt, *they <u>bowed their heads</u> and <u>worshipped</u> (va-yish'tacha-vu).*[506]

- At Mt. Sinai, God instructs Moses, *come up unto the Lord, you and Aaron, Nadab and Abihu, and seventy of the elders of Israel, and <u>worship</u> (ve-hish'tach-a-vitem) ye afar off.*[507]

- When Joshua son of Nun is in the vicinity of Jericho, he meets *the captain of the Lord's hosts,* and immediately *<u>fell on his face</u> to the earth and <u>worshipped</u> (va-yish'ta-chu).*[508]

- The Psalmist declares: *all the ends of the world shall remember and <u>turn unto the Lord</u>: and all the kindreds of the nations shall <u>worship</u> (ve-yish'tach-avu) before thee.* He also commands to *give unto the Lord the glory due unto his name; <u>worship</u> (hish'tach-avu) the Lord in the beauty of holiness.*[509]

Avoda

This second word for worship is based on the Hebrew root "Ayin, Bet/Vet, Dalet" (ד.ב.ע),[510] and mainly speaks of "service," "work of any

---

[506] See Ex. 12:27.

[507] See Ex. 24:1.

[508] See Josh. 5:14.

[509] See Ps. 22:27, 29:2. For other references, see Isa. 2:8, 2:20, 27:13, 36:7; 1 Kings 1:47, 1:53, 2:19; 2 Kings 2:15, 4:37; Neh. 8:6; Matt. 28:17; Lk. 24:52; Heb. 1:6; Rev. 4:10, 14:7.

[510] H5647 (Strong), `âbad. A primitive root; to *work* (in any sense); by implication to *serve, till,* (causatively) *enslave,* etc.: X *be, keep in bondage, be bondmen, bond-service, compel, do, dress, ear, execute, + husbandman, keep, labor (-ing man), bring to pass, (cause to, make to) serve (-ing, self), (be, become) servant (-s), do*

kind," "servant," "slave," "bondage," "bondservant," "ministering" and "office."

When you ask modern-day God-fearing religious Jews about their relationship with the Creator, they would hardly use the words *hishtach'vayah* or *halel.* Rather, they would use the word *avoda,* declaring, "I'm the servant of the Lord (*eved Adonai*), and whatever I do in life, from the moment I wake up in the morning to the moment I go to sleep at night, is in the service of God (avodat Hashem/Adonai)." To them, all that is done in their everyday life is an act of worship/*avoda* to the Creator.

Let us look at some scriptural references where the root "Ayin, Bet/Vet, Dalet" (ע.ב.ד) is used:

- Laban, when cheating Jacob, says *fulfill her week, and we will give you this one also for the* <u>*service*</u> *(Avoda) which you will* <u>*serve*</u> *(ta'avod) with me still another seven years.*[511]

- God calls Moses to go to Egypt and take His people out of there. He tells him, *when you have brought the people out of Egypt, you shall* <u>*serve*</u> (plural: *ta'avdun*) *God on this mountain.*[512]

(use) service, till (-er), transgress [from margin], (set a) work, be wrought, worshipper.

[511] See Gen. 29:27.

[512] See Ex. 3:12.

- Within the context of Israel perpetually keeping the Feast of Passover, Moses says, *and it shall be, when your children say to you, what do you mean by this* <u>*service*</u> *(h'avoda)?*[513]

- Within the context of granting permission to own slaves in the nation of Israel, God (through His servant Moses) says, *and if one of your brethren who dwells by you becomes poor, and sells himself to you, you shall not compel him to* <u>*serve*</u> *(avodat) as a* <u>*slave*</u> *(eved).*[514]

- Israel is called *the servant of God* (*eved Adonai* — or *avdi* — *my servant*).[515]

- Messiah is called *the servant of God* (*avdi/eved*).[516]

Halel

The third biblical Hebrew word for worship is based on the Hebrew root "Hey, Lamed, Lamed" (ה.ל.ל),[517] and as usual, the Hebrew language has more than one meaning. Here are only a few of them: "to be clear" (originally about sound, but usually about color), "to

---

[513] See Ex. 12:26.

[514] See Lev. 25:39

[515] See Isa. 41:8-9; 42:1, 19; 44:1-2, 21; 45:4.

[516] See Isa. 52:13, 53:11. For more references using this Hebrew root word, see Num. 3:26, 3:31; 1 Ch. 9:28; 2 Ch. 29:35, 31:2; Isa. 14:3; Jn. 16:2; Eph. 4:12; 2 Thes. 2:4; Heb. 9:1.

[517] H1984 (Strong), *hâllal*. A primitive root; to *be clear* (originally of sound, but usually of color); to *shine*; hence to *make a show*; to *boast*; and, thus, to *be* (clamorously) *foolish*; to *rave*; causatively to *celebrate*; also to *stultify:* (make) *boast (self), celebrate, commend, (deal, make), fool (-ish, -ly), glory, give [light], be (make, feign self) mad (against), give in marriage, [sing, be worthy of] praise, rage, renowned, shine.*

shine," "to boast" and thus "to be (clamorously) foolish," "to celebrate," "to be mad," "to sing," "to be worthy of praise."

I would like to elaborate on a few of the above meanings. We will start with the most familiar and obvious one:

Halel and Praise

- *Sing to the LORD, <u>praise</u> (hallelu) the LORD: for He has delivered the life of the poor from the hand of evildoers*[518]

- *I will declare Your name to My brethren: in the midst of the assembly, I will <u>praise</u> You (a'hallelcha).*[519]

- *<u>Praise</u> (Hallelu) ye. <u>Praise</u> (Hallelu), O servants of the LORD; <u>praise</u> (hallelu) the name of the LORD.*[520]

- *I will call upon the LORD, who is <u>worthy to be praised</u> (me-hu-llal)—so shall I be saved from my enemies.*[521]

Halel and "Madness"

- *So he changed his behavior before them, <u>pretended madness</u> in their hands (va-yit-hollel be-yadam) scratched on the doors of the gate, and let his saliva fall down on his beard.*[522]

---

[518] See Jer. 20:13.

[519] See Ps. 22:22.

[520] See Ps. 113:1.

[521] See 2 Sam. 22:4.

[522] See 1 Sam. 21:13.

- *And they will drink, and stagger and <u>go mad</u> (vehit'holalu) because of the sword that I will send among them.*[523]

Halel and Pride

- *So the king of Israel answered and said, tell him, let not the one who puts on his armor <u>boast</u> (yit'halel) like the one who takes it off.*[524]

- *Thus saith the LORD, let not the wise man glory (or <u>boast</u>— yit'halel) in his wisdom, let not the mighty man glory (or <u>boast</u>—yit'halel) in his might...*[525]

- *Whoso <u>boasteth himself</u> (mit'halel) of a false gift is like clouds and wind without rain.*[526]

Halel and... Satan!

Halel and Satan? Could this at all be possible? What's the connection? Many of you are probably familiar with the story of *the angel of light* or *the morning star* and/or, *the son of the dawn,* about which the prophet Isaiah spoke. Some English translations describe this figure as *Lucifer.* Here are Isaiah's own words: *How you are fallen from Heaven, <u>O Lucifer, son of the morning</u>. How you are cut down to the ground, you who weakened the nations?!*[527]

---

[523] See Jer. 25:16

[524] See 1 Kings 20:11

[525] See Jer. 9:23. See also Job. 4:18, where the use of the Hebrew root word *"Ha-Le-L"* is used for *folly,* or *to err.*

[526] See Prov. 25:14.

[527] See Isa. 14:3-20 (especially verse 12).

There are two facts worth noticing: (1) Isaiah was referring to the prideful king of Babylon; (2) the name *Lucifer* is <u>not</u> mentioned in the Hebrew manuscript! In Hebrew, *O Lucifer, son of the morning* is *Heilel ben Shachar* (הילל בן שחר). *Shachar* in Hebrew is *dawn*, while *ben* is *son*. The Hebrew name of this *son of the dawn, Heilel*, is connected to the very same root ("Hey, Lamed, Lamed" - ה.ל.ל), discussed above! So, how in the world did this *Heilel* become Lucifer? In Roman mythology (based on Greek mythology), Lucifer was known as "the god who carries the light." When the well-renowned Jerome translated Scripture for the first time into Latin,[528] he connected *the son of the dawn* to "the morning star"—Venus and then, Lucifer.

Later, in Christian theology, this fallen figure (*Heilel ben Shachar*) that was spoken of by the prophet, was connected to Yeshua's words— both in the Gospels and in the revelation given to John.[529] Yes, this figure in Isaiah was rightfully associated with boastfulness, pride and arrogance—all of which fit the description of Satan.

Now, of what was this *Heilel son of the dawn (or morning)* so boastful? As I understand it, the answer is contained in his special name. Prior to his rebellion against the Almighty, followed by his ejection from God's presence, the devil was probably <u>the greatest worship leader</u> in the heavenly Temple (see the connection between *hallel/praise* and *heilel*).

Worship is Much More than Singing Praise Songs

We can see that the biblical description of "worship has much deeper and broader meanings than just singing praises to the Lord and playing music! Worship is more about the <u>everyday lifestyle of the</u>

---

[528] *The Vulgate*. Fifth century CE.

[529] See Lk. 10:18 and Rev. 12:4&9.

<u>worshipper</u>, whether he/she leads the worship segment of the weekly gathering or not. It is more about seeing oneself as <u>a servant/slave</u> of the Almighty, having no special rights.[530]

Those who believe they are called to lead praise and worship in Yeshua's body need to be aware of the great responsibility they have before Him, as their calling is to actually bring people into His very presence![531] They can use the praise (*halel*) time in a good and pure manner, which brings glory to Him and to Him alone, or – God forbid – they can be boastful, prideful and (at times) also emotionally angry (or "mad"). Similar to a shepherd (*Ro'eh*—see above), who can abuse his calling and actually become an evil/bad shepherd (*Ra*), they – the *me-halelim* (worshipers/singers/musicians) can also be thrown out of God's very presence as a result of their choices—exactly as occurred with the former disobedient, evil worship leader—Heilel Ben Shachar!

How can true worship leaders lead their brethren into God's presence? I believe the following provides us with some good nuggets.

Three Levels of Worship

I would like to suggest that there are (primarily) three levels of worship, all of which are patterned after the three parts of the Tabernacle, and later the Temple in Jerusalem.

Worship in the Outer Court

In the Outer Court of the Tabernacle (and later in the Temple in Jerusalem), there was what I like to describe as the lowest and most basic level of holiness. In this court, there was a great deal of commotion and noise. Many people would bring their sacrifices to the

---

[530] See Lk. 17:5-10.

[531] See Ps. 22:3—*He loves to dwell in the praises of His people!* See also Ps. 9:11.

Levites and priests. Many would mingle together and speak to one another, etc.

I like to compare this outer court description to what I describe as easy, basic introductory worship that should start at the beginning of the weekly home fellowships. This can be done when people arrive and mingle with the other members, as well as in the beginning of the time frame allotted for worship. In my opinion, this easy and basic introductory worship should include the type of music that is light, happy, and exuberant.

Worship in the Holy Place

The second level of worship in Yeshua's body weekly gathering, should be patterned after the second part of the Tabernacle—the inner court called the Holy Place. This court was only accessed by priests—those who were called to come and serve closer to God's presence. In the same way that we are all called to be *a kingdom of priests,* I believe we are also called to this inner place; but we must understand that in this specific place, there was much less noise and commotion! There was instead reverence, respect, and a feeling of awe in the holy place!

Consequently, the next level of worship that worship leaders should help us all to enter, should be done with more meaningful, deeper, and slower types of songs and music—those which bring the worshipper into a greater personal interaction with God's Spirit and thus, into more awe and reverence to sense his beautiful presence!

Worship in the Holy of Holies

The very climax of our fellowship with God in worship, should, in my opinion, take place in the third and final level, which is patterned after the Holy of Holies, where God's very presence dwelt (symbolized by the Ark of the Covenant). Yes, this place represented God's throne in the heavenlies! In the Torah, this place was permitted only to one man, the High Priest, and only once a year - on the Day of Atonement - Yom Kippur!

Shaul the Apostle said that <u>by faith</u> we are already *sitting with Messiah, in the heavenlies...*[532] It is my suggestion that worship leaders at this third level, offer Him the deepest, quietest and most fully reverential type of music—the kind that brings both themselves and the brethren – the entire body of believers – into the only position possible at this stage—<u>fully prostrate</u> before the throne of God Almighty! I believe the following scriptures point to this kind of (Holy of Holies) presence:

- *Then the cloud covered the tabernacle of meeting, and the glory of the Lord filled the tabernacle, and <u>Moses was not able to enter the tabernacle of meeting</u>, because the cloud rested above it, and the glory of the Lord filled the tabernacle.*[533]

- *And Moses and Aaron went into the tabernacle of meeting and came out and blessed the people. Then the glory of the Lord appeared to all the people, and fire came out from before the Lord and consumed the burnt offering and the fat on the altar. When all the people saw it, they shouted <u>and fell on their faces</u>.*[534]

- *When all the children of Israel saw how the fire came down, and the glory of the Lord on the Temple, <u>they bowed their faces</u>*

---

[532] See Eph. 2:6.

[533] See Ex. 40:34-35.

[534] See Lev. 9:23-24.

> *to the ground on the pavement and worshipped and praised the Lord....*[535]

- *So, the priests could not continue ministering (in Hebrew, la'amod — "to stand") because of the cloud, for the glory of the Lord filled the house of the Lord.*[536]

Let us all strive to be true worshipers of the God of Israel - the only One deserving it - Amen!

---

[535] See 2 Ch. 2:3.

[536] See 1 Kings 8:11.

Appendix 5:
Suggested Order of Service

Needless to say, it was not my intention to cover every *jot and tittle* regarding the first century model in this book. This is true also regarding the order of service that I'm going to suggest in the following pages. I would like to stress: <u>The following is not something set in stone</u>! It is only my simple understanding regarding how each home fellowship should function. All I'm going to share in the following paragraphs are some principles to be interpreted and applied according to each person who has been led to a leadership position.

One True Supreme Leader

On the principal level, I believe the one who should be the real leader of each home fellowship is God's Holy Spirit! I suggest that leaders not have any kind of rigid written list of things that they feel should be included in the weekly service. Rather, they should let Him lead in the specific direction He wants to take His people at each of the local weekly fellowships.

Prayers & Supplications and Community Fellowship

First and foremost, everything should start with prayer and supplication for His perfect will to be done in a specific meeting. These prayers and supplications should start even before arriving at the private home in which the gathering is going to take place! As previously mentioned, each and every member should seek the Lord regarding what He wants him or her specifically to bring to the meeting, so that everyone can be edified.

I believe a relaxed time of fellowship and catching up with one another should also be considered.

Next, I believe there should be some time given to testimonies and specific prayer needs.

Praise, Worship and More...

Next, there should be a time set aside for worship with music. I do believe this specific component should <u>not</u> be constrained by time. I believe it is the responsibility of both the leaders and the musicians to be attuned to the Spirit in choosing the songs and in knowing when to stop and just be reflective in order to let the Spirit minister! I do believe that in this special spiritual atmosphere, words of knowledge, prophecies, and the like, should be shared, *all in Godly order* and with due respect given to the leaders and other members!

Reading & Teaching

Next, I believe there should be a short pertinent teaching, usually delivered by one of the leaders who has this gifting as well as a calling. It could be a 20–30-minute teaching or one without time constraints.[537] This might be an opportune occasion to also include some public readings. This is a time when the teaching and readings should include (at least) some of the specific, traditional Jewish readings from the Torah and Prophets.[538] There are a variety of ways to incorporate all of these things, and the possibilities are endless.

---

[537] I believe that the community of local Body should include Bible studies at different homes, with love feasts and communion shared there, as well as systematic study of Biblical books and/or topics.

[538] I do encourage home fellowships to include the traditional Jewish readings of the Torah portions and the *Haftarot* (portions from "the Prophets"), and the study thereof, in their services. We should all try and learn more about our Jewish

A Love Feast

I believe that the local home fellowship should end with what Scripture calls *a love feast,* a festive meal, which would also include communion. Members should be encouraged to bring some food with them, as they are financially able to do so.

May He bless us as we strive to get back to the model used by the first century body of Yeshua – Amen!

---

heritage and visit a synagogue whenever we can. See Lk. 4:16-19; Acts 13:15; 1 Tim. 4:13.

Appendix 6:
Yeshua's Body and the Torah

This appendix is dedicated to a subject which has been debated, I believe, since Yeshua's First Coming: How should true disciples of Israel's Messiah relate to the Five Books of Moses, known as *the Torah*? The following pages are an excerpt taken from my previous book, published in 2020,[539] with a few added modifications. As usual in this book, all excerpts and quotations are in a different font to make it easier on the respected reader to distinguish between the actual excerpt and my present content:

Many genuine followers of Messiah believe that Shaul, in his diverse writings, was "anti-Torah." And indeed, when reading some of his blunt statements regarding the Torah, it can lead to the impression that he had been teaching against it.[540] However, the problem with this notion is that it clearly contradicts Shaul's conduct which he displayed in his own life. Scripture clearly shows that he kept and observed the Torah.[541] So, what did the Apostle Shaul really want to convey to us regarding God's holy Torah?

In order to better understand Shaul's teachings on the Torah, we must first consider the following simple fact. Shaul did <u>not</u> function as a

---

[539] See again, *Moses Wrote About Me — Genesis, Appendix 1 – Shaul and the Torah,* pages 427-452: https://touryourroots.com/books-%26-articles

[540] See his statements in Gal. 2:17-21, 3:10-14; and Rom. 14:1-3, 5-6, 14.

[541] As already mentioned in the introduction, the first century believers, including Shaul himself, took Yeshua's words very seriously (including the ones recorded in Mt. 5:17-20). Thousands upon thousands were *zealous* for the Torah (Acts. 21:20); they observed it and cared for it with great love. See again Acts 15:21, 21:26, 22:3, 23:1, 24:11-14, 25:8, 28:17; and Rom. 3:31.

Christian theologian but rather as a Jewish rabbi, or teacher. All the truths he revealed in his writings were based on his knowledge and understanding of God's Word, which included the Torah.

Previously, I explained how Shaul used Hagar's story when relating to the Mt. Sinai Covenant. Through the continuation of Hagar's story, we can see more details that shed a greater light on Shaul's vital teachings which I call, 'the relationship between true followers of Messiah and the Torah.'

A Visitation, a Feast and a Separation, Followed by a New Beginning

Scripture repeatedly provides us with pictures, patterns and foreshadowing upon which the remainder of Scripture (including the New Covenant writings) rests. One of these patterns is what I call "the Principle of Clear Separation." This principle usually takes place within the context of a visitation, then a feast, followed by a new beginning or era. Here are a few examples of how this pattern works in the Scripture.

The Exodus from Egypt

God visited His people in Egypt, then He commanded them concerning the Feast of Passover, and lastly, He separated them from the Egyptians. All of this brought about a new beginning and a new era in their walk with Him.

The Wedding at Cana

Yeshua, His mother and His disciples visited a wedding Feast at the Galilean city of Cana. There, a certain separation started to take place relating to Yeshua and His mother's authority over Him. That separation marked <u>a new beginning and era</u> in His earthly ministry as the revealed Messiah of Israel.[542]

The Last Supper

Yeshua <u>visited</u> with His twelve disciples before the <u>Feast</u> of Passover while sharing their last supper before His crucifixion. At least two <u>separations</u> took place that evening: The separation between the true disciples and the one who would eventually betray Him and the separation between the eleven disciples and their beloved Rabbi, until shortly after His resurrection from the dead. Both <u>separations</u> marked <u>a new beginning</u>, or era, in the lives of the disciples and of Yeshua Himself.[543]

Yeshua's Glorious Return

In the future, there will be yet another <u>separation</u> which will involve <u>a visit</u>, <u>a Feast</u> and <u>a new era</u>. At His Second Coming, Yeshua will again visit His nation – Israel. Personally, I do believe, as many others, that since Yeshua's entire ministry was surrounded by the biblical feasts, His glorious return will also take place during one of these feasts. As an integral part of this Second Coming, Yeshua's followers will be <u>separated</u> from the rest of the non-believing world for a time, which will be followed by the wedding <u>feast</u> of the Lamb. This will mark yet another <u>new beginning</u> or era—the one-thousand-year kingdom.[544]

Separation and the Eighth Day

Previously, I discussed the symbolism of the number *eight* in Scripture. I state that it primarily symbolizes "new beginnings."

---

[542] See Jn. 2:1-4.

[543] See Matt. 26:20-30; Mk. 14:27, 49-52; Jn. 13:18-30.

[544] See Matt. 22:2-13 and others.

As mentioned above and discussed later in great detail, Isaac is a clear and important foreshadowing of the Messiah. Isaac is the first person who was recorded in Scripture as having his circumcision on *the eighth day.*

Messiah Himself was circumcised on *the eighth day,* as are all Jewish boys. Yet something else in Messiah's earthly ministry took place on *the eighth day.* It was something crucially important. It was an integral part of the salvation He offered to those who would follow Him. It was His resurrection from the dead! Without Messiah's resurrection on Sunday (which can be viewed as "the eighth day"), those who follow Him would have no hope and would still be lost in their sins.[545]

Messiah's resurrection marked His complete victory over death or better stated, His complete <u>separation</u> from Satan's grip and primary weapon, which is death. It marked an entirely <u>new beginning</u>, not only in Yeshua's ministry but also in the lives of those who followed Him.

Separation and the Havdalah

Torah-observant Jews practice a very interesting tradition called *Havdalah* ("separation" or "distinction"). It takes place every Sabbath (Saturday) at sundown, marking the end of the Sabbath and the beginning of the new week. What Jews actually do is separate or distinguish the seventh day (Sabbath) from the first day of the week which starts that evening.

Messiah's resurrection from the dead occurred on the *eighth* day—not long after the Jewish tradition of *Havdalah* had been held that Saturday evening. Thus, the resurrection (and the timing of it) marked a completely <u>new era</u> in human history.

---

[545] See 1 Cor. 15:12-19.

Considering this principle of <u>a visitation, a Feast</u> and <u>a separation followed by a new beginning,</u> we are better able to understand a few of Shaul's more blunt statements regarding the Torah.

Free Sons Through Rebekah and Isaac

Fulfilling His promises concerning *the son of promise,* God <u>visited</u> *Sarah.*[546] Following God's visitation, the birth of Isaac occurred, which was followed sometime later by <u>a feast</u> prepared by Abraham.[547]

It was during that <u>feast</u> that Ishmael scoffed at Isaac, and <u>a separation</u> between Hagar (along with her son Ishmael) and Sarah (along with her son Isaac) became inevitable.[548] This separation brought about <u>a new era</u> in Abraham's household. Hagar and Ishmael were no longer an integral part of Abraham's home; only Sarah and Isaac remained there.

Let us now focus on what this <u>new beginning</u> in Abraham's household truly meant, specifically as it concerns Isaac, a clear foreshadowing of Messiah.

In Galatians 4:21-31, Shaul uses this specific event related in the above Torah narrative, to speak about what true Torah observance actually entails. Shaul begins his rabbinic *midrash* this way, *tell me, you who desire to be under the law...* Notice that he does not say anything against the actual observance of the Law but rather against the *desire to be <u>under</u>* it.

In light of the above description of the <u>separation</u> followed by <u>a new era that took</u> place in Abraham's home, we need to ask, what did Shaul mean by using the words *under the Torah?*

---

[546] See Gen. 21:1.

[547] On the day Isaac was *about to be weaned* (Gen. 21:8).

[548] See Gen. 21:9-14; this separation process began already in the previous Torah portion (review Gen. 16:4-16).

True followers of Israel's Messiah are called *sons of Abraham.*[549] The Torah clearly teaches us that Ishmael and Isaac, both of whom were Abraham's sons, could <u>not</u> dwell <u>under</u> the same (Abraham's) roof! We are indeed *sons of Abraham,* but <u>not</u> through Ishmael! A complete <u>separation</u> between the two brothers had to occur. And indeed, this separation did eventually take place. Only Isaac remained in Abraham's home. So, Shaul is, in a way, asking the believers in Galatia (and other places as well), in which home and <u>under</u> which roof exactly do you desire to dwell?

As it was back then in Abraham's home, so it likewise needs to be in our day. A separation must take place in Abraham's (modern) dwelling place. In each home of true followers of Messiah, one needs to insist that Ishmael leave! Every household of true believers needs to be submitted to the one true inheritor of (Abraham's) blessings and promises! It is Isaac (foreshadowing Yeshua and "the new man" in us), as opposed to Ishmael (foreshadowing "the old man" or the deeds of the flesh). These two will never coexist in peace. They must be separated from each other. As long as both Ishmael and Isaac dwell <u>under</u> the same roof in someone's life, God's plans and promises cannot come to fruition and fulfillment. Without a complete separation between these two, there can be no <u>new beginning</u>, or a <u>new era</u> in the believer's life.

We are sons of Abraham through Isaac, who is *the son of the promise*, as opposed to Ishmael, who is *the son according to the flesh.* We are not Hagar's offspring, but Sarah's children. In Yeshua, we do not *walk after the flesh* (Ishmael) but rather, *after the Spirit* (Isaac)—or, more accurately stated, *according to God's election and promises.*[550]

---

[549] See Gal. 3:7, 4:22-23, 4:28.

[550] See Rom. 9:7-9.

Followers of the Messiah of Israel are called to be His bride. Who was Isaac's bride? Rebekah. She belonged to the family of Abraham, a descendant of Shem! Who was Ishmael's bride? An Egyptian, a descendant of Ham.[551] We are not Ishmael's bride. We are Isaac's (Yeshua's) bride. As such, we belong to the lineage of Shem, and thus are promise-inheritors. We are not slaves nor called to bondage! We are free sons and daughters and heirs of God's promises!

As you can see, Shaul's teachings are actually Torah-based teachings. Let us take a look at how all of the above applies to true Torah observance.

Mt. Sinai and Mt. Golgotha — Two Significantly Different Mountains

Shaul connects Hagar and Ishmael with Mt. Sinai, on the one hand, and Sarah and Isaac with the heavenly Jerusalem, on the other. Shaul does this to stress the key differences which exist between the Mt. Sinai Covenant and the New (as I prefer to call it) Mt. Golgotha Covenant. He uses the impossible match between the two well-known women and their sons to further illustrate the major differences between the two well-known covenants.

Now, before getting into the primary differences between the Mt. Sinai Covenant and the New Covenant, the following needs to be understood:

---

[551] See Gen. 21:21, 9:25-27, 10:6. Yes, Hagar took an Egyptian woman to be a wife for her son Ishmael. Hagar the Egyptian, the bondwoman (slave) picks another bondwoman, an offspring of Ham, to be Ishmael's wife. As mentioned before, wherever your English translations read *servant/s,* the Hebrew word translated is *eved/avadim*—which can mean both *servant/s* and *"slave/s"*.

The Connection Between Passover, Mt. Sinai and Shavuot

A careful reading of the Word shows a very important and interesting thing: It was during the Feast of Shavuot/Pentecost that both <u>the Torah</u> and <u>Holy Spirit</u> were given![552]

According to the Old Covenant writings, the event on Mt. Sinai would not have taken place if the exodus of God's people out of Egypt, which occurred during Passover, had not happened first. According to the New Covenant writings, the falling of the Holy Spirit on Shavuot, also would not have occurred without first experiencing the death, burial and resurrection of Israel's Messiah, all of which took place during the seven days of the Feast of Passover (including both the Feasts of Unleavened Bread and First Fruits).

Thus, we can see a clear connection between the Feast of Passover and the Mt. Sinai Covenant, as portrayed in the Torah, along with a connection between the Feast of Passover and the outpouring of God's Holy Spirit at Shavuot/Pentecost, in the New Covenant writings.

Mt. Sinai and the Levitical Order

The Mt. Sinai Covenant was the occasion and procedure by which God's holy Torah (His teachings, instructions, and different laws) was given. The understanding and observance of the Torah were directly connected to and mediated by the Levites. They and the priests (who were also from the tribe of Levi), taught and interpreted the Torah to the other tribes. The breaking of any of its commandments required the Levites and priests to mediate on behalf of transgressors through blood sacrifices. This was done in an earthly, man-made tabernacle. This Levitical order continued to function throughout the long journey in the wilderness as well as through the time when the two temples in Jerusalem existed. It ended when Jerusalem and the Temple were

---

[552] See Ex. 19:1 (*the third month* after the Passover event); and Acts 2:1.

destroyed by the Romans, about forty years after the death and resurrection of Yeshua.

Mt. Golgotha and the Order of Melchizedek

The New Covenant (or, "Mt. Golgotha Covenant") was the occasion and the procedure through which God's Holy Spirit was (and is still) given. Through the Holy Spirit, God inscribes His Torah on *the tablets of our hearts.*[553] While the understanding and actual observance of the Torah through the Mt. Sinai Covenant was mediated by <u>the Levitical order</u>, now, within this new framework (the New Covenant), the understanding <u>and observance of the Torah</u> is directly connected to and mediated by <u>the Holy Spirit,</u> rather than by flesh and blood. The Holy Spirit operates through a different order, an everlasting one — *the order of Melchizedek,* with its new and eternal High Priest, Messiah Yeshua![554]

The ancient Israelites were completely dependent upon the Levitical order, which operated in an earthly Temple, in order to truly understand and observe God's Holy Torah. True followers of Yeshua, when desiring to understand <u>and observe God's Holy Torah</u>, are now completely dependent upon the ministry of the Holy Spirit, to teach and mediate between them and God. This happens in a temple <u>not</u> made by man, but by God Himself—a heavenly one, which is now expressed and manifested physically in our own bodies—the body of believers - Messiah's members here on Earth.

The Two Covenants and the Two Men

As mentioned above, both Hagar and Ishmael are a picture of our "old man," the natural man, the one who was born into bondage. Sarah and

---

[553] Compare Jer. 31:33 with 2 Cor. 3:2-3, 6-11, 14-18.

[554] See Heb. 5–10, and see the detailed discussion concerning Melchizedek, King of Salem, in author's published book *Moses Wrote About Me.*

Isaac, by contrast, are a picture of the "new (spiritual) man," the one who is born into Messiah's freedom in accordance with God's promises and election.

As with Hagar and Ishmael as well as with Sarah and Isaac, so it is with the two covenants. The Mt. Sinai Covenant (again, operating through the Levitical order) specifically points and relates to "the old man," while the New Covenant (operating through the order of Melchizedek—through the working of the Holy Spirit) points and relates to the "new/spiritual man."[555]

The Holy Just Torah and Its Connection to Death

God's Torah, <u>when applied through the Levitical order</u>, awakens sin that dwells in the flesh. Consequently, sin provokes and brings about its inevitable consequences—death. To state it in Shaul's own words, *For I was alive without the law once, but when the commandment came, sin revived, and I died. And the commandment, which was ordained to life, I found to be unto death. For sin, taking occasion by the commandment, deceived me and, by it, slew me. Therefore <u>the law is holy</u>, and <u>the commandment holy</u>, <u>and just</u>, <u>and good</u>. Was then that which is good made death unto me? God forbid! But sin, that it might appear sin, working death in me by that which is good; that sin by the commandment might become exceeding sinful. For we know that <u>the law is spiritual</u>: but I am carnal, sold under sin.*[556]

When we enter into an agreement and sign a contract, we are automatically obligated to that contract. We put ourselves <u>under</u> its conditions. The very same thing happened with our fathers, the Israelites at Mt. Sinai. When they agreed to enter into a covenant relationship with God, they automatically put themselves <u>under</u>

---

[555] See Rom. 6:1-14; Gal. 2:20, 5:16-26; Heb. 7–12, especially 10:1 and 12:22-24.

[556] See Rom. 7:9-14.

specific stipulations which were included in that covenant.[557] The one major problem was that to this day, there has absolutely never been anyone who could observe, keep and obey <u>all</u> of the Mt. Sinai conditions! Thus, anyone <u>desiring to be under it</u> immediately finds themselves <u>under</u> its curses and judgments as well! And that's exactly the reason that the very heart of the Torah (operating through the Levitical order) was the earthly Temple, where numerous sacrifices were needed to cover sin each and every day of the year.

So, what was the main purpose for God's introduction of His holy Torah to His chosen ones at Mt. Sinai?

Shaul answers this question most thoroughly, and I back his words with a big Amen! *For God hath committed them <u>all</u> to disobedience, that he might have mercy upon <u>all</u>. Oh, the depth of the riches, both of the wisdom and knowledge of God! How unsearchable are his judgments, and his ways past finding out! For whom hath known the mind of the Lord? Or who hath been his counselor? Or who hath first given to him, and it shall be recompensed unto him again? For of him, and through him, and to him, are all things: to whom be glory forever. Amen!*[558]

When sin is awakened or exposed by the Torah, man's conscience feels an urgent need to cover and hide the sin, and if possible, to totally get rid of it! The Torah, which was given and mediated through the Levitical order on Mt. Sinai, supplied the Israelites with the sacrificial services at the Temple, but those could only <u>cover</u> sin—not completely remove it! According to the New Covenant writings, Messiah's precious blood not only covers and atones for our sins but completely removes them from us, cleansing and clearing our very consciences![559]

---

[557] See Ex. 19:8.

[558] See Rom. 11:32-36.

[559] See Heb. 9:9-15.

The Mt. Sinai Covenant's main role was to point (or *refer*) us to Messiah.[560] How did it accomplish this? Firstly, by showing us our complete inability to keep the law <u>in its entirety</u>, and secondly, by demonstrating the sad truth that animal sacrifices are not able to completely wash away or deal with our sins once and for all! After all, didn't the ancient Israelites need to continue sacrificing animals each day, each month and at each feast on an annual basis?

Being in such a state, the Torah indeed points us to the only one real solution - the Messiah, King and Redeemer! He, Yeshua, came and took the judgments and curses of the Torah upon Himself. He died on our behalf and signed God's New Covenant with His own blood![561] In this New Covenant, God's <u>holy, good</u> *and* <u>just Torah</u> is written on the tablets of our very hearts—<u>without</u> its curses and judgments![562]

The New Covenant (Mt. Golgotha) clarifies and exposes the differences between Ishmael (the old man) and Isaac (the new man) and the way true followers of Messiah should relate to them. Shaul's teachings on the differences between the two covenants clearly show that these two <u>must</u> be separated if we want to remain in the new beginning, or new era, which through His precious blood, the Messiah brought us into!

Torah Observance Within the Right Framework

Shaul was neither anti-Torah nor against its observance! Rather, he was against those who did not understand the crucially important differences between the two covenants and how they relate to the genuine <u>observance</u> of God's Torah. He spoke against those who tried (and taught others) to observe God's Holy Torah within and through

---

[560] See Gal. 3:23-24.

[561] In comparison to the blood of animals (see again Ex. 24:6-8; Heb. 9:11-22).

[562] See Rom. 7:12, 14; Jer. 31:31; Heb. 8:7-12; Gal. 3:10-14.

the old framework, the <u>Levitical order</u>, which is the wrong approach and method. Shaul insisted on <u>observing the Torah</u> through the new framework, *the order of Melchizedek*, which is the only correct framework and method.

What does this mean practically? In other words, how do we observe God's Holy Torah within the New Covenant framework? In order to answer this question, we may have to hit upon a controversial subject.

I would like to start by raising the following question: Could it be that some of the rituals, practices and laws included in the Mt. Sinai Covenant were actually <u>changed</u> in the new/Mt. Golgotha Covenant? It's possible that this may touch a nerve and the impulse to respond: "No way! Nothing in God's Holy Torah ever changes!"

My response to that specific view would be: I would encourage you to be open to increasing your knowledge of both God's Word and <u>some</u> traditional Jewish interpretations concerning the Torah.

The Law of Moses Versus the (New) Law of Messiah

A careful reading of Shaul's words to the believers in Corinth reveals a very interesting point, which, in my understanding, is strongly connected and relevant to our discussion:

For though I am free from all men, I have made myself a servant to all, that I might win the more; and to the Jews I became as a Jew, that I might win Jews; to those who are under the law, as under the law, that I might win those who are under the law. To those <u>who are without a law</u>, <u>as without law</u>—not being without law toward God, but <u>under law toward Christ</u>, that I might win those who are without law; to the weak, I became as weak, that I might win the weak. <u>I have become all things</u>

to all men, that I might by all means, save some. Now this I do for the gospel's sake, that I may be partaker of it with you[563] (emphases, mine).

The phrase, *under law toward Christ,* can be translated also as, *under the law of Messiah* (or *Messiah's law).*[564]

Now, we should ask the following inevitable question: Could it be that when Messiah comes, he will change parts in the law of Moses? But most importantly, could it be that Messiah has a different/new law that He is going to bring with Him when He comes?

Reading through some of the Jewish sages' writings reveals a very surprising answer. Some of them were brave enough to claim that it is very likely that the only answer to all of the above questions is yes![565]

I'm not suggesting that all the Jewish sages thought that way! In fact, there were endless arguments among them concerning the above questions as well as the Messianic Era in general! All I'm trying to say is that claiming the idea that the Messiah is going to bring a new law, a

---

[563] See 1 Cor. 9:19-23.

[564] See the NASB translation of this specific phrase. See also Gal. 6:2 and 2 Jn. 9 (here it is translated as *the doctrine of Messiah,* but it can also be translated as *the law of Messiah).*

[565] See a few examples: *The Holy One, blessed be His Name, sits and teaches a new law that He is going to give by/through the Messiah!* (Otiyot D'Rabbi Akiva, 1, 7, Yalkut Shimoni). *The Mitzvot (commandments) are going to end (or, be done with) in the future...* (Nida, 61, 72). *The forbidden foods (especially pig/swine!) will be allowed (to Jews) in the future...* (Vayikra Rabba, 13, 3) — see also *The Return of the Kosher Pig,* written by a personal friend of mine, Rabbi Tsachi Shapira. *The appointed times/Feasts will end in the future...* (Pirkei D'Rabbi Eliezer, 46. Midrash on Prov. 9:2). And lastly, *the sacrifices in the Temple will be done away with (cancelled) in the future* (R. Tanchuma, *Emor,* 14). For Hebrew readers, there is a book called, אוצרות אחרית הימים (*The Treasures of the Latter Days*), written by a modern rabbi named Rabbi Chayun (published in the city of B'nei B'rak, Israel, a few decades ago), which covers a lot of the Jewish traditions concerning Messiah and how things will look in his time.

better law (than that of Moses), a higher/deeper law (again, than that of Moses), is not a foreign concept to Jewish thought! It is not solely mentioned in the New Covenant writings but has been well-embedded in Jewish thought throughout the ages!

When I read my Bible, even given my limited understanding, I see it clearly demonstrates the above Jewish sages' way of thinking, as indeed, Scripture does tell us that *the Levitical order* was <u>changed</u> to *the order of Melchizedek,* and that when it changed, <u>other things changed as well</u>![566]

Furthermore, it must be asked: Can any of us keep the Sabbath, New Moons and Feasts with total precision, according to the ordinances and precepts specified in the Mt. Sinai Covenant? Is there any Temple that exists in Jerusalem today, where we can go and offer our sacrifices and show our faces before the Lord? Are there Levites and priests in modern Jerusalem who serve in a physical Temple according to *the letter of the Law?* Of course not!

So, my next question is: Do the changes I have just presented cancel or abolish the everlasting <u>principles</u> of God's holy Torah? I would vociferously repeat, <u>by no means!</u>

According to my understanding of Scripture, true followers of Messiah, who are "in Isaac" and not "in Ishmael," cannot and are not even

---

[566] See Heb. 7:11-19, especially verse 12. This is not the place to show it, but even the Mount Sinai covenant had a progressive revelation which required change! One good example is the permission given to slaughter animals in all places within the Promised Land and the *change* permitting it to happen only in one place—Jerusalem. Moreover, see how some of these Jewish sages thoughts regarding Messianic times are expressed by the New Covenant's Jewish writers: Rom. 14:20; 1 Cor. 8:8; Col. 2:16; Heb. 7:19, 9:10, 11:35. Remember, Messiah's job is to *exalt the law and make it honorable,* i.e., Messiah's job is not to leave the Torah and its (sometimes very wrong) interpretations as they remain; but rather to give new, deeper and exalted interpretations for it (Isa. 42:21).

supposed to try to keep or observe, God's holy Torah through Mt. Sinai's (Levitical) framework, but rather through the New Covenant (Melchizedek) framework. Here it is:

I Will Write It on Their Hearts

Jeremiah promised that God would write His Torah on the very tablets of our hearts and not on tablets of stone.[567] As previously stated, the Almighty does this through the ministry of His Holy Spirit.

Now the question all true seekers of God's truths must ask is: What exactly did God write on the tablets of our hearts?

Did He write all the 613 commandments (according to the traditional Jewish counting)? For example: Did He write the commandments regarding the building of the Tabernacle on our hearts? Did He write the commandments regarding animal sacrifices on our hearts? Did He write the commandments regarding the three-times-a-year pilgrimage to Jerusalem on our hearts? The list is endless…

What does God really write on the tablets of our hearts?

I believe it is His foundational, original Ten Commandments that He wrote with His own finger on the tablets of stone that He gave to Moses on Mt. Sinai! Yes. These Ten Commandments are the very heart of the entire Torah! Why? They point to and represent the very heart of God Himself!

One of the greatest descriptions of who God really is has been summed up in only one word: *LOVE!*[568] And indeed, the Ten Commandments which were uttered by God's own mouth on Mt. Sinai are the very best descriptions of who He, the only true God of the universe and of all Creation, really is! Carefully reading and meditating on the Ten

---

[567] See again Jer. 31:33 and 2 Cor. 3:3-6.

[568] See 1 Jn. 4:8, 16.

Commandments clearly reveals that all of them have to do with love! <u>Love</u> towards God (the first four), <u>love</u> towards parents (the fifth) and <u>love</u> towards one another (the last five)!

My friends, no matter how we look at it, it is absolutely clear that we <u>cannot</u> obey God's Holy Torah, *according to the letter of the law* of the Mt. Sinai Covenant (all 613 commandments)! Not only because the Levitical order and the Temple are no longer in existence but also because of the heavy burden—that actually no person other than Messiah Himself, not even the disciples, could bear.[569] God has *exposed all* (especially His chosen ones) *in disobedience* so that everyone (Jews and gentiles alike) would come to Him <u>only</u> through His Son, Messiah Yeshua – Melchizedek – with the help and through the ministry of the Holy Spirit![570]

God's Holy Torah — Simplified and Narrowed Down

True followers of Israel's Messiah Redeemer – when carefully looking at God's holy words through the new framework of the New Covenant writings – will discover some good news hidden in them. They will see that the *holy and just Torah,* which was delivered to us by Moses (the Mt. Sinai Covenant), has been narrowed down and simplified by God's own Spirit! Let me explain:

When asked, *teacher, which is the greatest commandment in the Law?* Israel's Messiah's answer was: *You shall love the Lord your God with all your heart, and with all your soul, and with all your mind. This is the first and great commandment. And the second is like it, you shall love your neighbor as yourself. <u>On these two commandments hang all the Law and the prophets</u>.* He also said: *Therefore all things whatsoever*

---

[569] See Acts 15:10.

[570] See Rom. 3:9-31; 7:7–8:11.

you would that men should do to you, do you even so to them: for this is the Law and the Prophets[571] (emphasis added).

No wonder Shaul stated something very similar: *For all the Torah is fulfilled in one word, even in this: You shall love your neighbor as yourself*[572] (emphases added).

Yes, my friends, the New Covenant writings bring what I prefer to define as "the Spirit behind the letter of the Torah," into the great light of God, who alone is holy, perfect and just. He is the One true God, who already from *before the foundation of the world* knew that His chosen ones could not, nor would ever be able to fully obey His holy requirements to perfection. Moreover, He gave all these letters of His holy Torah in order that He might *commit them all to disobedience* while already having the perfect plan in mind, which is salvation and redemption of <u>all</u> mankind through a *better covenant*. God said this *better covenant* would not be *according to the covenant that I made with their fathers in the day that I took them by the hand to bring them out of the land of Egypt.* Rather, God gave this *new* and *better covenant* in order to point to and focus on the only one, *the Son of Man*, who would be able to fully obey each and every letter of the holy requirements of the Mt. Sinai Covenant. And not only this. He would also take its punishments and judgments upon Himself and by doing so, would provide forgiveness and redemption to those who would enter His kingdom through this <u>New</u> *Covenant!*[573]

The Israelites who received the Torah at Mt. Sinai were on their way to the Promised Land. As we very well know, most of those who started

---

[571] See Matt. 22:36-40. Yeshua was not "an exception." Something very similar was said about seventy years before His time by a very famous rabbi, Rabbi Hillel. See also Matt. 7:12.

[572] See Gal. 5:14. See also Gal. 6:2; Rom. 13:8-10.

[573] See again Jer. 31:31-34; Heb. 8:6-13 and Rom. 3:9-31, 7:7–8:11 and 11:32.

the journey died before entering into their inheritance. Further, their great leader Moses was left on the other side of the river! The picture here should be clear to any true follower of Israel's Messiah who is sincerely seeking the truth.

Moses, who represents the Mt. Sinai Covenant, did <u>not</u> cross the river! Joshua was the one who ushered the new generation into their inheritance! The names *Yehoshua* (Hebrew for *Joshua*) and *Yeshua* come from the very same root — "Yod, Shin, Ayin" (י.ש.ע), meaning *salvation*! It was not Moses, via the Mt. Sinai Covenant, who led them into the Promised Land (representing the Kingdom of God), but rather, Joshua, representing Yeshua, the Messiah King and Redeemer of Israel! Moses only guided and pointed them (or, in Shaul's words, *tutored*) them into their inheritance. It was Joshua who brought them into their Promised Land.

God, in His great mercy and wisdom, does not put a heavy burden or yoke on His people![574] God is *LOVE* and as such, He wishes and desires to have a true <u>love relationship</u> with His followers!

The last question we should address in conclusion, is the following: What are the other commandments that are mentioned in God's holy Torah (other than the Ten Commandments which He has written on the tablets of our hearts) and how are we to keep them? In other words, now that we are <u>under a New Covenant</u> and in a love relationship with the very giver of this holy Torah, how should we relate to the other commandments given in the Mount Sinai Covenant?

As I understand it, each one of us should ask Him to lead us by the ministry of His Holy Spirit, regarding exactly what and how we should keep and observe the other commandments in His Torah. Once we are truly led in a certain direction, we should follow that leading as long as

---

[574] See Matt. 11:28-30.

we do not neglect the very heart of the Torah—the Ten Commandments (<u>LOVE</u>)!

Every one of us, as true followers of Yeshua, should keep ourselves from falling into the temptation and trap of judging others who may follow a different path. If the Spirit convicts and leads you to keep the commandments in a certain way, be humble, and give a bit of room to others who have not been convicted to do the same thing in the same way! After all, it is not an infraction which will jeopardize anyone's eternity.

On a more personal and practical level, my way of observing His holy Torah through the framework of the New Covenant is expressed in the following paragraphs:

I try to keep His holy Torah <u>at its principal level</u>! What do I mean by that? Knowing very well that I am incapable of observing His Torah, in its entirety, to the very last letter, I do try to at least remember and observe some of its <u>basic and fundamental commandments</u>. For example, I do my very best to love Him with all my heart, soul, and strength. I try not to have any idols and graven images inside of my mind and heart. I endeavor not to steal and not to fornicate. I try to remember and observe His holy day, the Sabbath. I also observe His (seven) feasts along with whatever else I feel His Spirit is guiding me to keep and observe.

How do I honor His Sabbath and His holy feasts? I try my best to draw a line, or make a clear <u>separation</u> (make holy) between these specific days and the other days of the week (or year, as far as the Feasts are concerned). On the Sabbath day and on each of God's seven feasts, which are also celebrated by Jews around the world, my family puts together a special feast in God's honor. It usually involves a joyful gathering of family and friends around the table with a very good meal. Speaking of food, we <u>try</u> as well to eat in accordance with God's dietary laws.[575] Another way to make this separation is by fellowshipping with local believers, reading and studying Scripture together, singing praises and simply being there for one another.

As uncomplicated as that, my friends! No heavy burdens, no condemnations, and no spiritual anxieties! Everything we do, we should do knowing that we would be unable to complete without His grace and lovingkindness. And thus, we should refrain from attempting to look at spiritual things in a legalistic way that puts us *under the letter of the law that kills* but rather as the *new creation,* under His New Covenant, which simplifies His holy Torah and narrows it down to the greatest and most fundamental commandments and principles.

But What About the Instructions of the Scribes and Pharisees?

There are sincere believers who claim we should keep God's holy Torah exactly as instructed by old and modern Jewish rabbis, who are actually the successors of the scribes and the Pharisees, of whom Messiah Yeshua declared: *The scribes and the Pharisees sit in Moses' seat. Therefore, whatever they tell you to observe, that observe and do...*[576] (emphasis added).

My response to this is: A central teaching, among these scribes and Pharisees back in Yeshua's time as well as the modern-day rabbis who succeeded them, is: Yeshua is not the Messiah of Israel! Most of them would define following Him as a form of idolatry! As quoted above, Yeshua said to *observe whatever they tell* us. So, should we follow this

---

[575] See Lev. 11; Deut. 14. We do it knowing that God never gives bad commandments. The exact reason why God gave these laws doesn't really matter (whether it pertains to health issues or something else which we don't know yet). We are just to trust that He knows what He is doing.

[576] See Matt. 23:2.

teaching, as well?! Should we leave Yeshua, His teachings, and His commandments, as some of His first century disciples did?[577]

It is my understanding that the above attitude is based on a lack of knowledge or ignorance of the full counsel of God's Word! I believe that we are no longer under Yeshua's specific (above) instruction, and that Yeshua expects us to follow the teachings He personally delivered to His disciples and apostles. After all, were they not the ones who eventually had been authorized by Him *to bind and loose* things and *to make disciples* (of Him, Yeshua, as opposed to the scribes and Pharisees) *of all nations?*[578]

False Freedom in Messiah

I would like to clarify one very important point, especially addressed to our dear non-Jewish brothers and sisters in Messiah. I sincerely do not think that God changed His mind concerning believers who, in the name of "freedom in Messiah," observe man-made traditions rather than scripturally based ones!

Observing and celebrating non-biblical feasts, whose origins emanate from paganism, does not bring glory to God, neither does it helps one to understand His Word and His prophetic master plan of salvation, which are clearly laid out in His biblical feasts. These non-biblical festive occasions also set a bad example and are a stumbling block for non-believing Jews. It adds further layers to the veil which is already over their hearts (or spiritual eyes) regarding their own Messiah

---

[577] See Jn. 6:66.

[578] See Matt. 18:18, which as understood in first century Judaism, had to do with interpretation and Jewish *Halacha* (law), based on God's holy Word. See also Acts 2:42, 4:13-19 (especially verses 19-20) and 5:27-29.

Redeemer. We should well remember what Yeshua said of those who place stumbling blocks before others.[579]

To those reading this book, it is my opinion that there is no better way to conclude this appendix on the relationship between true followers of Messiah and the Torah than by quoting one whom I personally consider to be the greatest Jewish rabbi ever, apart from Yeshua Himself—Shaul the Apostle. I hope you will join me in declaring amen to the following (Holy Spirit-inspired) words:

Now the purpose of the commandment is LOVE from a pure heart, from a good conscience, and from sincere faith. From which some, having strayed, have turned aside to idle talk; desiring to be <u>teachers of the law</u>; <u>understanding neither what they say, nor the things which they affirm</u>. But we know that <u>the law is good</u> <u>if one uses it lawfully</u>.

Knowing this, that <u>the law is not made for a righteous person</u>, but for the lawless and disobedient, for the ungodly and for sinners, for the unholy and profane, for murderers of fathers and murderers of mothers, for manslayers, for fornicators, for sodomites, for kidnappers, for liars, for perjurers, and if there is any other thing that is contrary to sound doctrine. According to the glorious gospel of the blessed God, which was committed to my trust.

And I thank Messiah, Yeshua our Lord, who has enabled me, because he counted me faithful, putting me into the ministry; although I was formerly a blasphemer, a persecutor, and an insolent man; but I obtained mercy, because I did it ignorantly in unbelief. <u>And the grace of our Lord was exceeding abundant, with faith and love which is in Messiah, Yeshua</u>.

This is a faithful saying, and worthy of all acceptance, <u>that Messiah Yeshua came into the world to save sinners</u>; <u>of whom I am chief</u>.

---

[579] See Matt. 18:7-9. See also Rom. 14:13-16; 2 Cor. 6:3-4.

However, for this reason I obtained mercy, that in me first , Yeshua the Messiah might show all long-suffering, as a pattern to those who are going to believe in him for everlasting life.

Now to the King eternal, immortal, invisible, to God who alone is wise, be honor and glory forever and ever. Amen![580] (emphasis added).

---

[580] See 1 Tim. 1:5-17.

GOD'S GREAT RESET:
Closing Words

Dear Reader:

Let me start by thanking you for taking the time to read my book! I'm sure that some of its content was very new to you and likely presented you with some challenges, which may have been a struggle.

The following are the main points I presented in this book:

- We are living at the end of what Scripture defines as *the latter days.*

- Covid-19 has been only a small portion of a much larger intentional maneuver.

- The recent pandemic was very well planned and executed by some of the global elites, who serve *the prince of the air*, who does his very best to replace the One true God of Scripture – YHVH, the God of Abraham, Isaac, and Jacob – the God of Israel.

- The international body of Yeshua is going to remain here on Earth during at least some of the Anti-Messiah's reign. Thus,

- It will need to get back to the first century model as very shortly it will no longer be able to use the present-day one.

I would like to ask you to prayerfully consider all that has been presented to you in this book, and to be open to adopting the parts His Holy Spirit is calling you to adopt and implement.

Another request is to hold me and my family in your prayers before His Throne, because this book might raise a great deal of opposition, which can be manifested both in the spiritual and physical realms.

Pray all those who read this book will make the needed preparations; spiritually, mentally, and physically, so that together we can all stand in that day of His great appearance; when He comes to finish <u>His Great Reset</u> that began already in the past few decades, with its climax being this recent Covid-19 crisis. Yes, we shall all look to the Lord who will soon establish *His* New World Order, here on Earth, for one thousand years!

Please feel free to recommend this book to others in your community, including those in leadership, if you do believe that it is relevant for the times in which we are living.

Lord Yeshua, please come – Maran Ata!

In His Great Love & Mercies,

Yosef Rachamim Danieli

Printed in the USA
CPSIA information can be obtained
at www.ICGtesting.com
BVHW040419090823
668345BV00002B/4